ISBN 978-0-266-15231-6
PIBN 10914887

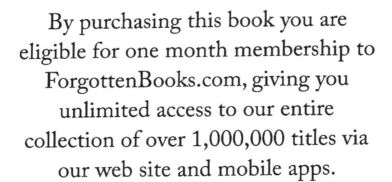

English
Français
Deutsche
Italiano
Español
Português

www.forgottenbooks.com

Mythology Photography **Fiction**
Fishing Christianity **Art** Cooking
Essays Buddhism Freemasonry
Medicine **Biology** Music **Ancient**
Egypt Evolution Carpentry Physics
Dance Geology **Mathematics** Fitness
Shakespeare **Folklore** Yoga Marketing
Confidence Immortality Biographies
Poetry **Psychology** Witchcraft
Electronics Chemistry History **Law**
Accounting **Philosophy** Anthropology
Alchemy Drama Quantum Mechanics
Atheism Sexual Health **Ancient History**
Entrepreneurship Languages Sport
Paleontology Needlework Islam
Metaphysics Investment Archaeology
Parenting Statistics Criminology
Motivational

COMMITTEE PRINT

S. Prt. 101-12
Vol. 7

A LEGISLATIVE HISTORY OF THE SUPERFUND AMENDMENTS AND REAUTHORIZATION ACT OF 1986 (PUBLIC LAW 99-499)

TOGETHER WITH

A SECTION-BY-SECTION INDEX

PREPARED BY THE

ENVIRONMENT AND NATURAL RESOURCES POLICY DIVISION

OF THE

CONGRESSIONAL RESEARCH SERVICE

OF THE

LIBRARY OF CONGRESS

FOR THE

COMMITTEE ON ENVIRONMENT AND PUBLIC WORKS U.S. SENATE

VOLUME 7

SEPTEMBER, 1990

Printed for the use of the Senate Committee
on Environment and Public Works

| 101st Congress
2d Session | COMMITTEE PRINT | S. Prt. 101–120
Vol. 7 |

A LEGISLATIVE HISTORY OF THE SUPERFUND AMENDMENTS AND REAUTHORIZATION ACT OF 1986 (PUBLIC LAW 99-499)

TOGETHER WITH

A SECTION-BY-SECTION INDEX

PREPARED BY THE

ENVIRONMENT AND NATURAL RESOURCES POLICY DIVISION

OF THE

CONGRESSIONAL RESEARCH SERVICE

OF THE

LIBRARY OF CONGRESS

FOR THE

COMMITTEE ON ENVIRONMENT AND PUBLIC WORKS U.S. SENATE

VOLUME 7

SEPTEMBER, 1990

Printed for the use of the Senate Committee
on Environment and Public Works

U.S. GOVERNMENT PRINTING OFFICE
23–507   WASHINGTON : 1990

(II)

CONTENTS

VOLUME 7

CONTENTS OF OTHER VOLUMES

VOLUME 1

IV

VOLUME 2

VOLUME 3

VOLUME 4

VOLUME 5

VOLUME 6

APPENDIX   I

EMERGENCY   FUNDING

(5391)

99TH CONGRESS
1ST SESSION **H. R. 3453**

To amend the Internal Revenue Code of 1954 to extend the Superfund taxes for 45 days.

IN THE HOUSE OF REPRESENTATIVES

SEPTEMBER 30, 1985

Mr. ROSTENKOWSKI (for himself and Mr. DUNCAN) introduced the following bill; which was referred to the Committee on Ways and Means

---

A BILL

To amend the Internal Revenue Code of 1954 to extend the Superfund taxes for 45 days.

1   *Be it enacted by the Senate and House of Representa-*

2 *tives of the United States of America in Congress assembled,*

3 SECTION 1. 45-DAY EXTENSION OF SUPERFUND TAXES.

4   (a) IN GENERAL.—Subsection (d) of section 4611 of the

5 Internal Revenue Code of 1954 (relating to termination of

6 environmental taxes) is amended by striking out "September

7 30, 1985" and inserting in lieu thereof "November 14,

8 1985".

9   (b) CONFORMING AMENDMENTS.—

2

1   (1) Subparagraph (D) of section 223(c)(2) of the

2   Hazardous Substance Response Revenue Act of 1980

3   is amended by striking out "September 30, 1985" and

4   inserting in lieu thereof "November 14, 1985".

5   (2) Section 303 of the Comprehensive Environ-

6   mental Response, Compensation, and Liability Act of

7   1980 is amended by striking out "September 30,

8   1985" and inserting in lieu thereof "November 14,

9   1985".

10   (c) EFFECTIVE DATE.—The amendments made by this

11   section shall take effect on September 30, 1985.

O

[From the Congressional Record, Oct. 1, 1985, pp. H7961-H7964]

LEGISLATIVE PROGRAM

(Mr. LOTT asked and was given permission to address the House for 1 minute.)

Mr. LOTT. Mr. Speaker, I have taken this time for the purpose of inquiring as to the schedule for the balance of the day and for the week, and I am happy to yield to the distinguished majority whip because, as I understand it, there have been some changes made in the schedule for the balance of the day and for the remainder of the week.

Mr. FOLEY. Mr. Speaker, I thank the distinguished Republican whip for yielding.

Mr. Speaker, we intend to take up under suspension of the rules this evening a bill, H.R. 3453, providing for an extension of the Superfund for 45 days, and following the consideration of that suspension the House will have concluded its business for today.

Tomorrow, the House will meet at 11 o'clock to consider the appropriation legislation for Health and Human Services for fiscal year 1986, and following that we will resume consideration of the agriculture bill. We will rise at 6 o'clock tomorrow night.

We will then continue to consider the agriculture bill on Thursday, hoping to complete consideration of the bill by Thursday evening. I would caution Members that it is our intention to attempt to conclude the bill Thursday night, and there may be a late session on Thursday for that purpose.

If we conclude the agriculture bill on Thursday night, we do not plan to schedule business for Friday. In the event that we do not complete the agriculture bill on Thursday night, a Friday session can be anticipated.

Mr. LOTT. Mr. Speaker, if the whip would allow me to intervene at that point while he is looking down at his schedule, I think we should emphasize again to our Members that the intention is to bring the agriculture bill back up for consideration tomorrow after we complete the Labor-HHS appropriation bill, or, if we do not have

any more time left tomorrow, the agriculture bill will be brought back up on Thursday, and the intention of the leadership is to complete consideration of the agriculture bill this week, is that correct? Whether it is Thursday night or Friday, the intention of the leadership is to complete the agriculture bill this week?

Mr. FOLEY. Yes, we intend to complete consideration of the agriculture bill Thursday night and, if necessary, to go late Thursday night for that purpose. If we do complete consideration of that bill on Thursday, as I have indicated, we do not intend to schedule business on Friday.

Mr. LOTT. Mr. Speaker, there were some other pieces of legislation on the schedule for this week, but they will be taken up at a later time, and I assume the Members will be notified of that; is that correct?

Mr. FOLEY. The gentleman is correct.

Mr. LOTT. Mr. Speaker, I thank the gentleman, and I yield back the balance of my time.

___

GENERAL LEAVE

Mr. DE LA GARZA. Mr. Speaker, I ask unanimous consent that all Members may have 5 legislative days in which to revise and extend their remarks on today's consideration of H.R. 2100.

The SPEAKER pro tempore. Is there objection to the request of the gentleman from Texas?

There was no objection.

___

SUPERFUND EXCISE TAX EXTENSION

Mr. ROSTENKOWSKI. Mr. Speaker, I move to suspend the rules and pass the bill (H.R. 3453) to amend the Internal Revenue Code of 1954 to extend the Superfund taxes for 45 days.

The Clerk read as follows:

[NOTE.-H.R. 3453 is previously reproduced and may be found at p. 5393]

The SPEAKER pro tempore. Is a second demanded?

Mr. ARCHER. Mr. Speaker, I demand a second.

The SPEAKER pro tempore. Without objection, a second will be considered as ordered.

There was no objection.

The SPEAKER pro tempore. The gentleman from Illinois [Mr. ROSTEN-KOWSKI] will be recognized for 20 minutes and the gentleman from Texas [Mr. ARCHER] will be recognized for 20 minutes.

The Chair recognizes the gentleman from Illinois [Mr. ROSTENKOWSKI].

GENERAL LEAVE

Mr. ROSTENKOWSKI. Mr. Speaker, I ask unanimous consent that all Members may have 5 legislative days in which to revise and extend their remarks on H.R. 3453, the bill presently under consideration.

The SPEAKER pro tempore. Is there objection to the request of the gentleman from Illinois?

There was no objection.

Mr. ROSTENKOWSKI. Mr. Speaker, I yield myself such time as I may consume.

Mr. Speaker, H.R. 3453 provides a short 45-day extension of the Superfund taxes the Congress enacted in 1980. The funding mechanism for the important Superfund Hazardous Waste Cleanup Program expired last night.

A short extension now is important so that the Congress can act in a deliberative manner to enact the 5-year reauthorization of Superfund without any loss of revenues to the trust fund during the debate. At a time when the EPA is severely reducing its cleanup efforts, we cannot afford to lose any money which we can collect.

Let me emphasize that this extension is only for 45 days so that the existing tax collecting mechanisms can continue in place. It is not a long-term extension into the next Congress. I would oppose a long politically motivated extension.

The Senate has already passed legislation to reauthorize the program and to expand the taxes associated with it. The House will soon consider similar legislation. It is probable that any legislation that is enacted will continue these original taxes at their preexisting rates or higher rates.

In the interest of avoiding an unwarranted disruption, I urge approval of H.R. 3453.

□ 1840

Mr. ARCHER. Mr. Speaker, I yield myself such time as I may consume.

Mr. Speaker, I support the bill, H.R. 3453.

I do so with some reluctance, however. I had hoped that our committee would be able to deal with Superfund legislation in a comprehensive way before today. Unfortunately, other committees of jurisdiction have not completed their work, and we had planned to take up the tax aspects of Superfund after the other committees had made their decisions on program changes.

In light of these timing problems, the termination of Superfund taxes at the end of the fiscal year—which was midnight—and difficulties with respect to getting our committee's deficit reduction bill to the floor, I think it would be wise to grant the additional 45 days in which to find workable resolutions.

I can assure my colleagues I will do everything I can to make certain that our committee does, indeed, deal promptly and comprehensively with Superfund legislation should the 45-day extension be approved by the Congress and signed by the President. If the bill before us today does not become law, I am frankly concerned that this might pave the way for both confusion and mischief. The Committee on Ways and Means, in seeking the extension, is not stalling; we want, instead, to buy some time to take responsible and expeditious action.

Mr. ROSTENKOWSKI. Mr. Speaker, I yield 2 minutes to the gentleman from Pennsylvania [Mr. KANJORSKI].

Mr. KANJORSKI. Mr. Speaker, I take this opportunity to commend the gentleman from Illinois for his leadership in the fight to renew the Superfund to clean up hazardous waste sites. As the gentleman is aware, my district includes the Butler Tunnel, an abandoned mine shaft, an illegal dump site in Pittston Township in Pennsylvania, which is one of only six toxic waste sites in the Nation to be declared clean by the EPA. Despite EPA's assurances in 1982 that the Butler Tunnel site was clean, last weekend's hurricane caused over 100,000 gallons of highly toxic waste to be discharged into the Susquehanna River, creating a 60-mile oil slick and threatening water quality all the way down the river to the Chesapeake Bay.

The EPA has already alerted communities as far south as Baltimore to be aware of the threat the discharge poses.

The Center for Disease Control in Atlanta urges area residents not to come in contact with the spill, which contains substances which can cause damage to the skin, respiratory tract, and gastrointestinal system problems.

Mr. Speaker, it is essential that this extension legislation be passed today so that projects like this, emergency projects caused during disaster times, can be undertaken with sufficient funding and sufficient activity by the EPA to act immediately.

We are talking here of the water quality that serves literally millions of Americans that has been put in jeopardy. I urge my colleagues in the House to support the leadership of the gentleman from Illinois by supporting this legislation.

Mr. ARCHER. Mr. Speaker, I yield 2 minutes to the minority whip, the gentleman from Mississippi [Mr. Lott].

(Mr. LOTT asked and was given permission to revise and extend his remarks.)

Mr. LOTT. Mr. Speaker, I thank the gentleman for yielding.

Mr. Speaker, I really question the need for this 45-day extension. I think the Members would like very much to get action on Superfund legislation, and that is my point. I would like for us to keep the pressure on and get this legislation to the floor as soon as possible.

Now, I realize that we have got three different committees at least involved here and that they all have actions that they are working on; but I would like to get some understanding that we are not going to see this thing dragged out again and again. We do not need 45 days. I do not see why we need even 20 days.

I would like to ask the chairman of the Ways and Means Committee, do we have some understanding that this thing is going to move forward expeditiously and that it will be brought up to the floor for consideration sometime in this month?

I yield to the gentleman.

Mr. ROSTENKOWSKI. I think there was an agreement with the leadership this afternoon that the Com-

mittee on Public Works and the Committee on the Judiciary are going to act quickly on this legislation. I believe the Committee on Energy and Commerce has already reported the legislation.

Immediately after the legislation is reported from the Public Works Committee and the Judiciary Committee, the Ways and Means Committee will consider the legislation. I am sure that the Committee on Ways and Means will be as expeditious as possible.

I am afraid that we on the Committee on Ways and Means want to see what the programming needs are before we fund them.

Mr. LOTT. Well, maybe I could address a question to members of the Public Works Committee, the chairman of the committee perhaps or the subcommittee could give us some information when the Committee on Public Works might report. Could we expect something within the next 10 days?

Mr. ROE. Mr. Speaker, will the gentleman yield?

Mr. LOTT. I am glad to yield to the gentleman from New Jersey.

Mr. ROE. Mr. Speaker, Chairman HOWARD of the Public Works Committee has sent out a formal notice now from the Public Works Committee, with the ranking member, the gentleman from Kentucky [Mr. SNYDER] that we will schedule to mark up the bill on Wednesday of next week in the subcommittee and Thursday in the full committee; so 95 percent of the work of the Committee on Public Works is completed. We will mark up the bill, that is the direction, next week, both in the subcommittee and in the full committee and report out the bill.

Mr. LOTT. Mr. Speaker, I thank the gentleman.

I wonder if maybe the chairman of the Committee on Energy and Commerce that has already acted would express himself on it. That committee has already taken action and I worry that 45 days is quite a delay.

The SPEAKER pro tempore. The time of the gentleman from Mississippi [Mr. Lott] has expired.

Mr. ARCHER. Mr. Speaker, I yield 1 additional minute to the gentleman from Mississippi.

Mr. DINGELL. Mr. Speaker, will the gentleman yield?

Mr. LOTT. I am happy to yield to the gentleman from Michigan.

Mr. DINGELL. Mr. Speaker, I thank the gentleman. I will try to respond briefly.

I was present in the meeting referred to. Our committee has already acted on this legislation. We are anxious to see it move.

My personal feeling is that 45 days are not needed, but I am willing to go along with it as long as it does not become an obstacle.

Mr. LOTT. Does the gentleman feel that he has a commitment that it will move quickly out of the Public Works Committee and through the Rules Committee and to the floor?

Mr. DINGELL. Well, the distinguished chairman of both the subcommittee and the full Committee on Public Works, the gentleman from New Jersey [Mr. HOWARD] and the gentleman from New Jersey [Mr. ROE] have indicated that it is their intention to have the bill out of their committees by a week from this next Friday.

The Judiciary Committee has indicated that they can meet approximately the same time limit and the Committee on Merchant Marine and Fisheries has acted this morning.

The Speaker has indicated that it is his intention to move this legislation as speedily as he knows how, so it is my hope that the matter can move speedily.

The gentleman from Illinois [Mr. ROSTENKOWSKI] of course, can speak for himself and for the Ways and means Committee and will have to do so, as I am not empowered to do so.

Mr. LOTT. Mr. Speaker, I appreciate the gentleman's remarks.

I would like to have some more specific commitment about when we can expect it in the Rules Committee and on the floor, but I recognize that we are dealing with several different committees and that is hard to do.

This is important legislation. I know the Members on both sides of the aisle have worked very hard on this in different committees and would like to see this legislation brought to the House for full consideration.

I would urge all the committees, all persons involved in the various committees, to get it to the Congress this month.

Mr. ROSTENKOWSKI. Mr. Speaker, I yield 5 minutes to the chairman of the Committee on Energy and Commerce, the gentleman from Michigan [Mr. DINGELL].

Mr. DINGELL. Mr. Speaker, I thank my distinguished friend, the gentleman from Illinois [Mr. ROSTENKOWSKI] for making this time available to me and I commend the gentleman for his comments made.

I share some of the concerns just raised by the distinguished minority whip, the gentleman from Mississippi [Mr. LOTT]. I do have reservation about taking this course, but I am willing to support the bill, in reliance on the pronouncements of the Speaker and others that this matter will go forward.

There is $130 million available at this time in the Superfund and there is not a desperate need for this extension. There is a sufficiency of moneys available according to the Administrator of the EPA that the process down there at EPA can go forward without any significant impairment during the time of the next 30 to 45 days.

Indeed, the spokesman for the New Jersey Department of Environmental Protection said yesterday that the gap would not hurt the program. He said as follows:

"We anticipate no interruptions. We already have $150 million appropriated and we are ready for it."

Similar comments have been made, as I mentioned, by the Administrator of the EPA.

The Governor of the State of Michigan has expressed particular concerns about the possibility of not enacting Superfund legislation during this year.

With this country having literally thousands, indeed, I have heard the figure of 100,000 Superfund sites which now are in need of cleanup, there is need for the most urgent speed, because this may perhaps be the largest single environmental and health problem now confronting the American people.

It should be noted that the Senate has passed a Superfund bill and for the House to delay further enactment of legislation of this kind would be indeed an action in which we could be charged with disregarding the public interest and in failing to carry forward on a matter of extreme and urgent importance.

As I mentioned, several committees having jurisdiction have met with the Speaker and all, including the Speaker, have agreed that the matter will move as expeditiously as possible. That is a judgment in which I concur and in reliance on those statements and in reliance on the urgent need to go forward with the least controversy, I am willing to support this legislation, even though I am aware that it is probably less than completely necessary.

I thank my dear friend, the gentleman from Illinois, for yielding to me.

Mr. ROSTENKOWSKI. Mr. Speaker, I have no further requests for time.

Mr. ARCHER. Mr. Speaker, I yield 8 minutes to the gentleman from New York [Mr. LENT].

Mr. LENT. Mr. Speaker, I thank the gentleman.

Mr. Speaker, it is with great reluctance that I rise to note my concern about a 45-day extension of the Superfund. I believe that the reauthorization of the Superfund is the most critical environmental program we will enact in this Congress. I am well aware that the taxing authority for Superfund ran out last night. I am concerned, however, that a 45-day extension will provide an easy out for those who for whatever reason are not able or are unwilling to face the important task of reauthorizing the Superfund now.

The Administrator of the Environmental Protection Agency put the cleanup program on hold in September due to uncertainty over funding. We must not be lulled into thinking that a 45-day extension will allow the EPA to continue its full cleanup activities.

A simple extension such as we are considering here tonight will provide only one-third of the moneys the EPA was expecting to have for fiscal year 1986. This lack of money, coupled with uncertainties about when the full funding might be put in place, will continue to cripple the Superfund cleanup program.

So rather than talk about a 45-day extension, we ought to be considering how much time is actually needed for us to reauthorize Superfund.

I know that the other body has sent us a reauthorization bill for our consideration in a timely manner. We heard from the chairman of the Energy and Commerce Committee that H.R. 2817 was reported 2 months ago. The Merchant Marine Committee to which this bill was referred reported H.R. 2817 today with only one negative vote. The Administrative Law Subcommittee of the Judiciary Committee marked up H.R. 2817 on Sep-

tember 11, and we hear that the full committee will mark up the bill next Tuesday. We learn from the press reports that the Ways and Means Committee is ready to mark up the bill, and the chairman of that committee has been quoted as saying it is simply a 1-day job. The chairman of the Committee on Public Works will report its Superfund bill to the House some time next week.

So it would seem to me all this being said that if all of the committees with jurisdiction are able to meet these commitments on this important subject, a subject considered at length in the last Congress, we could have Superfund reauthorized in a much shorter term than 45 days.

I would hope that the gentleman from Illinois [Mr. ROSTENKOWSKI], the sponsor of this legislation, might consider amending this legislation to extend the funding for 15 or perhaps 18 days so that we will not mask the urgency of the need to reauthorize, expand, and improve the Superfund Program.

Mr. Speaker, I yield 2 minutes to the gentleman from New York [Mr. ECKERT].

Mr. ECKERT of New York. Mr. Speaker, I thank my colleague.

Mr. Speaker, I also rise in opposition to the 45-day extension of Superfund. Such an extension will serve only to mask the critical problem facing our country, the cleanup of our hazardous waste dump sites. While a 45-day fund extension may have some surface appeal, it does not move the cleanup program forward.

As my colleague from New York mentioned, in September the Administrator of the EPA stopped work at 57 sites due to the uncertainty of the reauthorization of Superfund. The work that would have been undertaken in September was based on the expectation of an increase of funding by threefold. A simple 45-day extension will leave the funding two-thirds short.

Therefore, this 45-day extension will not enable additional cleanup to go forward in the proper manner.

I note as others have that the other body has concluded its work on this important legislation. I am embarrassed to tell my colleagues back home that I have not yet had the opportunity to vote on Superfund on the floor of this House despite the fact that the committee on which I serve, the

Energy and Commerce Committee, produced a carefully crafted bipartisan compromise measure by an overwhelming margin of 31 to 10.

We must spend our time working on permanent solutions to the Superfund, and I do not think we can tolerate any further delay.

I would hope that the commitments implied here tonight are honored and that we do not go beyond that 45 days, because even that is far too long.

Mr. ARCHER. Mr. Speaker, I have. no further requests for time, except that I would like to yield myself about 15 seconds to say in colloquy with the gentleman from New York that it certainly should not be necessary that any further extension be taken, that we do complete our work in 45 days. I personally would not favor any additional extension and I would hope that the chairman of our committee would agree with that.

Mr. ROSTENKOWSKI. Mr. Speaker, will the gentleman yield?

Mr. ARCHER. I yield to the gentleman from Illinois.

Mr. ROSTENKOWSKI. Mr. Speaker, I certainly expect immediately after the Committee on Ways and Means receives documents from the other various committees we will work on it and get it done hopefully within a week.

Mr. MARKEY. Mr. Speaker, I rise at this time to voice my support of this temporary extension of current Superfund legislation. Congress needs sufficient time to pass a tough and comprehensive Superfund bill. At this time I want to reiterate my objections to the Superfund legislation passed by the Energy and Commerce Committee. I feel this extension will allow me and my colleagues on other committees to pass a comprehensive Superfund bill. I have always been a strong supporter of Superfund, but we must make every effort to work to ensure that the bill that we finally pass is strong and effective and one that achieves the goal of cleaning up the worst hazardous waste sites on a thorough and expedited schedule.

Mr. ARCHER. Mr. Speaker, I yield back the balance of my time.

Mr. ROSTENKOWSKI. Mr. Speaker, I have no further requests for time, and I yield back the balance of my time.

The SPEAKER pro tempore. The question is on the motion offered by the gentleman from Illinois [Mr. ROS-TENKOWSKI] that the House suspend the rules and pass the bill, H.R. 3453.

The question was taken; and (two-thirds having voted in favor thereof) the rules were suspended and the bill was passed.

A motion to reconsider was laid on the table.

[NOTE.– The following excerpt from debate appeared in the Congressional Record on Oct. 2, 1985 at p. E4326.]

Mr. GALLO. Mr. Speaker, Congress has again forced itself into action. Faced with a deadline for reauthorizing Superfund, the Congress dragged its feet for 9 full months and has acted now to merely extend the Su. perfund for 45 days.

As a member of the Committee on Public Works and Transportation, one of the committees which has jurisdiction over the reauthorization of the Superfund, I am personally outraged by the necessity of this action. From the very first day of the 99th Congress, every Member in this body knew that we had a job to do. Every Member knew just how big that job was, and just how quickly we had to do it. In spite of this knowledge, the clock ran out on Superfund and, typically, we found ourselves in a position to have to take a Band-Aid approach to yet one more problem.

It almost seems like the bigger our problems are, the more willing this body is to use a Band-Aid approach to solve the problem. The debt ceiling, the budget, Superfund, these are all issues that deserve better solutions than this Congress has been willing to deliver.

I know that many of my colleagues have worked very hard for timely Superfund reauthorization. I have worked with members of my own committee and members of many of the other committees with jurisdiction over Superfund to see that we got our job done on time. I have joined with my own committee chairman and subcommittee chairman, and with the ranking members of the Public Works and Transportation Committee and the Subcommittee on Water Resources, in a complete commitment to accomplish a thorough and adequate reauthorization for the Superfund.

I am not sure that the commitment that we have made is pervasive throughout Congress, and I am very concerned that our temporary Band-Aid extension of Superfund might have taken the pressure off of those Members who do not share our commitment to protecting our environment.

In spite of the lack of progress that we, as a body, have made in the last 9 months, 45 days is more than enough time to accomplish an adequate reauthorization of the most important environmental program in our country, provided that we all dedicate ourselves to getting the job done. Without this dedication, there is not enough time.

Today I would like to take this opportunity to call upon all of the Members of this body, from all the States and from both parties to join in our commitment to do this job. To reauthorize Superfund, to do it right, and to do it now. Any further Band-Aid approaches are just not acceptable.

99TH CONGRESS
2D SESSION

H. J. RES. 573

Making a repayable advance to the Hazardous Substance Response Trust Fund.

IN THE HOUSE OF REPRESENTATIVES

MARCH 20, 1986

Mr. BOLAND introduced the following joint resolution; which was considered and passed

---

JOINT RESOLUTION

Making a repayable advance to the Hazardous Substance Response Trust Fund.

1   *Resolved by the Senate and House of Representatives*
2 *of the United States of America in Congress assembled,*
3 That language under the heading "Environmental Protection
4 Agency, Hazardous Substance Response Trust Fund" in
5 Public Law 99–160, is amended by deleting "as amended,
6 including sections 111 (c)(3), (c)(5), (c)(6), and (e)(4) (42
7 U.S.C. 9611), $900,000,000, to be derived from the Hazard-
8 ous Substance Response Trust Fund," and inserting in lieu
9 thereof "including sections 111 (c)(3), (c)(5), (c)(6), and (e)(4)
10 (42 U.S.C. 9611), $900,000,000, of which $750,000,000
11 shall be derived from the Hazardous Substance Response

2

1 Trust Fund and $150,000,000 shall be derived from an ad-
2 vance from the general fund of the Treasury to the Hazard-
3 ous Substance Response Fund to be repaid in accordance
4 with section 223(c)(3) of Public Law 96–510 and notwith-
5 standing section 223(c)(2)(D) of Public Law 96–510: *Provid-*
6 *ed,* That none of the $150,000,000 shall be available for obli-
7 gation after May 31, 1986,''.

O

5404

[From the Congressional Record, March 20, 1986, pp. H1533-H1534]

MAKING A REPAYABLE ADVANCE TO THE HAZARDOUS SUBSTANCE RESPONSE TRUST FUND

Mr. BOLAND. Mr. Speaker, I send to the desk a joint resolution (H.J. Res. 573) making a repayable advance to the Hazardous Substance Response Trust Fund, and ask unanimous consent for its immediate consideration.

The Clerk read the title of the joint resolution.

The SPEAKER pro tempore. Is there objection to the request of the gentleman from Massachusetts?

Mr. ECKART of Ohio. Mr. Speaker, I reserve the right to object.

On my reservation, Mr. Speaker, I yield to the gentleman from Massachusetts for purposes of explaining the bill.

Mr. BOLAND. Mr. Speaker, over the past 6 months, the reauthorization of Superfund has been hotly debated on both sides of this Capitol. What this program needs is a good, long-term bill and an assured source of funds.

Up until this point, the Committee on Appropriations has strenuously opposed all efforts to provide short-term extensions, in order to keep maximum pressure to reach some sort of an agreement on Superfund reauthorization.

Mr. Speaker, we have reached the point of a crisis, and we have passed that point, and still there is no solution in sight. Unless something is done soon, national Superfund contractors responsible for the actual work will have to be terminated and their staffs will have to be laid off.

If that should happen, it will take many months, maybe 12 to 18 months, to put the program back on track. We cannot allow that to happen to the Superfund Program.

So this resolution simply provides, out of the $900 million already appropriated for Superfund in 1986, that $150 million will be available from a repayable advance from the general fund to the Hazardous Substance Response Trust Fund.

These funds cannot be obligated after May 31, 1986. I understand that agreement has been reached by both sides and that the Committee on Ways and Means has no objection to it. Hopefully, they will be coming in with a solution to the tax problem.

My understanding is that the Committee on Energy and Commerce agrees to this. And CBO indicates that there are no additional outlays and no additional budget authority. The appropriation is already in place and this simply permits $150 million of that $900 million appropriated to be available now to continue this program.

Mr. ECKART of Ohio. Mr. Speaker, under my reservation of objection, I yield to the gentleman from New York [Mr. GREEN].

Mr. GREEN. Mr. Speaker, I would like to emphasize a couple of points to the House. First, this was adopted early this evening by the Committee on Appropriations by a voice vote. One addition, has been made to it, spelling out specifically the May 31st expiration date of the appropriation.

The other point that I think is very important is that there are no new obligations, no new budget authority in here, and no new outlays in here. This is all money that was in the HUD-independent agencies 1986 appropriation bill that has been adopted.

The only problem has been the hangup in the conference in the authorizing legislation. This emergency legislation will allow the program to keep going without contractors having to be terminated, and without the whole program collapsing. This will keep us going for 2 months while the conferees try to resolve their differences.

Mr. ECKART of Ohio. Continuing my reservation, Mr. Speaker, I yield to the gentleman from Minnesota [Mr. FRENZEL].

Mr. FRENZEL. May I ask the distinguished gentleman from Massachusetts: The resolution merely provides for borrowing; it does not provide for any particular rate of taxation?

Mr. BOLAND. The gentleman is absolutely correct. It provides an advance from the general fund and that will be repaid to the general fund when the money is available through the taxing process.

Mr. FRENZEL. I thank the gentleman for his explanation, and the gentleman from Ohio [Mr. ECKART] for yielding.

Mr. ECKART of Ohio. Mr. Speaker, I yield to the gentleman from New Jersey [Mr. ROE].

Mr. ROE. Just for the Members of the body, the Committee on Public Works, Representative HOWARD and myself, we support this action because it has to be done at this point.

Mr. ECKART of Ohio. Under my reservation of objection, Mr. Speaker, I yield to the gentleman from Pennsylvania [Mr. WALKER].

Mr. WALKER. I want to clear up a technical point. The unanimous consent was for consideration only? The question will be put on the resolution, is that correct?

Mr. ECKART of Ohio. It is my understanding that the question is consideration, and not passage.

The gentleman would have to proffer that question to the Speaker.

PARLIAMENTARY INQUIRY

Mr. WALKER. Mr. Speaker, the unanimous-consent request is for consideration, and the question will be put?

The SPEAKER pro tempore. That is correct.

Mr. BOLAND. Will the gentleman yield?

Mr. ECKART of Ohio. Under my reservation, I am happy to yield to my colleague from Massachusetts.

Mr. BOLAND. Mr. Speaker, I thank the gentleman from Ohio [Mr. ECKART] and the gentleman from New Jersey and everyone else involved in this, including the members of the Committee on Ways and Means and the Committee on Energy and Commerce.

This is a very serious problem with the Environmental Protection Agency. We completed 2 days of hearings yesterday with the EPA, and Lee Thomas, who in my judgment is probably one of the finest administrators that has ever been appointed, indicated to us the seriousness of the problem. He believes in a long-term solution. However, that is not possible within the timeframe within which these committees have been operating. So a short-term solution is the only solution to resolving the problems facing EPA today.

Mr. ECKART of Ohio. Last, Mr. Speaker, continuing my reservation, I understand there are no language or substantive provisions in this bill?

Mr. BOLAND. That is correct.

Mr. ECKART of Ohio. I understand that there are no future encumbrances in this bill.

Mr. BOLAND. There are no future encumbrances.

Mr. ECKART of Ohio. And that it can in no way be used for repayments or advances.

Mr. BOLAND. The gentleman is correct.

Mr. ECKART of Ohio. Mr. Speaker, I withdraw my reservation objection, and urge adoption of the joint resolution.

The SPEAKER pro tempore. Is there objection to the request of the gentleman from Massachusetts?

There was no objection.

The Clerk read the joint resolution, as follows:

[NOTE.—H.J. Res 573 is previously reproduced and may be found at p. 5402]

The joint resolution was ordered to be engrossed and read a third time, was read the third time, and passed, and a motion to reconsider was laid on the table.

[From the Congressional Record, March 21, 1986, pp. S3178-S3180]

HAZARDOUS SUBSTANCE RESPONSE TRUST FUND

The PRESIDING OFFICER. The Senator from Vermont is recognized.

Mr. STAFFORD. Mr. President, I have conferred with the Democratic leader, and I ask unanimous consent that the Senate turn to the consideration of House Joint Resolution 573, the Superfund extension.

The PRESIDING OFFICER. The House joint resolution will be stated by title.

The assistant legislative clerk read as follows:

A joint resolution (H.J. Res. 573), making a repayable advance to the hazardous substance response trust fund.

The PRESIDING OFFICER. Without objection, the joint resolution will be considered as having been read the second time by title.

Is there objection to the immediate consideration of the joint resolution?

There being no objection, the Senate proceeded to consider the joint resolution.

Mr. STAFFORD. Mr. President, in the brief time available to us, let me say that it was a decision of the Environment and Public Works Committee members who met in my office informally day before yesterday to endeavor to get temporary funding for EPA, and the Superfund Program over a 60-day period at a level of $150 million which is what the legislation in front of us now does in order to keep the Superfund Program going for a time with sufficient funding so that contracts will not have to be terminated, and at the same time to make it a short enough time so that pressure would remain on the conferees for the House and Senate who have been working hard for the last 3 or 4 weeks to solve this problem once and for all by agreeing on a conference report.

We are having a difficult conference. We had 730-some pages of differences between the House and the Senate. We are about halfway through the easier part of that.

This legislation will give us a reasonable opportunity to complete the work on that conference.

Having said that, and urging the Senate to adopt the bill which the House has sent over to us, in the terms I have described, 60 days, $150 million for Superfund, let me say that the point man for our committee, the man who has worked the hardest and certainly deserves great credit for helping to bring this off—he worked with absolutely enormous effort yesterday—is Senator LAUTENBERG of New Jersey who will follow me here in speaking for a moment.

Mr. President, I simply want to say additionally that without the cooperation of Senator GARN, chairman of the appropriate subcommittee of the Appropriations Committee here in the Senate, Senator HATFIELD, chairman of the full Committee on Appropriations, Senator LEAHY, who is the ranking member of Senator GARN's subcommittee, and on the House side Congressman BOLAND of Massachusetts, and the most able chairman of the Appropriations Committee, Congressman WHITTEN, we would not have been able to reach the point we have reached this morning in bringing this legislation before the Senate.

So I want to express my personal gratitude to all of the Members of the House and Senate. Let me not forget the staff of the committee on both sides of the aisle who have worked very hard with members to enable us to provide 60 more days to try to resolve the differences between the House and Senate on Superfund. I believe in that time we can.

I yield the floor to my friend and colleague from New Jersey, Senator LAUTENBERG.

Mr. BYRD. Mr. President, I yield my time remaining under the running order to Mr. LAUTENBERG for his control.

The PRESIDING OFFICER. The Senator from New Jersey.

Mr. LAUTENBERG. Thank you, Mr. President.

I thank my friend and chairman of the Environment and Public Works Committee very much for his continuous and constant support and guidance on many matters that concern each of us in terms of a better environment. I want to support House Joint Resolution 573, the bill that passed the House last night. It is a companion measure to S. 2212 which I introduced in the Senate yesterday.

Mr. President, this bill is very simple. It provides for interim funding for the Superfund Program through May 31 of this year. I was joined in introducing this bill by Senators STAFFORD and BENTSEN, chairman and ranking minority member of the Environment and Public Works Committee, Senator HATFIELD, chairman of the Appropriations Committee, Senator LEAHY, ranking minority member of the HUD-Independent Agencies Appropriations Subcommittee, and Senators CHAFEE, MITCHELL, DURENBERGER, BAUCUS, MOYNIHAN, HUMPHREY, BURDICK, BRADLEY, KENNEDY, and GORE.

Mr. President, I want to express my deep appreciation to the majority and minority leaders for making it possible to consider this measure so expeditiously.

I also want to take note of the cooperation, concern, hard work, and sensitivity displayed by the members who have joined me in this effort, particularly the leadership of the Appropriations and Environment and Public Works Committees.

I want to particularly mention Senator STAFFORD, Senator HATFIELD who is very helpful, Senator STENNIS, Senator GARN, Senator LEAHY, and Senator BENTSEN.

This proposal has been carefully considered and reviewed. After consultations, we arrived at a consensus that enjoyed widespread support in the Senate. I was deeply gratified last night, when Chairman WHITTEN and Congressman BOLAND moved this bill through the House of Representatives. I believe we can pass this measure here very quickly.

Taxing authority for the Superfund Program expired on September 30, 1985. The trust fund is virtually depleted. Without this bill, on April 1, the Environmental Protection Agency would have to begin to dismantle Superfund by terminating contracts with companies that are currently involved in clean up actions. Enforcement actions would be reduced by half and no new cases would be developed. Emergency removals would be curtailed by 80 percent. And, EPA would only be able to handle three or four major emergencies a month. Last month,

EPA began the process of furloughing its own employees.

We cannot permit this dismantling of the program to occur. It is not possible to start and stop a program the size and complexity of the Superfund Program without irreparable damage.

The House of Representatives and the Senate last year approved legislation reauthorizing the Superfund Program. The House bill provides for slightly over a $10 billion program. The Senate bill calls for $7.5 billion. But, these and other controversial issues separate the two Houses and the administration on this complicated legislation.

A House-Senate Superfund conference has been meeting regularly to resolve differences between the House and Senate bills since it convened late last month. Nevertheless, there is no realistic prospect that the conference will be able to complete its work prior to the congressional Easter recess. This legislation is designed to keep pressure on the conference to complete its work, but provide enough funding to protect the integrity of the Superfund Program until a 5-year reauthorization bill is enacted into law.

Time is of the essence. We have literally only hours to pass this bill. Without action, we would be leaving EPA to dismantle the Superfund Program. Along with my cosponsors, I strongly support a 5-year reauthorization bill to enlarge and strengthen the Superfund Program. But, we feel that while the conference continues to work on this bill, it would be irresponsible to permit the dismemberment of this program. If we do not provide this interim funding, Superfund will suffer serious and, perhaps, irreversible harm.

This bill would provide $150 million for the Superfund Program for 2 months, a level consistent with the annual rate of funding provided in the fiscal year 1986 HUD-Independent Agencies appropriations bill. This legislation is necessary because that money remains fenced, pending a reauthorization bill or further action by the Congress. Our legislation would unfence $150 million of the $861 million provided by that bill after the March 1 Gramm-Rudman sequester order.

The bill provides an emergency supplemental appropriation of $150 million from the general fund into the hazardous substance response trust fund. Under the bill, funds would be available immediately as repayable advances.

The objective of the bill is to keep Superfund intact and functioning effectively without removing the incentive to complete action on reauthorization of the program. This measure will infuse enough money into the trust fund to release 2 month's worth of the fiscal year 1986 Superfund appropriation.

Mr. President, there is no way to replace the knowledge, technical skill, and experience embodied in contractor project teams at a moment's notice. It takes time to build organizational resources of this kind. EPA Administrator Thomas testified last Wednesday before the HUD-Independent Appropriations Subcommittee that it would take at least a full year to get contractors back on board once their contracts were terminated. And that assumes that they would want to come back on board after having been cut off—a questionable proposition at best.

Passage of this measure should send a strong signal to EPA's employees and Superfund contractors that the conferees are determined to finish this job by May 31, and that we anticipate an expanded and strengthened Superfund Program.

Mr. President, once again, I thank the majority and minority leaders for their assistance in this effort. And, I thank my two chairmen, Senators HATFIELD and STAFFORD, and Senators BENTSEN, STENNIS, LEAHY and GARN, all of whom were essential to this effort.

Mr. President, I urge adoption of the bill.

Mr. BRADLEY. Mr. President, 2 years ago I asked this body to vote on the reauthorization of the Superfund. The Senate failed to take that action. Many of my colleagues maintained that there was plenty of time to consider the reauthorization. Last year the Senate finally did act on a bill, but once more we had no Superfund law because there was no agreement with the House on legislation.

Today we are considering a temporary extension because all time has run out. The Environmental Protection Administrator, Lee Thomas, has indicated that he will begin to lay off employees working on Superfund actions on April 1 unless Congress acts. Cleanup activities have already ground to a halt in many places. And in my own State of New Jersey, where we have the greatest number of sites slated for action, cleanup has only continued because our State environmental programs are loaning money to the Federal Government. This is simply intolerable. If government cannot protect the health and safety of the public then what is government for?

I am sorry that we have reached the point that this Superfund extension is now critical. Both Houses have passed new Superfund bills which can effectively address the issue of toxic waste cleanup. But we have wasted time. It took over 2 months from House and Senate passage of separate bills just to name conferees. With the recent Supreme Court ruling striking down the use of New Jersey's spill fund at EPA cleanup sites, the need for the Superfund reauthorization becomes even more urgent.

We are now at the 11th hour. This extension is critical and necessary. It is a stop-gap solution to a critical national problem. But the failure to act tonight would bring unthinkable results. I urge my colleagues to support this bill.

Mr. GARN. Mr. President, we have before us a very critical supplemental appropriations measure to provide additional resources needed to prevent the effective termination of the EPA Superfund Program.

Last year Congress, through the appropriations process, provided this program $900 million for fiscal year 1986. Unfortunately, this authority is not available unless the authorization and tax legislation for the program clears conference and is enacted into law.

At the time that Congress acted on the appropriations bill last fall, we were assured that prior year balances could maintain the Superfund core activities and technical infrastructure for several months—providing ample time for completion of the conference consideration of the authorization bill. We were wrong in predicting the difficulties and delays facing that conference.

We find ourselves now, 4 months later, facing the imminent collapse of the program. Not only will EPA have to begin RIF procedures, but equally critical contractors who directly implement hazardous waste cleanups are being told that their contracts will be terminated and their work force disbanded.

The years of effort to establish and develop an effective and aggressive program to clean up these hazardous waste dumps will all go down the drain unless additional funding is released immediately.

That is what the measure before us will do. House Joint Resolution 573 permits EPA to obtain a $150 million repayable advance from the Treasury to maintain program operations through May 31. This will allow the authorizing committees to conclude their conference on the necessary legislation.

Mr. President, I would also point out to my colleagues that we are confronting another very serious problem with respect to funding for the EPA Construction Grants Program. The underlying authorization bill for this program is also waiting conference action and funds we made available last year for the program are already being exhausted in some States.

I expect that we will be forced to address the construction grants issue shortly after we return from the recess and I would hope that the authorizing committees will have concluded their conference by that time so that we can relase the $1.8 billion appropriated last year.

Mr. GORE. Mr. President, I rise in support of S. 2212, legislation to provide stopgap financing for the Superfund Toxic Waste Cleanup Program. I joined Senator LAUTENBERG in sponoring the bill to keep Superfund alive long enough for Congress to work out a lasting compromise.

Superfund is in deep trouble. Funding expired last October, and the House and Senate have yet to agree on a bill to reauthorize the program. EPA has already had to curtail cleanup operations at 100 sites across the country, and may have to halt work at 200 others if it doesn't get more money by April 1. Lee Thomas, the EPA Administrator, said recently that the slowdown could turn into a shutdown, forcing him to furlough 1,500 Superfund employees.

This legislation makes a direct appropriation of $150 million as a repayable advance to keep the Superfund Program running for another 60 days. The bill would keep Superfund from going broke at a time when the coun-try needs it more than ever. The temporary extension would prevent a short-term shortfall from causing long-term damage to the program.

At the same time, a 60-day extension will keep Congress and the Superfund conferees on a short leash. We want to maintain the pressure and momentum to pass a bill that will secure Superfund's financial security for the next 5 years.

Let me also take this opportunity to ask my colleagues to join me in urging the Superfund conferees to find a compromise funding alternative to the manufacturer's excise tax. There is substantial bipartisan support in both Houses for a tax on those responsible for the hazardous waste problem, instead of an across-the-board value-added tax. We in the Senate would like a choice on how to pay for Superfund.

I think my colleagues recognize that we cannot afford to put off a compromise any longer. The Nation has already waited too long to clean up thousands of dangerous waste sites. The time bomb keeps ticking.

Mr. SIMPSON addressed the Chair.

The PRESIDING OFFICER. The Senator from Wyoming.

Mr. SIMPSON. Mr. President, may I just say I want to thank Senator LAUTENBERG for his patience last evening when we could have perhaps moved the measure from the House. I appreciate that. I want to particularly thank him for his work throughout the Superfund. And while the chairman of the Environment and Public Works Committee is on the floor, I think all should recognize his efforts with Superfund as one of the original sponsors. His great desire, drive, and energy to get a Superfund bill- is matched only by the Senator from New Jersey. I appreciate that very much.

We always have a good bipartisan move in the Environment and Public Works Committee. That is one of the touchstones of that committee, and proven once again.

I thank Senator LAUTENBERG, Senator STAFFORD, and their staffs. We will get a Superfund out of that conference, but we have to compete with other business. So it will be something I believe we can produce in a very few weeks.

I thank both of the Senators on the floor.

Mr. LAUTENBERG. Mr. President,

5410

if I may have one moment I wish to say thanks not only for the patience but the wisdom of the assistant majority leader in supporting our effort. It is always a pleasure to work with him, and to find us in agreement on occasion is especially pleasurable.

I thank the assistant majority leader for his assistance and guidance.

Mr. STAFFORD. Mr. President, once again I want to thank my able colleague, Senator LAUTENBERG, for helping us so materially to get this important issue through the Senate, and through the Congress.

Mr. President, I am prepared to yield the floor.

Mr. LAUTENBERG. Mr. President, I urge adoption of this joint resolution.

The joint resolution (H. J. Res. 573) was ordered to a third reading, read the third time, and passed.

Mr. STAFFORD. Mr. President, I move to reconsider the vote by which the joint resolution was passed.

Mr. LAUTENBERG. I move to lay that motion on the table.

The motion to lay on the table was agreed to.

99TH CONGRESS
2D SESSION
H. J. RES. 713

Making a repayable advance to the Hazardous Substance Response Trust Fund.

IN THE HOUSE OF REPRESENTATIVES

AUGUST 15, 1986

Mr. BOLAND introduced the following joint resolution; which was considered and passed

---

JOINT RESOLUTION

Making a repayable advance to the Hazardous Substance
Response Trust Fund.

1   *Resolved by the Senate and House of Representatives*

2 *of the United States of America in Congress assembled,*

3 That language under the heading "Environmental Protection

4 Agency, Hazardous Substance Response Trust Fund" in

5 Public Law 99–160, as amended by·Public Law 99–270, is

6 further amended by deleting "$750,000,000 shall be derived

7 from the Hazardous Substance Response Trust Fund and

8 $150,000,000 shall be derived from an advance from the

9 general fund of the Treasury to the Hazardous Substance

10 Response Trust Fund to be repaid in accordance with section

11 223(c)(3) of Public Law 96–510 and notwithstanding section

2

1 223(c)(2)(D) of Public Law 96–510: *Provided,* That none of

2 the $150,000,000 shall be available for obligation after

3 May 31, 1986, to remain available until expended: *Provid-*

4 *ed,"* and inserting in lieu thereof "$702,000,000 shall be de-

5 rived from the Hazardous Substance Response Trust Fund

6 and $198,000,000 shall be derived from advances from the

7 general fund of the Treasury to the Hazardous Substance

8 Response Trust Fund to be repaid in accordance with section

9 223(c)(3) of Public Law 96–510 and notwithstanding section

10 223(c)(2)(D) of Public Law 96–510: *Provided,* That none of

11 the $150,000,000 made available by Public Law 99–270

12 shall be available for obligation after May 31, 1986: *Provided*

13 *further,* That of the additional $48,000,000 made immediate-

14 ly available, $15,000,000 shall be obligated by Septem-

15 ber 30, 1986, for continuation of ongoing remedial and re-

16 moval site work and $19,000,000 shall be used only to con-

17 tinue ongoing contracts and to replace contracts for essential

18 services: *Provided further,* That all funds appropriated shall

19 remain available until expended, except as specified above:

20 *Provided further,"*.

O

[From the Congressional Record, Aug. 15, 1986, pp. H6341-H6343]

SHORT-TERM SUPERFUND EXTENSION

Mr. BOLAND. Mr. Speaker, I ask unanimous consent for the immediate consideration of the joint resolution (H.J. Res. 713) making a repayable advance to the Hazardous Substance Response Trust Fund.

The Clerk read the title of the joint resolution.

The SPEAKER. Is there objection to the request of the gentleman from Massachusetts?

Mr. GREEN. Mr. Speaker, reserving the right to object, I take this time only so the distinguished chairman of the HUD-Independent Agencies Subcommittee of the Committee on Appropriations can explain what we are doing in this joint resolution.

Mr. BOLAND. Mr. Speaker, will the gentleman yield?

Mr. GREEN. I am happy to yield to the distinguished chairman of the subcommittee.

Mr. BOLAND. Mr. Speaker, I ask unanimous consent that the joint resolution be considered as read and printed in the RECORD at this point.

The SPEAKER. Is there objection to the request of the gentleman from Massachusetts?

There was no objection.

The text of the joint resolution is as follows:

[NOTE.-H.J. Res 713 is previously reproduced and may be found at p. 5411]

Mr. BOLAND. Mr. Speaker, this joint resolution is virtually identical to the resolution passed last April to provide a short-term funding extension for Superfund. This resolution would make $48 million immediately available for Superfund. This is the minimum amount required to carry the program through September. It will avoid EPA having to send out contract termination letters to all Superfund contractors on September 1, and it will avoid terminating clean up work at sites.

This $48 million would be advanced from the general fund to the Superfund trust fund—to be repaid from Superfund taxes once they are enacted and collected. And this action requires no new budget authority and will result in no additional outlays.

However, it is important that all Members understand that this resolution is just another bandaid to carry the Superfund Program into September. Make no mistake about it—we need a long-term reauthorization bill for Superfund and for Superfund taxes now more than ever. I trust that the tax committees and the authorizing committees for Superfund will rapidly complete conference action—because it is critical that we have a Superfund reauthorization and tax bill signed by the President before September 30.

Mr. Speaker, I want to express my appreciation and compliments to the distinguished gentleman from New Jersey [Mr. FLORIO], who is one of the leaders in the House with reference to the Superfund Program, and to my distinguished colleague, the ranking minority member of the subcommittee dealing with the Department of Housing and Urban Development and various independent agencies, for their support and their interest in this matter.

I also want to compliment Members on the other side of this building. I commend the distinguished Senator from Vermont for his leadership and the Committee on Ways and Means.

Mr. WHITTEN. Mr. Speaker, will the gentleman yield?

Mr. GREEN. I yield to the chairman of the Appropriations Committee.

Mr. WHITTEN. Mr. Speaker, I would like to ask, how long would this money last? The Senator from Vermont, Senator STAFFORD, talked to me about it. This $48 million, would that take us to the beginning of the next fiscal year or beyond that?

Mr. BOLAND. No—this will last until the end of September.

Mr. WHITTEN. Mr. Speaker, I thank the gentleman very much.

The SPEAKER. Is there objection to the request of the gentleman from Massachusetts for the immediate consideration of the joint resolution?

Mr. FLORIO. Mr. Speaker, reserving the right to object, I will not object, and let me state first that I also commend the gentleman from Massachusetts [Mr. BOLAND] and the gentleman from New York [Mr. GREEN] for what they have done.

Mr. Speaker, I rise in support of the request of the gentleman from Massachusetts because I am concerned about the possibility based upon EPA's representations that unnecessary and potentially serious disruption of the already damaged Superfund Program may occur if emergency funds are not given to EPA now. I wish to make it clear, however, that this measure is at best a stopgap effort to postpone the current crisis until no later than September 30, 1986. At that time, we will be faced with the same crisis unless we enact a comprehensive, 5-year reauthorization of Superfund. So that we are clear about how EPA will use the $48 million in borrowing authority that is given under the legislation before us, I would ask the chairman of the subcommittee to explain how we are limiting the uses of the money we are providing.

Mr. BOLAND. Mr. Speaker, will the gentleman yield?

Mr. FLORIO. I yield to the chairman of the subcommittee.

Mr. BOLAND. Mr. Speaker, the legislation establishes $48 million in borrowing authority against the Treasury, to be repaid by future Superfund trust fund revenues. The $48 million is to be used for four specific purposes:

First, $10 million will be used to continue in force 14 "core" contracts which were identified in the EPA Administrator's letter dated August 13, 1986.

Second, $9 million will be used to exercise new options on three categories of replacement contracts, listed as items 4, 5, and 6 at page 4 of attachment A to the Administrator's August 13 letter.

Third, $14 million will be available to satisfy Anti-Deficiency Act requirements for newly obligated contracts.

Fourth, $15 million will be spent to conduct removal and remedial activities at sites specifically identified in attachment B of the Administrator's August 30 letter.

Mr. FLORIO. Can my colleague from Massachusetts also clarify for me the overall fiscal situation at EPA with regard to Superfund? Are there any other sources of money that could be used for purposes other than the ones you described earlier?

Mr. BOLAND. The basis for the Congress' decision to enact a second short-term extension of Superfund funding is that there is no other significant amount of money readily available to meet the purposes identified above. We have been informed by senior EPA officials that there are only two other sources of available funding and that each is negligible: First, money from the States under cooperative site agreements, if the States agree to release such funds; and second, a very limited amount of Superfund money which has been transferred to other Federal agencies and departments under interagency agreements and that could not easily be transferred back.

Because of these assumptions, we expect the effect of the $48 million extension to be that the circumstances described in the Administrator's August 13 letter will reoccur on September 30, 1986, unless Congress takes further legislative action.

Mr. FLORIO. Mr. Speaker, I thank the gentleman from Massachusetts [Mr. BOLAND] for his courtesy, and I withdraw my reservation of objection.

The SPEAKER. Is there objection to the request of the gentleman from Massachusetts for the immediate consideration of the joint resolution?

Mr. GREEN. Mr. Speaker, continuing my reservation of my right to object, I simply want to join my colleagues in impressing upon the House the urgency of adopting this measure.

Although the conference—and a very complicated conference it has been—has dealt with the substantive matters at issue, the fiscal matters have unfortunately not been concluded.

I want to say at this point that I have conferred with the ranking minority member of the Ways and Means Committee, and he has no objection to what we are doing here today.

But the failure to conclude the fiscal aspects of the conference leaves us at the point where the Administrator of EPA informs us that he must start delivering termination notices to contractors in the program, terminations for the convenience of the Government, by September 1; and he would also have to set in place reduction-in-force procedures within the EPA if we do not act.

Obviously the cost of terminations for the convenience of the Government and the costs of grinding this program to a halt and then restarting it some time from now would be much greater than the cost of what we are doing today.

So although this is somewhat of an interim step and we are not where we should like to be in terms of a completed conference report with a full appropriation for this operation, I think it is something we must do today in order to keep this program moving along, at least at a minimum level.

Therefore, Mr. Speaker, I withdraw my reservation of objection.

The SPEAKER. Is there objection to the request of the gentleman from Massachusetts [Mr. BOLAND] for the immediate consideration of the joint resolution?

Mr. LENT. Mr. Speaker, reserving the right to object, I am sorry that we are today providing only interim funding for the Superfund program. This very important environmental program has been limping along for 1 year now while Congress struggles with a reauthorization. I believe we are very close to reauthorizing the Superfund.

I do not plan to object to this interim funding measure because the amount of funds is sufficiently small, but Congress will have to turn its attention to Superfund authorization upon returning from the recess.

Mr. Speaker, I withdraw my reservation of objection.

The SPEAKER. Is there objection to the request of the gentleman from Massachusetts for the immediate consideration of the joint resolution?

There was no objection.

The joint resolution was ordered to be engrossed and read a third time, was read the third time, and passed, and a motion to reconsider was laid on the table.

[From the Congressional Record, Aug. 15, 1986, pp. S11824–S11830]

☐ 1510

SUPERFUND

The PRESIDING OFFICER. The Senator from Vermont.

Mr. STAFFORD. Mr. President, I ask unanimous consent that the Senate now turn to House Joint Resolution 713, Superfund, just received from the House. I ask for its immediate consideration.

The PRESIDING OFFICER. Is there objection?

Mr. HUMPHREY. Mr. President, reserving the right to object.

The PRESIDING OFFICER. The Senator from New Hampshire.

Mr. HUMPHREY. Will the Senator from Vermont and the floor managers be willing to enter into a time agreement or some stipulation of how much time they will consume so the rest of us who have been waiting to offer amendments will be aware of how long this will take?

Mr. STAFFORD. We do not intend to use any time. We plan to move immediately on it and ask for its. adoption.

The PRESIDING OFFICER. Is there objection? Without objection, it is so ordered. The clerk will report.

The legislative clerk read as follows:

A resolution (H.J. Res. 713), making a repayable advance to the Hazardous Substance Response Trust Fund.

The Senate proceeded to consider the joint resolution.

Mr. LEAHY. Mr. President, once again we find ourselves at a critical juncture in the Superfund Program.

The situation is very simple. If we do not enact a special appropriation bill today, the Superfund Program will be irreparably damaged.

The House has now acted. It is now our responsibility to act.

It is now clear that the Committee on Conference on the 1986 tax bill will not enact the taxes necessary to refill the depleted Hazardous Substances Response Trust Fund before we recess.

Now, we should all understand that the authorizing committee, led by my distinguished colleague, the Senior Senator from Vermont, has completed its work on this legislation. He has labored long and hard. The final bill is over 200 pages. It was only because of his outstanding leadership that the Conference Committee resolved the score of controversial issues in the Superfund bill. Once again he has shown the exemplary concern for the environment characteristic of his distinguished public career.

However, if the tax conference cannot address the Superfund issues before the August recess, the program will be damaged in two significant ways.

First, the core contractor capacity cannot be maintained. These contractors are absolutely essential to respond to emergencies, to control hazardous sites, and to develop cleanup programs at toxic dumps.

Second, at 76 sites, the work needed to control and remove toxic waste would be halted and at 12 sites, removal actions would end as of September 30.

Therefore, 2 days ago Senator STAFFORD and I introduced a special appropriation bill to provide $60 million so that the members of the tax committees can complete action on the taxes in September without disrupting the Superfund Program. (S. Res. 393)

Because of concerns raised by the Senator from New Jersey, Senator LAUTENBERG, the resolution introduced yesterday has now been refined. The total has been lowered to $48 million. Second, all remedial action funds and removal funds will have to be committed by September 30. All funds provided for contract continuation could only be used for that purpose. They would not be a kitty that the agency could use to keep the program going absent a Superfund tax bill.

This resolution was greatly improved as we resolved the excellent issues raised by my friend, Senator LAUTENBERG.

Mr. President, I want to say a few words about Senator LAUTENBERG's leadership on the Superfund issue.

Last March we faced this same situation. It was only because of the outstanding efforts of the Senator from New Jersey, Senator LAUTENBERG, that an emergency appropriation was passed at that time. Without his dynamic leadership, Superfund would have been shut down months ago, the Superfund conference would have collapsed, and we would not have the strong Superfund bill we do today. Thus, I look forward to working closely with him in keeping this program—which is vital to his State and the Nation—operating.

Finally, I want to thank the chairman of the HUD Subcommittee, JAKE GARN, for his cooperation on this resolution. As usual he has bent over backward to make sure that these essential programs are not disrupted.

I urge the passage of the resolution.

I ask unanimous consent that materials describing the amendment be included in the RECORD.

There being no objection, the material was ordered to be printed in the RECORD, as follows:

STATEMENT ON SHORT-TERM SUPERFUND EXTENSION

The legislation establishes $48 million in borrowing authority against the Treasury, to be repaid by future Superfund trust fund revenues. The $48 million is to be used for four specific purposes:

1. $10 million will be used to continue in force fourteen "core" contracts which were identified in the EPA Administrator's letter dated August 13, 1986.

2. $9 million will be used to exercise new options on three categories of replacement contracts, listed as Items 4, 5 and 6 at page 4 of Attachment A to the Administrator's August 13 letter.

3. $14 million will be available to satisfy Anti-Deficiency Act requirements for newly obligated contracts.

4. $15 million will be spent to conduct removal and remedial activities at sites specifically identified in Attachment B of the Administrator's August 30 letter.

The basis for the Congress' decision to enact a second short-term extension of Superfund funding is that there is no other significant amount of money readily available to meet the purposes identified above. We have been informed by senior EPA officials that there are only two other sources of available funding and that each is negligible: (1) money from the states under cooperative site agreements, if the states agree to release such funds; and (2) a very limited amount of Superfund money which has been transferred to other federal agencies and departments under Interagency Agreements and that could not easily be transferred back.

Because of these assumptions, we expect the effect of the $48 million extension to be that the circumstances described in the Administrator's August 13 letter will reoccur on September 30, 1986 unless Congress takes further legislative action.

Mr. GARN. Mr. President, we have before us a very critical supplemental appropriations measure to provide additional resources needed to prevent the effective termination of EPA's Superfund Program.

Last year, Congress, through the appropriations process, provided this program $900 million for fiscal year 1986. Unfortunately, this authority is not available unless the authorization and tax legislation for the program clears conference and is enacted into law.

At the time that Congress acted on the appropriations bill last fall, we were assured that prior year balances could maintain the Superfund core activities and technical infrastructure for several months. But due to the delay of the conference consideration of the authorization bill, in April, we had to do such an emergency measure to provide EPA with the funds necessary to keep the Superfund going until September 30 without disrupting the contract infrastructure. Now we are again faced with a delay of the authorizing bill action and the possible termination of EPA's Superfund Program. Contractors who directly implement hazardous waste cleanups are being told that their contracts will be terminated and their work force disbanded.

The years of effort to establish and develop an effective and aggressive program to cleanup these hazardous waste dumps will all go down the drain unless additional funding is released immediately.

That is what the measure before us will do. House Joint Resolution 713 permits EPA to obtain a $48 million repayment advance from the Treasury.

Of the $48 million, $15 million shall be obligated by September 30, 1986, for the continuation of ongoing remedial and removal site work and $19 million shall be used only to continue ongoing contracts and to replace contracts for essential services. All the funds appropriated shall remain available until expended except the $15 million which must be obligated by September 30, as I stated earlier. This emergency action will, we hope, allow the authorizing committees to conclude their conference on the necessary legislation.

I urge immediate adoption of this bill.

Mr. MITCHELL. Mr. President, I am pleased that we are considering legislation providing stopgap funding for the Superfund Program. The pending resolution would provide the Federal Environmental Protection Agency with $48 million for Superfund activities through September 30, 1986.

The conferees for the substantive provisions of Superfund have reached agreement. The only remaining issue is the kind of tax that will be used to fund the program. I am hopeful that the Superfund tax conferees will conclude work on their title of the bill shortly after we return from the Labor Day recess. Once all the conferees have reached agreement, the Superfond Program can be funded at the level envisioned by the conferees: $7.5 billion over a 5-year period.

In the interim, the program faces grave funding problems that this resolution is designed to alleviate.

The money we are providing today should permit EPA to maintain its major contracts and to continue some work at Superfund sites. We support the continuation of these activities.

Fifteen million dollars is provided for remedial activity. We do not anticipate that this money will be used by EPA to sign records of decisions so that compliance with new and more complex cleanup standards agreed to by the Superfund conferees on June 13, 1986, can be avoided. In fact, EPA should be using the time until the reauthorization bill is signed to fully implement the new cleanup standards upon enactment.

I am pleased that further funding for the Superfund Program can be made available. The unfortunate pace of the Superfund conference has delayed the infusion of funds that is so badly needed. The money we provide today is not sufficient to fully fund the program, but it will prevent virtual shutdown of the program.

I urge my colleagues to support this resolution.

SUPERFUND EXTENSION URGENTLY NEEDED

Mr. STAFFORD. Mr. President, I hope that the Senate can approve this resolution immediately, because it provides money which is urgently needed by the Superfund Program.

As many Members probably know, the conferees on the nontax aspects of the Superfund legislation have reached agreement and the report will soon be ready for signature. Unfortunately, the tax conferees have not yet reached agreement, so there is no money available for this Program because the tax supporting it expired last September 30. This resolution will provide $48 million to the Superfund program, enough to keep it running at a minimal level until September 30. This should provide time for the tax differences to be worked out.

Mr. President, I would like to say that this extension would not have been possible without the assistance and perseverance of the Senator from New Jersey, Senator LAUTENBERG. He has been a steadfast supporter of this program and has worked at every turn to assure that it continues to operate as well as possible under these very difficult circumstances. I would also like to thank my fellow Senator from Vermont, Senator LEAHY, for his help. He has worked closely with our counterparts on the House side to assure that we were able to reach an understanding agreeable to both bodies. Bringing the many different parties together on a matter as contentious and complex as this law is no small feat and both Senators LAUTENBERG and LEAHY deserve credit for their efforts.

Finally, Mr. President, I would like to assure that the Senator from Delaware, Senator ROTH, is included as a cosponsor of this resolution, as it was introduced in the Senate yesterday as Senate Joint Resolution 399. Although not a member of the Committee on Environment and Public Works or the Committee on Appropriations, he has been a steadfast supporter of this program, for which I express my appreciation.

Mr. President, I hope we can dispose of this matter quickly and urge my colleagues to support it.

The PRESIDING OFFICER. The Senator from New Jersey.

Mr. LAUTENBERG. Thank you, Mr. President.

I intend just to speak for a few minutes, and ask unanimous consent to submit a colloquy between the junior Senator from Vermont and myself and the full text of my remarks. In the interests of moving things along, I will just briefly summarize these remarks.

I rise to express some concerns about the interim funding measure for Superfund before us.

Two weeks ago, conferees on the programmatic portion of the Superfund Conference reached final agreement on the nonrevenue parts of the Superfund reauthorization bill. After months of tough and enormously complex negotiations we approved a vastly enlarged and strengthened Superfund bill. I felt a deep sense of satisfaction at what we had accomplished.

We came out of the negotiations with a fivefold increase in the size of the Superfund Program and we approved a bill with very stiff new requirements that we all hope will lead to a better program.

Mr. President, when we completed our deliberations on the Superfund, I believed that we would complete action on the conference report accompanying the bill before the recess that we are about to begin. However, because of the continuing conference on the tax title we obviously do not have a bill to send to the White House. Due to the work on several tax reforms, the tax conferees apparently will not be able to get to this until after the recess.

I want to say that I commend my very distinguished colleagues, the chairman of the Environment and Public Works Committee, Senator STAFFORD, and the ranking member of the HUD and Independent Agencies Subcommittee on Appropriations for their concerns over the fiscal crisis Superfund is facing, concerns which have led them to support this interim funding measure for Superfund. It is designed to be strictly a stop-gap, short-term measure. The point that I would like to make here is that I hope that with all the effort, all the commitment, and all the work that went into fashioning and crafting a Superfund bill that had teeth and had appropriate resources behind it, that we will not permit these efforts to be lost. That we will not take the pressure off Congress to complete action on Superfund.

So, Mr. President, I support keeping the pressure on, and I feel the need to raise concerns about the interim funding measure. I support ensuring that Congress get the job done on Superfund, and have some questions about the measure before us. I am first and foremost behind enactment of the Su-perfund reauthorization, and hope that all of us here will recognize that the Environmental Protection Agency and the Superfund Program will have to get on with the task of cleaning up this Nation's toxic waste sites as quickly as we give them the resources to do so.

Mr. President, I rise to speak with some degree of ambivalence.

Two weeks ago, conferees on the programmatic portion of the Superfund Conference reached final agreement on the nonrevenue parts of the Superfund reauthorization bill. After months of tough and enormously complex negotiations, we approved a vastly enlarged and strengthened Superfund bill. I felt a deep sense of satisfaction at what we had accomplished. We came out of those negotiations with a fivefold increase in the size of the Superfund Program. And, we approved a bill with stiff new requirements that I hope will lead to a better program.

Our bill provides for the first Federal right-to-know requirements, to make sure that communities and emergency response personnel know about the chemicals nearby, and how to respond in case of an emergency. I authored those provisions and fought long and hard to keep them in conference, against a lot of opposition.

Our bill also established Federal clean up standards, to avoid quick fixes at Superfund sites, and gives citizens the right to sue when EPA is not doing its job. It provides, for the first time, health assessments at Superfund sites, and meaningful Federal participation in cleaning up contaminated ground water.

Mr. President, when we completed our deliberations on the Superfund bill, I believed that we would complete action on the conference report accompanying the bill before the recess that begins today. However, due to continuing disagreement over the tax title, we cannot send a bill to the White House today. Because of their work on the tax reform bill, the tax conferees have been distracted from this task.

Mr. President, while there had been some optimisim that the conference on the tax reform bill was nearing conclusion, it appears that the conferees will not complete action before recess. This will make it doubly hard for them to work on Superfund legislation. I have joined with the two Senators from Vermont in writing to Senator PACKWOOD and Congressman ROSTENKOWSKI, chairmen of the Finance and Ways and Means Committees, asking for prompt resolution of this issue when we reconvene in September.

Mr. LAUTENBERG. Mr. President, it is this impasse over the tax title of the bill that is the genesis of this interim funding measure for Superfund. In March, I sponsored a $150 million interim funding measure for Superfund, which was enacted into law, to keep the Superfund Program intact during a very sensitive 60-day period of the Superfund Conference. At that time, many of us considered it a close call whether or not we should provide interim funding for Superfund. Ultimately, many of my colleagues, including the two Senators from Vermont, joined in a modest, short lived, interim funding measure to keep the program afloat during this period of time.

We wanted to keep pressure on the conference, and the administration, to work constructively toward a reauthorized program. However, we did not want to destroy the integrity of the Superfund Program. We wanted to make sure that Superfund employees at EPA were not fired. We wanted to make sure that Superfund contracts were not cancelled, and that work at sites continued. We wanted to make sure that adequate funds existed for emergency actions.

So, Mr. President, we arrived at what we considered just the right balance. We pumped enough funding into the program—$150 million for 2 months—to keep Superfund employees on board, and Superfund contractors intact. We provided enough money to keep clean up projects going and adequate funds available for emergency actions and removals.

With the failure of the Congress to enact a conference report on Superfund today, we again face the threat of serious disruption to the program. The Administrator of EPA, Lee Thomas, has notified Congress in a letter dated August 13, has discussed the fiscal situation of Superfund. I ask unanimous consent that this letter be inserted in the RECORD following my remarks.

The PRESIDING OFFICER. Without objection, it is so ordered.

(See exhibit 1.)

Mr. LAUTENBERG. Mr. Thomas states that if no further interim funding is provided, he will have to send out termination notices for cleanup contracts on September 1. Critical cleanup work will be sharply curtailed. That is not a pleasant prospect.

This situation, Mr. President, is the genesis of the bill before us. And, I compliment the two Senators from Vermont. They are a good team for their State, one of the most environmentally conscious in our Nation. The senior Senator from Vermont, Senator STAFFORD, is the able chairman of the Environment and Public Works Committee, on which I serve. The junior Senator from Vermont is the ranking minority member of the Appropriations Subcommittee which oversees environmental programs. They have worked in close cooperation on this measure, in an effort to avoid damage and disruption to the Superfund Program. They have been responsible and I commend them for their concern and leadership.

Mr. President, my reservations about the bill go to the question of timing on the rest of the Superfund Conference, and the prospects that the President will veto the Superfund bill.

This measure would add an additional $48 million to existing funding for the Superfund Program. These funds will be used to fund core Superfund projects and conduct removal and remedial actions at specific Superfund sites. I join with my colleagues from Vermont in supporting funding for these endeavors. My only concern is that providing these funds could reduce pressure on the conferees to finish their work on the Superfund tax title, playing into the hands of an administration that has already threatened to veto this bill.

Mr. President, I earnestly hope that this interim funding measure does not take pressure off the conferees on the tax portion of the conference to come to a timely agreement on a financing mechanism for the Superfund Program. It would be tragic if the work of the programmatic conferees, work that produced a stronger and better Superfund bill, were to be lost because of delay in coming to agreement on the rest of the legislation.

But, Mr. President, the greater danger is that delay in completing action on Superfund legislation will make possible a pocket veto of this bill by the President. If interim funding takes the pressure off Congress to complete action, we may not vote on a conference report until late September. With Congress scheduled to recess on October 3, President Reagan will be in a position to kill Superfund by inaction. He could pocket veto the bill and Congress would not be in session to override it.

Mr. President, the White House and Department of the Treasury have already threatened a veto of the Superfund bill unless the Congress scales the program way back, and raises revenues for it according to the President's lights.

As my colleagues well know, the conferees authorized a $9 billion Superfund Program, including the Underground Storage Tank Program. But, the administration has consistently said it would veto a Superfund bill larger than $5.3 billion. Further, the administration has said it will veto a bill which incorporates the Senate's broad-based tax to finance the program. This tax would broaden the base of the financing mechanism for Superfund, taking into account the large range of industrial and commercial users of products with toxic byproducts. I support this broad based tax. And it has overwhelming support in the Senate. But, the President has said he will veto any bill that includes a financing mechanism that broadens the tax for this program.

Mr. President, I think that President Reagan misreads the American public and their concern about the environment. In my home State of New Jersey, public opinion polls show environmental protection is the No. 1 priority. A recent national poll by NBC and the Wall Street Journal indicates that 67 percent of the American people viewed cleaning up toxic wastes as more important than tax reform. Another poll by CBS and the New York Times indicated that 67 percent of the American people agreed that requirements for cleaning up toxic wastes cannot be too high, regardless of the costs. This is quite a mandate for a strong, well funded Superfund.

If the President is willing to ignore this mandate, we are entering another very sensitive window on Superfund legislation. The threat of a Presidential veto must be taken seriously. And, as we get closer to our adjournment date, it gets more and more likely that the President could veto a bill without giving the Congress a chance to override that veto.

Today I contacted Lee Thomas to seek what assurances I could that he would recommend that the President sign the reauthorization legislation. In response to my call, Mr. Thomas has sent up a letter underscoring his concern that the Superfund Program be reauthorized as quickly as possible. Mr. President, let me quote from this letter:

The Superfund Program is again at a crisis point—Superfund is near collapse. It is crucial that Congress complete a full reauthorization of Superfund as soon as possible. I cannot overemphasize the urgency I place on swift congressional action. Interim funding represents nothing more than a stop-gap means for maintaining the Superfund's infrastructure during the final days of debate. In no way does it eliminate or diminish the urgency of the situation.

I ask unanimous consent that a copy of this letter be inserted in the RECORD.

Mr. President, this does not sound like a veto message to me. When our bill lands on the President's desk, I hope he heeds the words of his chief environmental steward about the urgency or enacting this legislation into law. And, in the days ahead, I hope he does not use his leverage of a veto threat to try and weaken the bill, or reduce the funding which will be available in the years ahead to clean up toxic wastes.

Mr. President, to address these concerns I have raised, I would like to engage in a brief colloquy with the junior Senator from Vermont about the scope and intent of this interim funding measure.

Mr. LAUTENBERG. Mr. President, I would like to ask the Senator from Vermont about the necessity and scope of the measure before us. What is the status of available funds for the Superfund Program?

Mr. LEAHY. Mr. President, as Lee Thomas stressed in his August 13 letter, the Superfund Program will be facing a fiscal crisis on September 1. Notices of termination will have to be sent to cleanup contractors. Removal and remedial actions will be severely curtailed. In fact, according to Mr. Thomas, work at some 76 remedial projects, 10 of which are in New Jersey, will stop at the end of September, if we do not respond with interim funding. In sum, the program, already operating at a reduced level will be pushed to the brink of no longer being able to respond to the serious hazardous waste problems we are facing. I am convinced that this interim funding measure is necessary.

Mr. LAUTENBERG. Mr. President, can the distinguished Senator clarify whether there are any other sources of money available to EPA to respond to the needs you have described?

Mr. LEAHY. Mr. President, according to EPA, the Agency lacks any other sources of funding sufficient to address the urgent needs facing the Superfund Program.

Mr. LAUTENBERG. Mr. President, the Senator from Vermont has outlined a real crisis in the Superfund Program if we do not pass this legislation. Could the Senator explain how the measure before us responds to this crisis, without taking the pressure off Congress to achieve prompt final passage of the Superfund reauthorization?

Mr. LEAHY. Mr. President, I should begin my response by making it clear that the measure before us has been carefully tailored to achieve this goal. It provides only $48 million, enough funds to postpone a real crisis through the month of September but not so much so as to carry the program for any extended length of time. Even with this funding measure, contract termination notices must issue on October 1. So let there be no doubt, the pressure will remain on Congress to complete action on reauthorization as soon as possible in September.

Let me describe the details of just how carefully structured this measure is. First, it places a date certain for the obligation of $15 million for removal and remedial actions. This sum must be obligated by September 30. Fifteen million dollars is the amount that EPA has deemed necessary to carry on the remedial and removal activities at the sites specifically identified in attachment B of Lee Thomas' August 13 letter.

Second, $19 million is explicitly designated to continue ongoing contracts and to replace contracts for essential services. This money is intented to be used to continue action on the 14 cleanup contracts identified in Mr. Thomas' letter as being subject to termination notices on September 1, and to replace the three categories of contracts, listed as items 4, 5, and 6 on page 4 of attachment A of this letter.

Third, $14 million is appropriated to satisfy the Anti-Deficiency Act requirements for cleanup contracts. This is the sum that EPA has indicated it is required by law to have to cover the termination costs associated with such contracts.

Fourth, the measure explicitly prohibits EPA from reobligating any of the $150 million of the previous interim funding measure.

Thus, the measure before us today has been crafted to avert the crisis for 30 days, to ensure that EPA obligates the money for its essential needs, and to keep the pressure on for Congress to complete action on the bill with all deliberate speed.

Mr. LAUTENBERG. Mr. President, the Senator from Vermont has cross referenced the obligation of specific sums to specific sites, contracts, and contract categories noted in Lee Thomas' August 13 letters. I would inquire whether EPA has assured the Senator that such sums will be obligated at such sites and for such contracts?

Mr. LEAHY. Mr. President, EPA has assured us that the sums specified in the legislation will be obligated for the sites, contracts, and contract categories I have cross referenced to Mr. Thomas' letter. They have also assured us that the designated sums are the minimum amounts to achieve these specified purposes.

Mr. LAUTENBERG. Mr. President, I thank the Senator for his clarifications. As ranking minority member of EPA's Appropriations Subcommittee, he had to make a tough call. He had to decide whether to move to provide interim funding now, or to wait until September to see whether we could conclude action on the conference, before taking this step.

The Senators from Vermont are both concerned about the Superfund Program, and I share their concern. I commend the two Senators for their concern. It is always a pleasure to do business with them on the environment and public works and appropriations committees.

Mr. President, I think the President would be making a terrible mistake if he were to veto the Superfund bill. The Congress has spent more than 2 years working on this legislation. There is a strong consensus in the Congress that this is a good bill, desperately needed. The American people want these waste sites cleaned up. The Congress has written a good, strong bill to improve this program. Mr. President, I urge the tax conferees on the Superfund bill to move promptly on the tax title when we return from recess, so that we can spend a bill to the White House in time to respond to a veto, should one be sent to the Congress.

(Conclusion of later proceedings.)

EXHIBIT 1

ENVIRONMENTAL PROTECTION AGENCY
Washington, DC, August 15, 1986.
Hon. FRANK LAUTENBERG,
U.S. Senate,
Washington, DC.

DEAR SENATOR LAUTENBERG: As you and I have discussed several times, the Superfund program is again at a crisis point, while we have all struggled during the past year and one half to craft a strong and workable reauthorization, we at EPA have also worked very hard to maintain the integrity of the Superfund program itself. We have succeeded in keeping the program intact with limited resources, but even those funds are now virtually exhausted. Superfund is near collapse.

It is crucial that Congress complete a full reauthorization of Superfund as soon as possible. We must get on with the strong national cleanup effort that was underway a year ago when the original law expired.

The Superfund legislation which emerged from the Conference Committee will greatly expand our cleanup program. While we may disagree about certain provisions in the final compromise, I think the new law, if enacted, will enable us to get back to our priority task quickly.

But before we can proceed with the aggressive cleanup effort we all want, Congress must complete the reauthorization. I cannot overemphasize the urgency I place on swift Congressional action.

Interim funding represents nothing more than a stop-gap means for maintaining Superfund's infrastructure during the final days of debate. In no way does it eliminate or diminish the urgency of the situation.

I appreciate your support on this matter. And I urge you to continue to push for a full reauthorization of Superfund.

Sincerely,

LEE M. THOMAS,
Administrator.

Mr. LAUTENBERG. Mr. President, I ask unanimous consent that there may be printed in the RECORD at this point certain letters relating to this matter.

There being no objection, the letters were ordered to be printed in the RECORD, as follows:

COMMITTEE ON ENVIRONMENT
AND PUBLIC WORKS,
Washington, DC, August 14, 1986.
Hon. DAN ROSTENKOWSKI,
Chairman, Committee on Ways and Means, Longworth House Office Building, Washington, DC.
Hon. BOB PACKWOOD,
Chairman, Committee on Finance, Dirksen Senate Office Building, Washington, DC.

DEAR MESSRS. CHAIRMEN: This is to urge you, in the strongest possible terms, to turn to the question of how to finance the Superfund program immediately upon your return from the August recess.

Attached is a letter from Lee Thomas, Administrator of the Environmental Protection Agency, describing the current status of the Superfund program due to lack of funding. His letter focuses primarily on the impact of a funding loss on contractors. What should not be lost is the fact that this is merely the latest development in steady program deterioration that began over one year ago when it became apparent that there was a Congressional impasse.

The non-tax conferees have now reached agreement on the several hundred issues which separated the House and Senate bills. The papers can soon be signed. All that will remain to be done is reach agreement on a revenue mechanism.

There have been repeated assurances that such an agreement could be reached between the two revenue Committees almost immediately upon resolution of the non-tax issues. If that is so, attendance to the Superfund issues should divert attention from the tax reform bills for no more than a few hours. This would be a small sacrifice for the sake of guaranteeing the rest of the Congress and the American public that the Superfund program will once again, and for the forseeable future, be on sound footing.

With every passing day, the chance of the thousands of hours spent on the non-tax issues having been wasted increases because of the possibility that agreement might not be reached on tax matters. It is fair to say that each and every Member of the non-tax conference considers this to have been the most difficult legislative challenge they have ever undertaken or witnessed. It would be a tragedy if, having come so far, it were all to be for nought.

We understand that general tax reform is uppermost in your minds. We also understand that the delay in extending the Superfund tax may have been due in no fault of the revenue committees. Nevertheless, we hope that Superfund can be made the first and only order of business after the recess so that a bill can be sent to the President for signature with no delay.

Thank you in advance for your consideration of this request.

Sincerely,

ROBERT T. STAFFORD,
PATRICK J. LEAHY,
MAX BAUCUS,
GARY HART,
FRANK R. LAUTENBERG.

U.S. ENVIRONMENTAL PROTECTION
AGENCY,
Washington, DC, August 13, 1986.

Hon. ROBERT STAFFORD,
Chairman, Committee on Environment and Public Works, U.S. Senate, Washington, DC.

DEAR MR. CHAIRMAN: Your leadership and the involvement of the many Members of the Superfund Conference have now led to resolution of the program portion of the legislation. It is clear, of course, that the legislation will not be acted upon before Congress recesses until September. I am hopeful Congress will act soon after returning. However, unless additional interim funding is received before Congress leaves, I will have to take actions that will impair the long term viability of the Superfund program. This will delay even further the return to a fully expanded cleanup effort to protect the public health and environment of our Nation.

Current funding levels will only support our contracts through the end of September. Unless interim funding is provided, I will be sending notices to contractors on September 1 which will result in fully terminating two of our contracts and partially terminating another twelve contracts as of September 30. Over 40 sub-contractors and 600 contractor personnel will be affected by this decision. Attachment A provides a list of contractors that will receive these notices. The direct costs of these terminations is estimated at $6 million. The costs of delay, loss of talented staff and contractors will be much higher, both in dollars and public protection.

Other contracts will also be affected. Without further funding, we will not be able to award new contracts to replace those which normally expire in September. Even those contracts which we do not legally need to terminate will be of little use to us because we will not have adequate funding to support ongoing work. This will have a serious impact on their personnel also. In our contract lab program alone, over 1,000 people will be affected. These disruptions will place enormous pressures on contractors who are striving to maintain the integrity of their staffs during this period of uncertainty.

We have already taken drastic steps to avoid these actions. We have tried to stretch our funding by all possible means. We have minimized our emergency response program to respond to only the most significant and immediate threats to human health or the environment. We have managed our contracts to conserve funding to the maximum extent possible without jeopardizing site work. We have closely scrutinized our contract balances to deobligate and reuse any unexpended funds. As a last ditch effort, we are deobligating site work that would continue past September 30 in order to redirect those funds into our absolutely critical program needs. However, even these actions fall far short of providing the funding necessary to support our contract infrastructure beyond September 30.

Due to the lack of funding, critical site work in both the removal and remedial program is being sharply curtailed. Work will cease at approximately 76 projects by September 30 as funding runs out. Starting in October, another 46 projects will also begin phasing out as remaining funds are used up. Our emergency removal program, which is already operating at a reduced level, is also facing devastating cutbacks. We have already been forced to demobilize our ongoing efforts at 29 removal actions so far this year. These sites have been stabilized at this stage, but are not yet completed. Without additional funding, we will be forced to leave work uncompleted at another 12 actions before the end of September. For your information, Attachment B provides a list of these affected sites.

I must also consider taking actions to plan for an extended employee furlough under reduction-in-force procedures. Even though I have allotted sufficient funding to retain our staff through the end of December, we need adequate leadtime to initiate open discussions with employees, establish retention registers, and allow employees to exercise their options.

The process is a lengthy and complicated one which must be executed with great sensitivity. It affects not only Superfund employees, but employees throughout the entire Agency. It is a virtual certainty that Superfund employees will displace other Agency employees from positions for which they are eligible. As good managers, it is incumbent upon us to conduct the process with utmost professionalism.

Throughout the year we stretched our funding while Congress worked on Superfund reauthorization. Congress provided $150 million in interim funding in April which enabled us to continue the program. However, we are now at a crucial impasse. We can no longer maintain, even at the current minimum levels, the entire Superfund program as an integrated response to abandoned and uncontrolled hazardous sites. Unless reauthorization is enacted or interim funding is received prior to the upcoming Congressional recess, I am now faced with dismantling the program, piece by piece, beginning in two weeks and continuing over the next 30 to 45 days.

Given the gravity of the situation and the short time remaining before Congress goes on recess, I urge that you actively support an interim funding measure to avoid lasting disruption to the program's performance.

Sincerely,

LEE M. THOMAS.

ATTACHMENT A.—CONTRACTS TO BE TERMINATED ON 9/30/86 DUE TO CERCLA REAUTHORIZATION DELAYS

Contract No.	Contract title	Prime contractor	Subcontractors	Complete (C) or partial termination
68-01-6939	REM II	Camp Dresser & McKee (CDM)	Woodward Clyde.	P
			ICF.	
			Clement Association.	
			Roy F. Weston.	
			C.C. Johnson.	
68-01-7050	Superfund policy support	CH₂M Hill	Versar.	P
			ICF.	
			Environ.	
			Envire. Law Institute.	
68-01-7250	REM III	Ebasco Services, Inc.	Engineering & Economics Research, Inc.	P
			E.C. Jordan.	
			Environmental Science & Engineering.	
			ICF.	
			NUS Corp.	
			AEPCO.	
			C.C. Johnson.	
			Techno, Inc.	
			Westor Geophysical Corp.	
			Environmental Testing & Certification Corp.	
68-01-7251	REM IV	CH₂M Hill	Aqualisc, Inc.	P
			Ecology & Environment	
			Planning Research Corp.	
			Black & Veatch.	
68-01-7054	National Priorities List Program	The MITRE Corp.	ICF.	P
68-01-7104	Evidence audit and case file preparation assistance	Techlaw, Inc.	N.A.	C
68-01-7753	Contract lab program management	Viar	N.A.	C
68-01-7159	QA/QC support for contract lab program	University of Las Vegas	N/A.	C
68-01-3161	Aerial imagery interpretation and analysis	Bionetics.	N/A.	C
68-01-3255	Emergency environmental response unit	Enviresponse, Inc.	NUS Corp.	C
68-01-3249	Collection and analysis of environmental samples.	Lockheed Engineering & Management Services Co (LEMSCO)	Princeton Aqua Science.	P
			N/A.	
68-01-3245	Remote Sensing	Camp, Dresser & McKee.	Versar, Inc.	P
68 01-7331	Technical enforcement support at hazardous waste sites [FTS 3]		Booz Allen & Hamilton, Inc.	P
			PRC Environmental Management, Inc.	
			TechLaw, Inc.	
			Label Anderson, Inc.	
			Priekt Sedgwick, Inc.	
			Geoscience Consultants Ltd.	
			SRA Technologies, Inc.	
			Life Systems, Inc.	
			Hydraulic & Water Resources Engineers, Inc.	
			AEPCO, Inc.	
			Sobotka & Co. Inc.	
			Geo Resources, Inc.	
			Lee Wan & Associates, Inc.	
			Putnam, Hayes & Bartlett, Inc.	
68-03-3206	Hazardous sample repository	Northrop	N/A.	P

Note.—Contracts in the Contract Laboratory Program (CLP) would not be terminated as we have met our minimum obligations under these contracts. However, additional work up to the contracts' maximums would not be ordered. This would significantly and adversely affect the 94 laboratories in CLP.

NEW CONTRACTS WHICH CANNOT BE AWARDED BY 9/30/86 DUE TO CERCLA REAUTHORIZATION DELAYS

Contract title	Potential contract value
1. Transportation and disposal services at Schaffer site	$800,000
2. Technical assistance teams (TAT) for removal program—zone I	150,000,000
3. Technical assistance teams (TAT) for removal program—zone II	100,000,000
4. Field investigation teams (FIT) for remedial program—zone I	115,000,000
5. Field investigation teams (FIT) for remedial program—zone II	160,000,000
6. Technical enforcement services (TES IV)	60,000,000
7. Evidence audit and case file preparation	11,000,000

ATTACHMENT B—REMEDIAL PROJECTS WHERE WORK WILL STOP ON SEPTEMBER 30, 1986

REGION I

Yaworski Lagoon, CT.
Charles George Reclamation, MA.
Iron Horse Park, MA.
Re-Solve, MA.
Davis Liquid, RI.

REGION II

Chemical Control, NJ.
De Rewal Township, NJ.
Fried Industries, NJ.
Lang Property, NJ.
Lipari Landfill, NJ.
Lone Pine Landfill, NJ.
Myers Property, NJ.
Reich Farms, NJ.
Tabernacle Drum Dump, NJ.
Waldick Aerospace, NJ.
Katonah Well, NY.
Robintech/Nat'l Pipe, NY.
Sarney Farm, NY.

REGION III

Kane & Lombard, MD.
Sand Gravel & Stone, MD.
Southern Maryland Wood, MD.
Amchem/Ambler, PA.
L.A. Clarke, VA.

REGION IV

Mowbray Engineering, AL.
Zellwood Groundwater, FL.
SCRDI Dixiana, SC.
Wamchem, SC.

REGION V

Byron Salvage Yard, IL.
Kerr-McGee, IL.
American Chemical, IN.
Envirochem Corp., IN.
Fisher-Calo, IN.
Fort Wayne Reduction Dump, IN.
Main Street Wellfield, IN.

Marion (Bragg) Dump, IN.
Midco I, IN.
Midco II, IN.
Northside Landfill, IN.
Butterworth #2 Landfill, MI.
G&H Landfill, MI.
Ionia City Landfill, MI.
K&L Avenue Landfill, MI.
Mason County Landfill, MI.
Packaging Corp., MI.
Tar Lake, MI.
Verona Wellfield, MI.
Industrial Excess, OH.
Miami City Incinerator, OH.
Pristine, Inc., OH.
Skinner Landfill, OH.
South Point Plant, OH.
United Scrap Lead, OH.
Eau Claire Wellfield, WI.
Master Disposal, WI.
Mid-State Disposal, WI.
Moss American, WI.
Schmalz Dump, WI.

REGION VI

United Nuclear Corp., NM.
Motco, TX.

REGION VII

Cherokee County, KS.
Doepke Holliday, KS.
Fulbright Landfill, MO.
Hastings Ground Water, NE.
Waverly Ground Water, NE.

REGION VIII

Broderick Wood, CO.
Central City, CO.
East Helena Site, MT.
Monticello Radioactive, UT.

REGION IX

Atlas Asbestos Mine, CA.
Coalinga Asbestos, CA.
Operating Industries, CA.
San Fernando, CA.
Stringfellow Acid Pit, CA.
Ordot Landfill, GU.

REGION X

Comm. Bay/Nearshore, WA.
Comm. Bay/S. Tacoma Channel.

REMOVAL ACTIONS WHERE WORK WILL STOP ON SEPTEMBER 30, 1986

REGION I

South Bank, NH.
Tibbetts Rd., NH.
Auburn, NH.

REGION II

Madison Wireworks, NY.
Fulton Terminals, NY.

REGION III

East Kane Tar Pit, PA.
North Road Landfill, PA.
Paoli Railyard, PA.
Son of Lansdowne, PA.

REGION V

Carter Industrial, MI.

REGION VII

Minker/Stout/Romaine Creek, MO.

REGION VIII
Montana Pole, MT.

REMOVAL ACTIONS WHERE WORK WAS
STOPPED DUE TO FUNDING CONSTRAINTS
BEFORE COMPLETION

REGION II
Shirley-Broadway, NY.
Friendship Drive, NY.
Gozzola Drive, NY.
Honeyoe Falls, NY.

REGION III
Walsh Landfill, PA.
Ryeland Road, PA.
Rotunda Drive, PA.
Roanoke River Drugs, VA.
Shaffer Site, WV.
Howard Rogers Prop., PA.
Pagan Road, PA.
Johnson Bronze, PA.
Sandonelle, PA.

REGION IV
Naomi Drug Site, GA.
Aberdeen Pesticides, NC.

REGION V
International Disk Corp, MI.
Laskin Poplar, OH.
Midco II, IN.
Conservation Chemical, IN.
Greiners Lagoon, OH.
Commercial Oil, OH.

REGION VI
Filling Station, TX.
FM 518, TX.
Heritage/Laurel, TX.
Dempsey/Holly, TX.

REGION VII
Castle Wood Community, MO.

REGION IX
Garvey Ave., CA.

REGION X
Pallister Paint, WA.
Standard Steel, AK.

Mr. STAFFORD. Mr. President, I move the adoption of the joint resolution.

The PRESIDING OFFICER. The question is on the third reading and passage of the joint resolution.

The joint resolution (H.J. Res. 713) was ordered to a third reading, was read the third time and passed.

Mr. STAFFORD. Mr. President, I move to reconsider the vote by which the joint resolution was passed.

Mr. LEAHY. I move to lay that motion on the table.

The motion to lay on the table was agreed to.

IA

99TH CONGRESS
2D SESSION **H. J. RES. 727**

Making repayable advances to the Hazardous Substance Response Trust Fund.

IN THE HOUSE OF REPRESENTATIVES

SEPTEMBER 16, 1986

Mr. WHITTEN introduced the following joint resolution; which was referred to the Committee on Appropriations

JOINT RESOLUTION

Making repayable advances to the Hazardous Substance Response Trust Fund.

1   *Resolved by the Senate and House of Representatives*

2 *of the United States of America in Congress assembled,*

3 That language under the heading "Environmental Protection

4 Agency, Hazardous Substance Response Trust Fund" in

    Public Law 99–160, as amended by Public Law 99–270 and

    Public Law 99–411, is further amended by deleting

5 "$702,000,000 shall be derived from the Hazardous Sub-

8 stance Response Trust Fund and $198,000,000 shall be de-

9 rived from advances from the general fund of the Treasury to

10 the Hazardous Substance Response Trust Fund to be repaid

11 in accordance with section 223(c)(3) of Public Law 96–510

1 and notwithstanding section 223(c)(2)(D) of Public Law 96–

2 510: *Provided*, That none of the $150,000,000 made avail-

3 able by Public Law 99–270 shall be available for obligation

4 after May 31, 1986: *Provided further*, That of the additional

5 $48,000,000 made immediately available, $15,000,000 shall

6 be obligated by September 30, 1986, for continuation of on-

7 going remedial and removal site work and $19,000,000 shall

8 be used only to continue ongoing contracts and to replace

9 contracts for essential services:" and inserting in lieu thereof

10 "$102,000,000 shall be derived from the Hazardous Sub-

11 stance Response Trust Fund and $798,000,000 shall be de-

12 rived from advances from the general fund of the Treasury to

13 the Hazardous Substance Response Trust Fund to be repaid

14 in accordance with section 223(c)(3) of Public Law 96–510

15 and notwithstanding section 223(c)(2)(D) of Public Law 96–

16 510: *Provided*, That none of the $150,000,000 made avail-

17 able by Public Law 99–270 shall be available for obligation

18 after May 31, 1986: *Provided further*, That of the

19 $48,000,000 made available by Public Law 99–411,

20 $15,000,000 shall be obligated by September 30, 1986, for

21 continuation of ongoing remedial and removal site work and

22 $19,000,000 shall be used only to continue ongoing contracts

23 and to replace contracts for essential services: *Provided fur-*

24 *ther*, That none of the additional $600,000,000 advanced to

25 the Hazardous Substance Response Trust Fund by this joint

3

1 resolution shall be available for obligation until Superfund

2 taxing authority is enacted:".

○

99TH CONGRESS 2d Session	HOUSE OF REPRESENTATIVES	REPORT 99–830

MAKING REPAYABLE ADVANCES TO THE HAZARDOUS SUBSTANCE RESPONSE TRUST FUND

SEPTEMBER 16, 1986.—Mr. Whitten introduced the following joint resolution; which was referred to the Committee on Appropriations

SEPTEMBER 16, 1986.—Committed to the Committee of the Whole House on the State of the Union and ordered to be printed

Mr. WHITTEN, by direction of the Committee on Appropriations, submitted the following

REPORT

[To accompany H.J. Res. 727]

The accompanying joint resolution provides a repayable advance of $600,000,000 from the general fund of the Treasury to the hazardous substance response (Superfund) trust fund. None of these additional funds made available to the hazardous substance response trust fund shall be available for obligation by the Environmental Protection Agency until after enactment of Superfund taxing authority.

This joint resolution addresses a technical problem. If the Superfund authorizing legislation and taxing authority is not enacted by September 30, 1986, approximately $600,000,000 of the remaining 1986 appropriation will expire. This measure will protect those funds and allow them to be carried over into 1987 and beyond, as originally intended in the 1986 HUD-Independent Agencies Appropriations Act.

This joint resolution provides no new budget authority and no additional outlays. The advance from the general fund will be repaid from future Superfund taxes as they are enacted. The Committee emphasizes that no additional funds would be made available by this joint resolution until the Superfund program and its taxes are reauthorized. The Committee also assures that this measure would in no way breach the $8.5 billion 5-year authorization level agreed to by the Superfund conferees over the fiscal year 1987–91 period.

Finally, the Committee wants to emphasize that time is of the essence in the execution of the repayable advance authorized by this joint resolution. It is essential that the $600,000,000 be advanced to and deposited in the hazardous substance response trust fund by September 30, 1986. The Committee expects the Administration to take all necessary steps to expedite this advance and to assure that it is completed by the September 30, 1986, deadline.

COMPLIANCE WITH RULE XIII—CLAUSE 3

In compliance with Clause 3 of Rule XIII of the Rules of the House of Representatives, changes in existing law made by the bill, as reported, are shown as follows (existing law proposed to be omitted is enclosed in black brackets, new matter is printed in italic, existing law in which no change is proposed is shown in roman):

Language under the heading "Environmental Protection Agency, Hazardous Substance Response Trust Fund" in Public Law 99-160, as amended by Public Law 99-270 and Public Law 99-411, is further amended as follows:

HAZARDOUS SUBSTANCE RESPONSE TRUST FUND

For necessary expenses to carry out the Comprehensive Environmental Response, Compensation, and Liability Act of 1980, including sections 111 (c)(3), (c)(5), (c)(6), and (e)(4) (42 U.S.C. 9611), $900,000,000, of which [$702,000,000 shall be derived from the Hazardous Substance Response Trust Fund and $198,000,000 shall be derived from advances from the general fund of the Treasury to the Hazardous Substance Response Trust Fund to be repaid in accordance with section 223(c)(3) of Public Law 96-510 and notwithstanding section 223(c)(2)(D) of Public Law 96-510: *Provided,* That none of the $150,000,000 made available by Public Law 99-270 shall be available for obligation after May 31, 1986: *Provided further,* That of the additional $48,000,000 made immediately available, $15,000,000 shall be obligated by September 30, 1986, for continuation of ongoing remedial and removal site work and $19,000,000 shall be used only to continue ongoing contracts and to replace contracts for essential services:] *$102,000,000 shall be derived from the Hazardous Substance Response Trust Fund and $798,000,000 shall be derived from advances from the general fund of the Treasury to the Hazardous Substance Response Trust Fund to be repaid in accordance with section 223(c)(3) of Public Law 96-510 and notwithstanding section 223(c)(2)(D) of Public Law 96-510: Provided, That none of the $150,000,000 made available by Public Law 99-270 shall be available for obligation after May 31, 1986: Provided further, That of the $48,000,000 made available by Public Law 99-411, $15,000,000 shall be obligated by September 30, 1986, for continuation of ongoing remedial and removal site work and $19,000,000 shall be used only to continue ongoing contracts and to replace contracts for essential services: Provided further, That none of the additional $600,000,000 advanced to the Hazardous Substance Response Trust Fund by this joint resolution shall be available for obligation until Superfund taxing authority is enacted: Provided further, That all funds appropriated shall remain available until expended, except as specified above: Provided further, That funds appropri-*

3

ated under this account may be allocated to other Federal agencies in accordance with section 111(a) of Public Law 96-510: *Provided further*, That for performance of specific activities in accordance with section 104(i) of Public Law 96-510, the Comprehensive Environmental Response, Compensation, and Liability Act of 1980, $21,000,000 shall be made available to the Department of Health and Human Services, to be derived by transfer from the Hazardous Substance Response Trust Fund, of which no less than $5,125,000 shall be available for toxicological testing of hazardous substances. For necessary expenses to carry out the Comprehensive Environmental Response, Compensation, and Liability Act of 1980, as amended, not to exceed $90,000,000 shall be available for administrative expenses.

INFLATIONARY IMPACT STATEMENT

Pursuant to clause 2(l)(4), Rule XI of the House of Representatives, the Committee states that in its opinion this resolution, as proposed, will have no overall inflationary impact over the broad spectrum of the Nation's economy.

O

[From the Congressional Record, Sept. 16, 1986, pp. H6948–H6951]

□ 1725

REQUEST FOR CONSIDERATION OF HOUSE JOINT RESOLUTION 727, MAKING REPAYABLE ADVANCES TO THE HAZARDOUS SUBSTANCE RESPONSE TRUST FUND

Mr. WHITTEN. Mr. Speaker, I ask unanimous consent to take from the Speaker's table the joint resolution (H.J. Res. 727) making repayable advances to the Hazardous Substance Response Trust Fund, and ask for its immediate consideration.

The Clerk read the title of the joint resolution.

The SPEAKER pro tempore. Is there objection to the request of the gentleman from Mississippi?

Mr. CONTE. Mr. Speaker, reserving the right to object, I yield to the gentleman from Mississippi to explain what is being attempted here.

Mr. WHITTEN. I thank the gentleman for yielding to me.

Mr. Speaker, the resolution will take care of what is essentially a technical problem in regard to the Superfund. It is my understanding that this has been cleared by the affected authorizing committees on both sides of the aisle. I am told that all parties in the issue are in agreement that this needs to be done.

At the end of this month there will be about $600 million remaining of the 1986 Superfund appropriation, which EPA has not obligated because the trust fund is out of money. The Appropriations Committee intended these funds to be carried over into 1987—and we specifically provided that the funds remain available until expended.

However, both OMB and GAO recognize that if there is no cash balance in a trust fund during the year of the appropriation—the appropriation expires. That is exactly the situation we face in Superfund—if new taxing authority and reauthorization is not enacted before September 30, $600 million will be lost on October 1.

This resolution will take care of the problem. It will permit the $600 million to be advanced from the general fund to the Superfund trust fund—so that it can be carried over into 1987. This action provides no new budget authority and no additional outlays. Finally, language has been included to fence these funds so that EPA cannot make any obligations until after taxing authority has been enacted.

This $600 million is essential to provide for an expanding Superfund Program in 1987 and 1988. The 1987 HUD bill provides $861 million, assuming substantial funds would carry over. If this $600 million is lost, it cannot be replaced within our 302 allocation, so the Superfund Program will suffer in 1987 and beyond.

Without a doubt, the Superfund Program is now suffering from a severe shortage of funds. However, the solution must be a long-term reauthorization bill—not another Band-Aid. Most members of the authorizing committees and supporters of Superfund believe that making additional funds available at this point would backfire and actually work to undermine or delay passage of reauthorizing and tax legislation.

Finally, let me say that this will in no way breach the $8.5 billion authorization total. This concerns the other side of the ledger—the Appropriations Committee's problem in preserving the budget authority to provide the levels of funds anticipated in the legislation. We will not exceed the $8.5 billion total for Superfund during the 1987–91 period.

Mr. FLORIO from the legislative committee is in agreement and other Members are too.

To correct that situation, I hope that we can pass this this afternoon so we can save this $600 million from expiring at the end of this fiscal year.

Mr. CONTE. Mr. Speaker, further reserving the right to object, I yield to the gentleman from New Jersey [Mr. FLORIO].

Mr. FLORIO. I thank the gentleman for yielding to me.

Mr. Speaker, I would just say that I support the motion of the chairman of the Appropriations Committee. I hasten to point out that the action that is being taken is important to take so that we do not in any way lose the opportunity to use the $600 million that has already been appropriated that will lapse on the 30th of September.

It should in no way, however, detract from the urgency of our getting an authorization before the end of this year because this step is an important step to take, but we still at the end of this period of time will have no money in the authorization. This language is quite clear that this money will be available in fiscal 1987 subject to the establishment of an authorization bill which is yet to be done this year.

I thank the gentleman and rise in support of the gentleman's motion.

Mr. CONTE. Mr. Speaker, further reserving the right to object, I yield to the gentleman from New York [Mr. GREEN].

Mr. GREEN. I thank the gentleman for yielding to me.

Mr. Speaker, I want to join the gentleman from New Jersey in his explanation of this situation. As I understand the technicalities of the matter, without this action the trust fund would expire on September 30 and this $600 million would be lost and given the budget situation in which we find ourselves it would, in all probability, be lost irretrievably. So that the effect of what we are doing is to preserve this $600 million for future use.

However, as the gentleman from New Jersey has said, that in no way reduces the need for proceeding with the resolution of the revenue issues relating to the Superfund and the resolution is so drawn as to make it clear that this money shall not be available for obligation until the new legislation with regard to the Superfund taxing authority is enacted.

So we must do this to preserve the $600 million. It should be understood that our doing this in no way reduces the urgency of resolving the revenue issues and enacting the new Superfund legislation.

Mr. CONTE. Mr. Speaker, I strongly support my chairman.

(Mr. CONTE asked and was given permission to revise and extend his remarks.)

Mr. CONTE. Mr. Speaker, I withdraw my reservation of objection.

The SPEAKER pro tempore. Is there objection to the request of the gentleman from Mississippi?

Mr. PICKLE. Mr. Speaker, I reserve the right to object.

(Mr. PICKLE asked and was given permission to revise and extend his remarks.)

Mr. PICKLE. Mr. Speaker, this motion catches me by surprise. I am sure it was unintentional and I do not question the motives. I am concerned that what you are doing here is either transferring money from one or two sources and putting it into some kind of mythical fund to use in case the authorization finally comes through.

Let me remind the chairman and the Members of the House: We have had quite a battle on the Superfund. You will recall that earlier in this Congress the Ways and Means Committee voted that the Superfund would be funded by a broad-based tax, which was passed after a very heated debate within the committee. When we got to the floor the funding was changed because the House labeled the broad-based tax as a value-added tax.

Many debates were had on it; it was not a very becoming debate. The Superfund excise tax was not a value-added tax at all; it was just an excise tax.

You have extended the Superfund, on either one or two occasions since that date. There is still considerable discussion and argument about how it is to be funded. Those people who represent States with oil and gas and chemical industries are very distressed that we cannot seem to get an equitable resolution on funding in spite of the fact that our committee voted that we would have a broad-based tax.

The onus on paying for the cleanup fund now and in the House bill is on the oil and gas industry and on the chemical industry. I see my friend from New Jersey standing here. There is more waste in sites in New Jersey then there is in any State in the United States, and yet those of us from about 4 or 5 States are paying anywhere from 60 to 90 percent of the cost. We are asking that that be spread on an equitable basis.

Now, if I understand this amendment offered today, it seems to me that what you are doing is transferring some money and then you are going to renew the Superfund again for another 30 to 60 or 90 days. If that is the case we will not have resolved this question about the Superfund again.

It is not right for us to be faced with another funding mechanism if in fact this is a back door way to avoid settling the tax issue. I am told that this does nothing but just take some money from one fund to be used just in case it is needed.

In conclusion, I fear you are just getting money from somebody else's pocket. Then you are going to renew this Superfund again just as we have before and we will never have given this House a chance to vote on it.

□ 1735

That is not right. I do not know that that is what the gentleman intends, but that is my concern. If you trot this out of chute 1 here today without us having any notice about it, we get concerned about it.

Mr. WHITTEN. Mr. Speaker, will the gentleman yield?

Mr. PICKLE. I yield to the gentleman from Mississippi.

Mr. WHITTEN. Mr. Speaker, others may want to discuss some of the specifics. The Appropriations Committee spent the afternoon on the continuing resolution before we found out that the Congress has fenced itself in a thousand ways here: The budget resolution; the fact that the other body is controlled by outlays, which is in reality controlled by the executive branch. We have been wrestling with that all afternoon, knowing what it does.

So what this joint resolution does from the viewpoint I have is that this $600 million dips into this year's budget resolution, dips into what we have already appropriated. Unless we do this, it will be out of place in the coming resolution.

I do not know whether the gentleman realizes how we have tied our hands with Gramm-Rudman and other things. So what is involved here is whether the Appropriations Committee loses it or not. It is not a case of taking it from one place to another.

My friend, the gentleman from New Jersey [Mr. FLORIO], can discuss the detailed questions that you bring up better than I can, but that is the situation so far as this $600 million is concerned.

Mr. PICKLE. Mr. Speaker, let me ask the gentleman, does the present extension for Superfund expire on September 30?

Mr. WHITTEN. On the first of October, this $600 million will expire.

Mr. PICKLE. Then if you were to get $600 million from some other source, then you could renew it again for another 30, 60 or 90 days. That is what I suspect is going to happen.

Mr. FLORIO. Mr. Speaker, will the gentleman yield?

Mr. PICKLE. I yield to the gentleman from New Jersey.

Mr. FLORIO. Mr. Speaker, by way of clarification, if I in any way had any thought that this was a back-door way of funding Superfund, I would stand shoulder-to-shoulder with the gentleman in opposition to it. That is not what this is.

The legitimate policy consideration that the gentleman raises with regard to who is to pay the amount that this bill, this basic Superfund bill, would authorize are yet to be resolved.

What the gentleman is doing, and I think commendably so, is providing for the elimination of the problem that results from the expiration of the authority to use the $600 million, which has already been appropriated, after October 1, of September 30 of this year.

That money cannot be used, absent a specific authorization by this Congress, which has not yet been forthcoming.

All we are doing is preserving the right of the Congress to utilize that money when we determine how it is that it is going to be utilized. The difficulty that the gentleman is going to have if this does not take place is that $600 million less toward the $9 billion that the Congress has already approved is going to have to be made up somewhere else.

Mr. PICKLE. If the gentleman contends that this is not back-door support and it is only getting the money to use once the authorization is effected, my question to you, then, is why does the gentleman not go and get the authorization out? Why do we not know what the vote is, instead of carving out $600 million, or whatever this sum amounts to, so we can continue the program?

I think I have one of the most reliable records on environmental matters as anybody in this Congress. Of course I think we ought to continue the Superfund.

I am willing to go for the higher sum, but I will tell the gentleman what is going to happen. If the gentleman takes this $600 million, whatever it is, to be used if it is authorized, as you say, I will tell the gentleman what is going to happen. You are going to renew the program again by September 30, probably, on the same basis as before, and you are going to be funding Superfund at about $1 to $2 billion instead of the $8.5 billion that has been agreed on between the House and the other body.

You are going to buy about one-fourth of a good program if you fail to face the question of having an authorization.

For some reason or another, you do not do it. You want to have an authorization, but you cannot handle the funding question because there is such opposition among some people here; so much so that they are going to call this broad base funding plan a value-added tax. It is not a value-added tax, although everybody can make their own choice.

I am just saying to you that what you are doing is creating a little mechanism here so you have this fund to be used once the authorization comes through. If you cannot get an authorization, then you just extend it for another 30 or 60 or 90 days. That is what you have done twice this year.

I think this is a repetition again of the same thing.

It seems to me that this is not the appropriate time to do it, certainly without some kind of notice.

Mr. CONTE. Mr. Speaker, will the gentleman yield?

Mr. PICKLE. I yield to my friend, the gentleman from Massachusetts.

Mr. CONTE. Mr. Speaker, I want the gentleman to listen carefully. We are not taking this money, $600 million, from some other place.

At the end of this month there will be about $600 million remaining of the 1986 Superfund appropriation, which EPA has not obligated because the trust fund is out of money. The Appropriations Committee intended these funds to be carried over into 1987—and we specifically provided that the funds "remain available until expended."

However, both OMB and GAO recognize that if there is no cash balance in a trust fund during the year of the appropriation—the appropriation expires. That is exactly the situation we face in Superfund—if new taxing authority and reauthorization is not enacted before September 30, $600 million will be lost on October 1.

This resolution will take care of the problem. It will permit the $600 million to be advanced from the general fund to the Superfund trust fund—so that it can be carried over into 1987. This action provides no new budget authority and no additional outlays. Finally, language has been included to fence these funds so that EPA cannot make any obligations until after taxing authority has been enacted.

Why is the $600 million so important? This $600 million is essential to provide for an expanding Superfund Program in 1987 and 1988. The 1987 HUD bill provides $861 million, assuming substantial funds would carry over. If this $600 million is lost, it cannot be replaced within our 302 allocation, so the Superfund Program will suffer in 1987 and beyond.

Why not let EPA use the funds immediately? Without a doubt, the Superfund Program is now suffering from a severe shortage of funds. However, the solution must be a long-term reauthorization bill—not another band-aid. Most members of the authorizing committees and supporters of Superfund believe that making additional funds available at this point would backfire and actually work to undermine or delay passage of reauthorizing and tax legislation.

Will this resolution bust the budget? This resolution provides no new budget authority and no additional outlays. The original $900 million 1986 appropriation has already been scored by CBO for BA and outlays. This resolution simply provides an advance from the general fund, which will be repaid from Superfund taxes as soon as they are enacted.

Will this resolution increase the $8.5 billion authorization agreed to by the Superfund conferees? No. This will in no way breach the $8.5 billion total. This concerns the other side of the ledger—and the Appropriations Committee's problem in preserving the budget authority to provide the levels of funds anticipated in the legislation. We will not exceed the $8.5 billion total for Superfund 1987-91.

Mr. PICKLE. Mr. Speaker, let me respond to the gentleman [Mr. CONTE].

The problem here is that we do not have an authorization for a Superfund and that we do not have a decision on the taxing mechanism.

Mr. CONTE. If the gentleman will yield, we agree on that.

Mr. PICKLE. Mr. Speaker, that has been delayed all this year and is still hanging in the balance.

Mr. CONTE. We agree on that, Mr. Speaker.

Mr. PICKLE. Mr. Speaker, what is the gentleman going to do that at the last minute, the gentleman from Massachusetts [Mr. CONTE], representing the Committee on Appropriations, to try to have funds to keep the Superfund so it can continue? That is your purpose, is it not?

Mr. CONTE. Mr. Speaker, the gentleman is right.

Mr. PICKLE. Mr. Speaker, so the gentleman wants to sack up money from different agencies just to have in case.

Mr. CONTE. Mr. Speaker, if the gentleman will yield further, we are not taking this from any other agency. We have already appropriated this money for the Superfund.

Mr. PICKLE. It is being redirected. It is not a new appropriation. But it is money that you are going to use and I am saying to the gentleman, the more straightforward way to do it is to settle this authorization and have a vote on it and to settle this funding question, the taxing question.

Mr. CONTE. Mr. Speaker, I could not agree with the gentleman any more. I agree with the gentleman.

However, this is money that we appropriated, $600 million for the Superfund. Because of an interpretation by OMB and GAO, we cannot spend this money. So all we are saying is that we are going to comply with you; we are going to take this $600 million that we have appropriated for the Superfund, and we are going to put it in a trust fund.

Mr. GREEN. Mr. Speaker, will the gentleman yield?

Mr. PICKLE. I yield to the gentleman from New York.

Mr. GREEN. Mr. Speaker, let me try to explain, perhaps, in a little more detail as ranking minority member of the Subcommittee on HUD-Independent Agencies of the Committee on Appropriations, which appropriates for EPA, the difficulty in which we find ourselves and why we are asking for this accommodation.

I want to represent, first off, to the gentleman that we have not the slightest intention of trying to short-circuit the conference on the Superfund or the Committee on Ways and Means on this issue.

□ 1745

Mr. PICKLE. That is comforting.

Mr. GREEN. The problem we face is that we have $600 million which was appropriated for fiscal year 1986 which will lapse on September 30 unless this resolution is dealt with and passed.

We do not have enough budget authority left to our subcommittee under the 302(b) process to fund the Superfund operations for fiscal year 1987 at the $1½ billion level, unless we can take advantage of this $600 million. If this $600 million lapses on September 30, even if the gentleman's conference thereafter succeeds, as I hope and pray it will in resolving the fiscal issues involved in the Superfund, our subcommittee will be unable to respond and operate the Superfund at a $1½ billion level unless we can keep this $600 million for fiscal year 1986 alive. That is all we are trying to do.

We are not trying to short-circuit the gentleman's negotiations in the conference. We are not trying to run an end run around the authorizing process. We are, simply, given the budget constraints under which we are operating, trying to keep ourselves able when the gentleman resolves his problems to fund the program next year at the $1½ billion level and we will not be able to do that if this resolution does not pass.

PARLIAMENTARY INQUIRY

Mr. PICKLE. Mr. Speaker, I have a parliamentary inquiry.

The SPEAKER pro tempore (Mr. MONTGOMERY). The gentleman will state it.

Mr. PICKLE. Mr. Speaker, is the motion by the gentleman from Mississippi a unanimous-consent request?

The SPEAKER pro tempore. That is correct.

Mr. WHITTEN. Mr. Speaker, will the gentleman yield to me?

Mr. PICKLE. I yield to the gentleman from Mississippi.

Mr. WHITTEN. May I say finally that language has been included to fence these funds so that the EPA cannot make any obligations until after Superfund taxing authority has been enacted. Those who handled it in the subcommittee under no circumstances would agree to the prior release of these funds.

Mr. PICKLE. Mr. Speaker, I would like to get more familiar with this. I would like to know the plans we have for a vote on the Superfund and the funding of it. I will try to cooperate with the leadership; but at this point I object, Mr. Speaker.

The SPEAKER pro tempore. Objection is heard.

5439

[From the Congressional Record, Sept. 18, 1986, pp. H7214-H7215]

MAKING REPAYABLE ADVANCES TO THE HAZARDOUS SUBSTANCE RESPONSE TRUST FUND

Mr. WHITTEN. Mr. Speaker, I ask unanimous consent for the immediate consideration of the joint resolution (H.J. Res. 727) making repayable advances to the hazardous substance response trust fund.

The Clerk read the title of the joint resolution.

The SPEAKER pro tempore. Is there objection to the request of the gentleman from Mississippi?

Mr. CONTE. Mr. Speaker, I reserve the right to object.

(Mr. CONTE asked and was given permission to revise and extend his remarks.)

Mr. WALKER. Mr. Speaker, will the gentleman yield?

Mr. CONTE. I yield to the gentleman from Pennsylvania.

Mr. WALKER. Mr. Speaker, I just want to confirm for the record that what we are doing here is taking money that was previously appropriated in this year and transferring it into the Superfund trust fund so that it has sufficient money with which to operate; but we are not coming up with any new dollars, and there is no dificit add-on involved in this particular appropriation bill.

Mr. CONTE. Mr. Speaker, the gentleman is absolutely right.

Mr. Speaker, I rise once again in support of this joint resolution on Superfund.

As I explained in great detail during Tuesday's debate, when we had first attempted to bring this up, what we are trying to do here is save about $600 million in Superfund appropriations. That's $600 million that we appropriated last November but that we will lose if we don't pass this resolution.

Let me emphasize for my colleagues that this action provides no new budget authority and no additional outlays. None. It simply transfers in a manner of speaking the $600 million already in the Superfund account to the trust fund where it can be used when we have a Superfund reauthorization enacted.

We are trying to address a technical problem here, but it is not a small one. We can't afford to lose $600 million because of a technicality. The Superfund Program can't afford to lose it, either. Lee Thomas—the Administrator of EPA—will tell you that. He's been pinching pennies for over a year waiting for a reauthorization bill. The Office of Management and Budget, and the General Accounting Office recognize that if there is no cash balance in a trust fund during the year of an appropriation, then the appropriation expires. That is the situation we are facing with the Superfund trust fund. That fund is broke. If new taxing authority and reauthorization is not enacted by September 30—12 days from now—the $600 million we have already appropriated will vanish.

Now, perhaps some of our conferees on the reauthorization bill can assure us that they will have a new bill enacted in 12 days. I haven't received any such assurances. But, as a member of the Appropriations Committee, my interest is to ensure that these funds are available as we intended them to be for the Superfund Program, whenever it is resuscitated.

Even though Superfund is gasping right now, none of this $600 million is available for expenditure under the provisions of this bill. It is fenced off. We still need the taxing authority and the reauthorization before a penny of this money can be spent. The same fence applies to the $861 million in our 1987 bill passed on Friday.

If we lose the $600 million, there's no way we'll be able to replace it in our 302(b) allocation. The big losers are going to be all of our communities with Superfund sites.

I don't like these bandaid approaches to maintaining one of the most vitally important health and environmental issues of our time. I regret that our Appropriations Committee must tai e this action today. But we have no choice.

I hope that my colleagues will support this resolution, and urge our friends on the Superfund conference to complete action on the reauthorization bill.

Mr. CONTE. Mr. Speaker, I withdraw my reservation of objection.

The SPEAKER pro tempore. Is there objection to the request of the gentleman from Mississippi?

There was no objection.

The Clerk read the joint resolution, as follows:

[NOTE.–H.J. Res 727 is previously reproduced and may be found at p. 5428]

The SPEAKER pro tempore. The gentleman from Mississippi [Mr. WHITTEN] is recognized for 1 hour.

(Mr. WHITTEN asked and was given permission to revise and extend his remarks.)

Mr. WHITTEN. Mr. Speaker, I yield myself such time as I may consume.

Mr. Speaker, this resolution will take care of what is essentially a technical problem in regard to the Superfund issue.

At the end of this month there will be about $600 million remaining of the 1986 Superfund appropriation, which EPA has not obligated because the trust fund is out of money. The Appropriations Committee intended these funds to be carried over into 1987—and we specifically provided that the funds "remain available until expended."

However, both OMB and GAO recognize that if there is no cash balance in a trust fund during the year of the appropriation—the appropriation expires. That is exactly the situation we face in Superfund—if new taxing authority and reauthorization is not enacted before September 30, $600 million will be lost on October 1.

This resolution will take care of the problem. It will permit the $600 million to be advanced from the general fund to the Superfund trust fund—so that it can be carried over into 1987. The action provides no new budget authority and no additional outlays. Finally, language has been included to "fence" these funds so that EPA cannot make any obligation until after taxing authority has been enacted.

This $600 million is essential to provide for an expanding Superfund program in 1987 and 1988. The 1987 HUD bill provides $861 million, assuming

substantial funds would carry over. If this $600 million is lost, it cannot be replaced within our 302 allocation. So the Superfund program will suffer in 1987 and beyond.

Without a doubt, the Superfund program is now suffering from a severe shortage of funds. However, the solution must be a long-term reauthorization bill—not another bandaid. Most members of there authorizing committees and supporters of Superfund believe that making additional funds available at this point would backfire and actually work to undermine or delay passage of reauthorizing and tax legislation.

This will in no way breach the $8.5 billion authorization total. This concerns the other side of the ledger—and the Appropriations Committee's problem in preserving the budget authority to provide the levels of funds anticipated in the legislation. We will not exceed the $8.5 billion total for Superfund during the 1987-91 period.

It is my understanding that this has been cleared with the affected authorizing committees, on both sides of the aisle. I am told that all parties to this are in agreement that this needs to be done.

Mr. FLORIO. Mr. Speaker, will the gentleman yield.

Mr. WHITTEN. I yield to the gentleman from New Jersey.

(Mr. FLORIO asked and was given permission to revise and extend his remarks.)

[Mr. FLORIO addressed the House. His remarks will appear hereafter in the Extensions of Remarks.]

Mr. WHITTEN. Mr. Speaker, I urge the adoption of the joint resolution and I yield back the balance of my time.

The joint resolution was ordered to be engrossed and read a third time, was read the third time, and passed, and a motion to reconsider was laid on the table.

[NOTE. – Mr. Florio's remarks never appeared in the Extensions of Remarks.]

APPENDIX   II

ADDITIONAL   BILLS

(5441)

SUPERFUND LEGISLATION

COMMUNICATION

FROM

THE PRESIDENT OF THE UNITED STATES

TRANSMITTING

A DRAFT OF PROPOSED LEGISLATION TO AMEND THE COMPRE-
HENSIVE ENVIRONMENTAL RESPONSE, COMPENSATION, AND LI-
ABILITY ACT OF 1980 TO ASSURE ADEQUATE FUNDING FOR THE
CLEANUP OF ABANDONED HAZARDOUS WASTE SITES, AND FOR
OTHER PURPOSES

FEBRUARY 26, 1985:—Referred jointly to the Committees on Energy and
Commerce, Public Works and Transportation, Merchant Marine
and Fisheries, the Judiciary, and Ways and Means
and ordered to be printed

U.S. GOVERNMENT PRINTING OFFICE
WASHINGTON : 1985

THE WHITE HOUSE,
Washington, February 22, 1985.

Hon. THOMAS P. O'NEILL, Jr.,
Speaker of the House of Representatives,
Washington, DC.

DEAR MR. SPEAKER: I am pleased to send you proposed legislation of critical importance to every American, the Administration's proposal for improving the Comprehensive Environmental Response, Compensation, and Liability Act of 1980 (better known as Superfund) and for extending the taxing authorities which support it, now due to expire on September 30, 1985.

My Administration has been moving forcefully to implement the Superfund program, expanding the national priorities list from the statutorily mandated minimum of 400 sites to 756 sites, greatly augmenting the money available for the program, and, most importantly, beginning the cleanup process at an ever increasing number of sites. The danger to public health and the environment presented by releases and threatened releases of hazardous substances from inactive waste sites persists, however, and we must not lose the momentum we have achieved.

The Administration's proposed legislation will more than triple the size of the existing program, from $1.6 billion to $5.3 billion. In order to fund this three-fold increase, we are requesting the Congress to extend for another five years the existing tax imposed on the manufacture of certain chemicals and to enact a fee, which will go into the dedicated trust fund, on the disposal and treatment of hazardous waste. These taxes and fees will raise approximately $1 billion per year over the next five years, which should provide adequate, stable, and equitable financing for the program. I strongly believe that funds used to pay for the program should be generated entirely through these dedicated sources, not the general treasury.

In addition to the expansion of the Superfund, we are requesting other authorities which will allow us to build on our momentum and will strengthen our ability to respond to the health and environmental threats emanating from abandoned hazardous waste sites. These authorities will allow us to:

Continue a comprehensive but focused Federal response program;

Strengthen our existing enforcement tools to ensure that responsible parties undertake or pay the costs of cleanup;

Enhance the Federal-State partnership needed for effective response action; and

Actively involve citizens in the cleanup decisions that will affect them.

To help ensure prompt enactment of responsible legislation, I have instructed Lee Thomas, Administrator of the Environmental

2

Protection Agency, to make reauthorization of this important legislation his highest priority.
    Sincerely,

RONALD REAGAN.

5446

A BILL

To .amend the Comprehensive Environmental Response, Compensation, and Liability Act of 1980 to assure adequate funding for the cleanup of abandoned hazardous waste sites, and for other purposes.

Be it enacted by the Senate and House of Representatives of the United States of America in Congress assembled,

SHORT TITLE AND TABLE OF CONTENTS

Section 1. This Act, together with the following table of contents, may be cited as the "Comprehensive Environmental Response, Compensation, and Liability Act Amendments of 1985".

TABLE OF CONTENTS

4

AMENDMENT OF CERCLA

Sec. 2. Except as otherwise expressly provided, whenever in Title I, II, or IV of this Act an amendment or repeal is expressed in terms of an amendment to or repeal of a section or other provision, the reference shall be considered to be a reference to a section or provision of the Comprehensive Environmental Response, Compensation, and Liability Act of 1980 (42 U.S.C. §9601 et seq.).

5

STATEMENT OF FINDINGS AND PURPOSES

Sec. 3.(a) The Congress hereby finds that --

(1) Releases and threats of releases of hazardous substances continue to pose a serious threat to public health and the environment; and

(2) A major source of such threat is uncontrolled hazardous waste facilities, where hazardous substances have been disposed of in a manner that has resulted in, or that may in the future result in dangerous releases.

(b) In order to adequately protect human health and the environment from such releases, the Congress further finds it necessary to:

(1) continue a comprehensive Federal program focused on the cleanup of hazardous waste sites and releases or threatened releases of hazardous substances into the environment;

6

(2) strengthen existing enforcement authority so that responsible parties will bear responsibility for cleanup costs;

(3) create a viable and effective Federal-State partnership for cleanup efforts; and

(4) ensure that citizens be informed of and have an opportunity to comment on cleanup activities taking place within their community.

DEFINITIONS

Sec. 4. Section 101(14)(C) is amended by striking "hazardous waste" and inserting "substance" in lieu thereof, and by inserting "whether or not that substance would be considered a solid waste under the Act" after "Act" the first time that word appears.

TITLE I--PROVISIONS RELATING PRIMARILY TO RESPONSE
AUTHORITY TO RESPOND: SCOPE OF PROGRAM

Sec. 101.(a) Section 104(a)(1) is amended to read as follows:

"(a)(1) Whenever any hazardous substance is released or there is a substantial threat of such a release into the

environment which may present a risk to public health or
the environment, the President is authorized to act, consistent
with the national contingency plan, to remove or arrange for
the removal of, and provide for remedial action relating to
such hazardous substance at any time (including its removal
from any contaminated natural resource), or take any other
response measure consistent with the national contingency
plan which the President deems necessary to protect the
public health or the environment. The President shall give
primary attention to those releases which he deems may present
a public health threat. The President, in his discretion,
may authorize the owner or operator of the vessel or facility
from which the release or substantial threat of release
emanates, or any other responsible party, to perform the
response action if the President determines that such removal
or remedial action will be done properly by the owner, operator,
or other responsible party.".

(b) Section 104(a) is further amended by striking
paragraph (2) and inserting in lieu thereof the following:

"(2) The President shall not respond under this Act
to a release or threat of a release:

(A) resulting from the extraction, beneficiation, or
processing of ores and minerials which are covered under the
Surface Mine Control and Reclamation Act of 1977;

(B) resulting from the lawful application of a pesticide product registered under Section 3, permitted under section 5, or exempted under Section 18 of the Federal Insecticide, Fungicide, and Rodenticide Act;

(C) to the extent it affects residential dwellings, business or community structures, or public or private domestic water supply wells, unless the release or threatened release emanates from a vessel or facility used for the deposition, storage, processing, treatment, transportation, or disposal of hazardous substances;

(D) of a naturally occurring substance in its unaltered form, or altered solely through naturally occurring processes or phenomena, from a location where it is naturally found; or

(E) covered by and in compliance with a permit, as that term is defined in section 101(10), if such hazardous substance was specifically identified, reviewed, and made part of the public record in issuing the permit and the permit was designed to limit such substance.

(3) Notwithstanding paragraph (2) of this subsection, the President may respond to any release or threat of release of a hazardous substance in any form if he determines, in his discretion, that the release or threat of release constitutes a major public health or environmental emergency and that no other person has the authority or capability to respond to the emergency in a timely manner.".

(c) Section 104(b) is amended by striking the phrases, ", pollutant, or contaminant" and ", pollutants or contaminants" whenever they appear.

(d) Section 105 is amended by striking ", pollutant and contaminants,".

STATUTORY LIMITS ON REMOVALS

Sec. 102. Section 104(c)(1) is amended by striking "six months" and inserting "one year" in lieu thereof and inserting before "obligations" the following: "or (C) continued response action is otherwise appropriate and consistent with permanent remedy,".

PERMANENT REMEDIES

Sec. 103.(a) Section 104(c)(4) is amended by adding at the end thereof the following sentence: "For determining whether a remedy is cost-effective, the President may consider the permanence of such remedy.".

(b) Section 105(3) is amended by inserting before the semicolon at the end thereof the following: ", taking into account the permanence of any remedial measures".

OFFSITE REMEDIAL ACTION

Sec. 104. Section 101(24) is amended by striking the last sentence of the paragraph; striking the period after "welfare" the third time that word appears, and inserting a semicolon in lieu thereof, striking "or" before "contaminated materials" and inserting "and associated" in lieu thereof; and inserting before the period after "environment" the third time that word appears, the following: ", as well as the offsite transport and offsite storage, treatment, destruction, or secure disposition of hazardous substances and associated contaminated materials.".

NATIONAL CONTINGENCY PLAN

Sec. 105.(a) Section 105(8)(B), is amended by striking "at least four hundred of" when it appears.

(b) Section 105(8)(B) is further amended by striking the phrase "at least" following the word "facilities" the second time it appears and by inserting "A State shall be allowed to designate its highest priority facility only once." after the third full sentence thereof.

COOPERATIVE AGREEMENTS

Sec. 106.(a) Section 104(d)(1) is amended to read as follows:

"(d)(1) Where the President determines that a State or political subdivision thereof has the capability to carry out any or all of the actions authorized in this section, the President, in his discretion and subject to such terms as he may prescribe, may enter into a contract or cooperative agreement covering a specific facility or facilities with such State or political subdivision to take such actions in accordance with criteria and priorities established pursuant to section 105(8) of this title and to be reimbursed from the Fund for reasonable response costs incurred pursuant to such contract or cooperative agreement. Any contract or cooperative agreement made hereunder is subject to the cost-sharing provisions of subsection (c) of this section.".

(b) Section 101(25) is amended by striking "and" and by inserting before the semicolon at the end thereof the following: ", and enforcement activities related thereto".

PUBLICLY OPERATED FACILITIES

Sec. 107. Section 104(c)(3)(C)(ii) is amended to read as follows:

"(ii) at least 75 per centum or such greater amount as the President may deem appropriate, taking into account the degree of responsibility of the State or political subdivision, of any sums expended in response to a release from a facility, that was operated by the State or a political subdivision thereof, either directly or through a contractual relationship or otherwise, at the time of any disposal of hazardous substances therein. For purposes of this clause only, "facility" does not include navigable waters or the beds underlying those waters.".

SITING OF HAZARDOUS WASTE FACILITIES

Sec. 108. Section 104(c) is amended by adding at the end thereof the following new paragraph:

"(5)(A) Effective two years after the date of enactment of this paragraph, the President shall not initiate any response actions pursuant to this section, except for the provision of alternative drinking water supplies or the temporary relocation of affected individuals from their residential dwellings, neither to exceed one year, unless the State in which the release occurs first provides assurances deemed adequate by the President that the State will assure the availability of hazardous waste treatment or disposal facilities, either within that State or pursuant to a regional agreement, acceptable to the President with adequate capacity for the treatment, or disposal of all hazardous wastes that are reasonably expected to be generated within that State during a period of time specified by the President by regulation.

(B)(i) Notwithstanding subparagraph (A) of this paragraph, the President may take response action under this section if he determines, in his discretion, that a major public health or environmental emergency exists.

(ii) Notwithstanding subsection (c) of this section, the President shall not provide alternative drinking water supplies or the temporary relocation of affected individuals from their residential dwellings pursuant to subparagraph (A) of this paragraph or response pursuant to subparagraph (B)(1) of this paragraph, unless the State in which the release occurs provides assurances that the State will pay or assure payment of 40 percent of those costs, or at least 80 percent of those costs for actions related to facilities operated by the State or a political subdivision thereof, either directly or through a contractual relationship or otherwise, at the time of any disposal of hazardous substances therein.

(C) Effective on the date of enactment of this paragraph, in addition to the cost share required by paragraph (3) of this subsection, the State shall pay all additional costs associated with any out-of-State or, if the State is party to a regional agreement for the treatment or disposal of hazardous substances, out-of-region transportation of hazardous substances resulting from response actions taken pursuant to this section.".

COMMUNITY INVOLVEMENT

Sec. 109. Section 104(c) is amended by adding after new paragraph (5) the following new paragraph:

"(6) Before selection or approval of any remedial action to be undertaken by the United States or a State or any other person under this section or section 106 of this Act, notice of and an opportunity to comment on the proposed action shall be afforded to the public.".

HEALTH RELATED AUTHORITIES

Section 110.(a) Section 104(i) is amended by inserting "(1)" after "(i)"; striking the remaining part of the sentence following "Registry", and inserting a period in lieu thereof; inserting "(A)" before the second sentence of subsection (i); and adding the following:

": (i) in support of response actions and because of the immediate need to protect public health in the event of a release or threatened release of a hazardous substance, and upon request of the Administrator of the Environmental Protection Agency, State officials, or local officials, may provide health consultations, health assessments, and other technical assistance relating to the health effects of exposure to hazardous substances; and

14

(ii) to improve the ability to render future public health judgments and recommendations, and to further scientific knowledge of the health effects of hazardous substances, develop and conduct epidemiological studies, including pilot studies.".

(b) Section 104(i) is further amended by inserting "(B)" before the third sentence thereof, striking "In addition," capitalizing "said", and striking all of paragraph (1) and inserting in lieu thereof the following:

"(i) in cooperation with the States, Indian tribes, and with other Federal and local officials, establish and maintain appropriate registries of serious diseases and illnesses or registries of persons exposed to hazardous substances through the environment, whenever their inclusion in such registries would be scientifically appropriate or valuable for specific scientific studies or for long-term follow-up;".

(c) Section 104(i) is further amended by striking "(2)" and inserting "(ii)" in lieu thereof, striking "(3)" and inserting "(iii)" in lieu thereof, and striking all of paragraph (4) and inserting in lieu thereof the following:

"(iv) in cases of public health emergencies caused or believed to be caused by exposure to toxic substances, assist, and consult with private or public health care providers in the provision of medical care and testing of exposed individuals, including the collection and laboratory analysis of specimens as may be indicated by the specific exposure incident or any other assistance appropriate under the circumstances; and ".

15

(d) Section 104(i) is further amended by striking "(5)" and inserting "(v)" in lieu thereof and striking the last sentence of the paragraph.

(e) Section 104(i) is further amended by adding the following new paragraph:

"(vi) All results of studies conducted under this subsection (other than health assessments) shall be reported or adopted only after appropriate peer review established by the Administrator of the Agency. Existing peer review systems may be used where appropriate.

(f) Section 104(i) is further amended by adding the following new paragraph at the end thereof:

"(2) The Administrator of the Environmental Protection Agency, or the head of the Agency to which response authority has been delegated, in his discretion, may perform exposure and risk assessments at a release for the purpose of determining appropriate action adequate to mitigate the public health threat. For purposes of this paragraph, "exposure and risk assessment" means the process for characterizing the potential risk from exposure to hazardous or toxic substances at a specific site, based upon hazard identification, dose-response assessment, exposure assessment, and risk characterization."

COMPLIANCE WITH OTHER ENVIRONMENTAL LAWS

Sec. 111. Section 104(c)(4), as amended by section 103(a) of this Act, is amended by inserting "(A)" after "(4)" and adding the following new subparagraph at the end thereof:

16

"(B)(i). When revising the national contingency plan pursuant to section 105, the President shall specify the extent to which removal or remedial actions selected under this section or secured under section 106(a) should comply with applicable or relevant standards and criteria of other Federal, State, or local environmental and public health laws. When making this determination, the President shall consider, among other factors, the following: the level of health or environmental protection provided by applicable or relevant standards and criteria; the technical feasibility of achieving such standards and criteria for different types of releases; the interim or permanent nature of particular response actions; the need for expeditious action; and the need to maintain availability of amounts from the Fund to respond to other releases which present or may present a threat to public health or the environment.

(ii) No permit shall be required under Federal, State, or local law for removal or remedial action selected under this section or secured under section 106(a).

(iii) Removal or remedial actions selected or taken under this section or secured under section 106(a) that have voluntarily met the provisions of section 102 of the National Environmental Policy Act of 1969 (Public Law 91-190, 83 Stat. 852) need not comply with any further public participation requirements which may be provided under this Act.

ACTIONS UNDER THE NATIONAL CONTINGENCY PLAN

Sec. 112. Section 107(d) is amended by inserting "response costs or" before "damages" both times that word appears and by inserting after "person" the second time that word appears the following: "and shall not alter the liability of any person who is liable or potentially liable under subsection (a) of this section who subsequently undertakes a response action.".

NATURAL RESOURCE DAMAGE CLAIMS

Sec. 113.(a) Section 107(f) is amended by inserting "(1)" after "(f)" and by adding at the end thereof the following new paragraphs:

"(2)(A) The President shall designate in the national contingency plan published under section 105 of this Act the Federal officials who shall act on behalf of the public as trustees for natural resources under this Act and section 311 of the Clean Water Act. Such officials shall assess damages to natural resources for the purposes of this Act and section 311 of the Clean Water Act for those resources under their trusteeship, and may upon request of and reimbursement from a State and at the Federal officials' discretion, assess damages for those natural resources under a State's trusteeship.

(B) The Governor of each State shall designate the State officials who may act on behalf of the public as trustees for natural resources under this Act and section 311 of the Clean Water Act and shall notify the President of such designations. Such State officials shall assess damages to natural resources for the purposes of this Act and section

311 of the Clean Water Act for those resources under their trusteeship.

(C) Any determination or assessment of damages to natural resources for the purposes of this Act and section 311 of the Clean Water Act made by a Federal or State trustee in accordance with the regulations promulgated under section 301(c) of this Act shall have the force and effect of a rebuttable presumption on behalf of the trustee in any judicial proceeding under this Act or section 311 of the Clean Water Act."

(3) With respect to Federal facilities, Federal agencies with custody and accountability for those facilities shall be the only trustees of natural resources on, under, or above these facilities for purposes of the Act.".

(b) Section 111(b) is amended by inserting a period after "title" the first time that word appears and striking all that follows.

(c) Section 111(c) is amended by striking paragraphs (1) and (2) and renumbering the following paragraphs accordingly.

(d) Section 111(e)(1) is amended by inserting "pursuant to subsection 111(a)(2)" after the word "Fund" the first time it appears.

(e) Section 111 is amended by striking subsections (d), (h), and (i) and relettering the remaining subsections accordingly.

(f) Section 111(a) is amended by striking paragraph (3) and renumbering the following paragraph.

(g) Section 111(e)(4) is amended by striking "Paragraphs (1) and (4) of subsection (a) of" and by replacing "t" with "T" in "this" when it appears.

RESPONSE CLAIMS

Sec. 114.(a) Section 111(a)(2) is amended to read as follows:

"(2) payment of any claim for necessary response costs incurred by any other person as a result of carrying out the national contingency plan established under section 311(c) of the Clean Water Act and amended by section 105 of this title: Provided, however, that such costs must be approved under said plan and certified by the responsible Federal official prior to the taking of any action for which costs may be sought; and".

(b) Section 112 is amended by striking subsection (a) and inserting in lieu thereof the following:

"(a) No claims may be asserted against the Fund pursuant to section 111(a)(2) of this title unless such claim is presented in the first instance to the owner, operator, or guarantor of the vessel or facility from which a hazardous substance has been released, if known to the claimant, and to any other person known to the claimant who may be liable under section 107 of this title. In any case where the claim has not been satisfied within sixty days of presentation in accordance with this subsection, the claimant may present the claim to the Fund for payment; provided, that no claim against the Fund may be considered during the pendency of an action in court to recover costs which are the subject of the claim.".

20

(c)   Section 112(b) is amended by striking "$5,000" in paragraph (1) and inserting "$25,000" in lieu thereof; and by striking all of paragraphs (2), (3) and (4) and inserting in lieu thereof the following:

"(2)   The President may, if he is satisfied that the information developed during the processing of the claim warrants it, make and pay an award of the claim; provided, no claim may be awarded to the extent that a judicial judgment has been made on the costs that are the subject of the claim. If the President declines to pay all or part of the claim, the claimant may, within thirty days after receiving notice of the President's decision, request an administrative hearing.

(3)   In any proceeding under this subsection, the claimant shall bear the burden of proving his claim.

(4)   All administrative decisions made hereunder shall be in writing, with notification to all appropriate parties, and shall be rendered within ninety days of submission of a claim to an administrative law judge, unless all the parties to the claim agree in writing to an extension or unless the President, in his discretion, extends the time limit for a period not to exceed 60 days.

(5)   All administrative decisions hereunder shall be final, and any party to the proceeding may appeal a decision within thirty days of notification of the award or decision. Any such appeal shall be made to the Federal district court for the district where the release or threat of release took place.   In any such appeal, the decision shall be considered binding and conclusive, and shall not be overturned except for arbitrary or capricious abuse of discretion.

21

(6) Within twenty days after the expiration of the appeal
period for any administrative decision concerning an award,
or within twenty days after the final judicial determination of
any appeal taken pursuant to this subsection, the President
shall pay any such award from the Fund. The President shall
determine the method, terms, and time of payment.".

(d) Section 112 is amended by striking subsection (d)
and relettering the following subsection.

INDIAN TRIBES

Sec. 115. (a) Section 101 is amended by striking "and"
at the end of paragraph (31), striking the period at the end
of paragraph (32) and inserting a semicolon in lieu thereof,
and adding the following new paragraphs:

"(33) "Indian tribe" means any Indian tribe, band, nation,
group, pueblo, or community for which, or for the members of
which, the United States holds lands in trust; and

(34) "Indian lands" means lands, title to which is
held by the United States in trust for an Indian or an Indian
tribe or lands title to which is held by an Indian or an Indian
tribe subject to a restriction against alienation.".

(b) Section 104(c)(3), as amended by section 107 of
this Act, is amended by inserting "or Indian tribe" after the
word "State" the first four times that word appears and after
phrase appears, and by adding a new sentence at the end
thereof to read as follows: "The assurances required by this
paragraph with respect to Indian lands may be made by the
Department of the Interior if the Secretary of the Interior
determines that an Indian tribe cannot provide those assurances.".

(c) Section 104(d), as amended by section 106(a) of this Act, is amended by inserting "or Indian tribe" after the phrase "political subdivision thereof" wherever that phrase occurs, and by inserting "or Indian tribe" after the phrase "political subdivision.".

(d) Section 103(a) is amended by striking the period at the end thrreof and inserting, ", or to any affected Indian tribe."

(e) "Section 104(c)(2) is amended by adding, "or Indian tribe" after "States."

(f) Section 105(8)(B), as amended by section 105 of this Act, is further amended by inserting "or Indian tribe" after "State" the first time that word appears and after the phrase "established by the States"; and inserting "or Indian lands" after "State" the second time that word appears.

PREEMPTION

Sec. 116. Section 114 is amended by striking subsection (c) and relettering the following subsection accordingly.

STATE COST SHARE

Sec. 117. Section 104(c)(3)(C)(i) is amended by striking "10" and inserting "20" in lieu thereof.

TITLE II--PROVISIONS RELATING PRIMARILY TO ENFORCEMENT

CIVIL PENALTIES FOR NON-REPORTING

Sec. 201. Section 103(b)(3) is amended by striking "$10,000", inserting "$25,000" in lieu thereof, and inserting before the last sentence the following: "Any such person also shall be liable to the United States for a civil penalty of not more than $10,000 for each violation of this subsection.

23

Any civil penalty for violations of this subsection in excess
of $25,000 may be assessed in an action brought by the Attorney
General in a United States district court pursuant to section
113. The Administrator may assess any penalty under this
subsection for less than $25,000, and such assessment shall
become final unless, no later than 30 days after notice of
the penalty is served, the person or persons named in the
notice request a public hearing. Upon such request, the
Administrator shall promptly conduct a public hearing. In
connection with any proceeding under this section the Administrator
may issue subpoenas for the attendance and testimony of
witnesses and the production of relevant papers, books, and
documents and may promulgate rules for discovery procedures.".

CONTRIBUTION AND PARTIES TO LITIGATION

Sec. 202. Section 107, as amended by section 205 and
Title III of this Act, is amended by adding a new subsection
to read as follows:

"(k)(1) In any civil or administrative action under
this section or section 106, any claims for contribution or
indemnification shall be brought only after entry of judgment or
date of settlement in good faith.

(2) After judgment in any civil action under section 106
or under subsection (a) of this section, any defendant held
liable in the action may bring a separate action for contribution
against any other person liable or potentially liable under
subsection (a). Such action shall be brought in accordance
with section 113 and shall be governed by Federal law. Except
as provided in paragraph (4) of the subsection, this subsection
shall not impair any right of indemnity under existing law.

24

(3) When a person has resolved its liability to the United States or a State in a judicially approved good faith settlement, such person shall not be liable for claims for contribution under paragraph (2) of this subsection regarding matters addressed in the settlement. Such settlement does not discharge any of the other potentially liable persons unless its terms so provide, but it reduces the claim against the others to the extent of any amount stipulated by the settlement.

(4) Nothing in this subsection shall affect or modify in any way the rights of the United States, a State, or any person that has resolved its liability to the United States or a State in a good faith settlement to seek contribution or indemnification against any persons who are not party to the settlement. In any such contribution or indemnification action, the rights of a State or any person that has so resolved its liability shall be subordinate to the rights of the United States. Any contribution action brought under this paragraph shall be brought in accordance with section 113 and shall be governed by Federal law.".

ACCESS AND INFORMATION GATHERING

Sec. 203. Section 104(e) is amended by striking "(2)" and inserting "(3)" in lieu thereof and by striking all of existing paragraph (1) and inserting in lieu thereof the following:

"(1) For the purposes of determining the need for response, or choosing or taking any response action under this title, or otherwise enforcing the provisions of this

title, any officer, employee, or representative of the President,
duly designated by the President, or any duly designated
officer, employee, or representative of a State under a
contract or cooperative agreement, is authorized where there is a
reasonable basis to believe there may be a release or threat
of release of a hazardous substance --

(A) to require any person who has or may have information
relevant to (i) the identification or nature of materials
generated, treated, stored, transported to, or disposed of at
a facility, or (ii) the nature or extent of a release or
threatened release of a hazardous substance at or from a
facility, to furnish, upon reasonable notice, information or
documents relating to such matters. In addition, upon reasonable
notice, such person either shall grant to appropriate representatives access at all reasonable times to inspect all
documents or records relating to such matters or shall copy
and furnish to the representatives all such documents or
records, at the option of such person;

(B) to enter at reasonable times any establishment or other
place or property (i) where hazardous substances are, may be,
or have been generated, stored, treated, disposed of, or
transported from, (ii) from which or to which hazardous
substances have been or may have been released, (iii) where
such release is or may be threatened, or (iv) where entry is needed
to determine the need for response or the appropriate response
or to effectuate a response action under this title; and

(C) to inspect and obtain samples from such establishment
or other place or property or location of any suspected
hazardous substance and to inspect and obtain samples of any

containers or labeling for suspected hazardous substances. Each such inspection shall be completed with reasonable promptness. If the officer, employee, or representative obtains any samples, prior to leaving the premises, he shall give to the owner, operator, tenant, or other person in charge of the place from which the samples were obtained a receipt describing the sample obtained and, if requested, a portion of each such sample. If any analysis is made of such samples, a copy of the results of the analysis shall be furnished promptly to the owner, operator, tenant, or other person in charge, if such person can be located.

(2)(A) If consent is not granted regarding a request made by a duly designated officer, employee, or representative under paragraph (1), the President, upon such notice and an opportunity for consultation as is reasonably appropriate under the circumstances, may issue an order to such person directing compliance with the request, and the President may ask the Attorney General to commence a civil action to compel compliance.

(B) In any civil action brought to obtain compliance with the order, the court shall, where there is a reasonable basis to believe there may be a release or threat of a release of a hazardous substance: (i) in the case of interference with entry or inspection, enjoin such interference or direct compliance with orders to prohibit interference with entry or inspection, unless under the circumstances of the case the demand for entry or inspection is arbitrary and capricious, an abuse of discretion, or not in accordance with law; and (ii) in the case of information or document requests, enjoin interference with such information or document requests or direct compliance with orders to provide such information or documents, unless under the circumstances of the case the demand for information or documents is arbitrary and capricious, an abuse of discretion, or not in accordance with law. The court may assess a civil penalty not to exceed $10,000 against any person who unreasonably fails to comply with the provisions of paragraph (1) or an order issued pursuant to paragraph (2).".

(3) Nothing in this subsection shall preclude the President from securing access or obtaining information in any other lawful manner.

(4) Notwithstanding this subsection, entry to locations and access to information properly classified to protect the national security may be granted only to any officer, employee, or representative of the President who is properly cleared.".

ADMINISTRATIVE ORDERS FOR SECTION 104(b) ACTIONS

Sec. 204.(a) Section 104 is amended by adding a new subsection at the end thereof to read as follows:

"(j)(1) If the President determines that one or more responsible parties will properly carry out action under subsection (b) of this section, the President may enter into a consent administrative order with such party or parties for that purpose.

(2) The United States district court for the district in which the release has occurred or threatens to occur shall have jurisdiction to enforce the order, and any person who violates

or fails to obey such an order shall be liable to the United States for a civil penalty of not more than $10,000 for each day in which such violation occurs or such failure to comply continues.".

(b) Section 107(c)(3) is amended by striking "104 or".

NON-TRUST FUND AND PRÉ-TRUST FUND EXPENDITURES

Sec. 205. Section 107(a)(4) is amended by striking "and" from the end of subparagraph (B), striking the period from the end of subparagraph (C) and inserting "; and" in lieu thereof, and adding a new subparagraph at the end thereof to read as follows:

"(D) All other costs incurred by the United States Government subsequent to the enactment of the Resource Conservation and Recovery Act of 1976, in response to a release or threatened release of a hazardous substance from a facility used for the storage, treatment, or disposal of hazardous substances, where such person knew or should have known of the response action and the costs are not inconsistent with the response actions provided for in subsections 101(23) and (24) of this Act.".

STATUTE OF LIMITATIONS

Sec. 206. Section 113, as amended by sections 207 and 208 of this Act, is amended by adding at the end thereof the following new subsection:

"(h)(1) No claim may be presented nor may an action be commenced under this title for recovery of the costs referred to in subsection (a) of section 107 more than six years after the date of completion of the response action. Provided, however, that within the limitation period set out herein a

State or the United States may commence an action under this title for recovery of any cost or costs at any time after such cost or costs have been incurred.

(2) No action may be commenced for damages under this title more than three years from the date of discovery of the loss.

(3) No action for contribution may be commenced under section 107 more than three years after the date of judgment or the date of the good faith settlement.

(4) No action based on rights subrogated pursuant to section 112 by reason of payment of a claim may be commenced under this title more than three years after the date of payment of such claim.".

PRE-ENFORCEMENT REVIEW

Sec. 207(a). Section 113(b) is amended by adding "s" to the word "subsection" and inserting "and (e)" after "(a)".

(b) Section 113 is further amended by adding at the end thereof the following new subsections:

"(e) No court shall have jurisdiction to review any challenges to response action selected under section 104 or any order issued under section 104, or to review any order issued under section 106(a), in any action other than (1) an action under section 107 to recover response costs or damages or for contribution or indemnification; (2) an action to enforce an order issued under section 106(a) or to recover a penalty for violation of such order; or (3) an action for reimbursement under section 106(b)(2).

30

(f) In any judicial action under section 106 or 107, judicial review of any issues concerning the adequacy of any response action taken or ordered by the President shall be limited to the administrative record. The only objection which may be raised in any such judicial action under sections 106 or 107 is an objection to the response action which was raised with reasonable specificity to the President during the applicable period for public comment. In considering such objections, the court shall uphold the President's decision in selecting the response action unless the decision was arbitrary and capricious or otherwise not in accordance with law. If the court finds that the President's decision in selecting the response action was arbitrary and capricious or otherwise not in accordance with law, the court shall award the response costs or damages or other relief being sought to the extent that such relief is not inconsistent with the national contingency plan. In reviewing alleged procedural errors, the court may disallow costs or damages only if the errors were so serious and related to matters of such central relevance to the action that the action would have been significantly changed had such errors not been made.".

(c) Section 106(b) is amended by inserting "(1)" after "(b)" and adding a new paragraph at the end thereof to read as follows:

"(2)(A) Any person who receives and complies with the terms of any order issued under subsection (a) may, within sixty days of completion of the required action, petition the

President for reimbursement from the Fund for the reasonable costs of such action, plus interest. Any interest payable under this paragraph shall accrue on the amounts expended from the date of expenditure at the same rate that applies to investments of the Fund under section 223(b) of this Act.

(B) If the President refuses to grant all or part of a petition made under this paragraph, the petitioner may within thirty days of receipt of such refusal file an action against the President in the appropriate United States district court seeking reimbursement from the Fund. To obtain reimbursement, the petitioner must establish by a preponderance of the evidence that it is not liable for response costs under section 107(a) and that costs for which it seeks reimbursement are reasonable in light of the action required by the relevant order. Provided, however, that a petitioner who is liable for response costs under section 107(a) may recover its reasonable costs of response to the extent that it can demonstrate, on the administrative record, that the President's decision in issuing the order was arbitrary and capricious or otherwise not in accordance with law. In any such case, the court may award to petitioner all reasonable response costs incurred pursuant to the portions of the order found to be arbitrary and capricious or otherwise not in accordance with law.".

NATIONWIDE SERVICE OF PROCESS

Sec. 208. Section 113, as amended by section 207 of this Act, is amended by adding after new subsection (f) the following new subsection:

"(g) In any action by the United States under sections 104, 106, or 107, process may be served in any district where the defendant is found, or resides, or transacts business, or has appointed an agent for the service of process.".

ABATEMENT ACTION

Sec. 209. Section 106(a) is amended by striking the phrases "or welfare" and "and welfare".

FEDERAL LIEN

Sec. 210. Section 107 is amended by adding after new subsection (1) the following new subsection:

"(1)(1) All costs and damages for which a person is liable to the United States under subsection (a) of this section shall constitute a lien in favor of the United States upon all real property and rights to such property belonging to such person that are subject to or affected by a removal or remedial action.

(2) The lien imposed by this subsection shall arise at the time costs are first incurred by the United States with respect to a response action under this Act and shall continue until the liability for the costs (or a judgment against the person arising out of such liability) is satisfied or becomes unenforceable through operation of the statute of limitations provided in section 113(h).

(3) The lien imposed by this subsection shall not be valid as against any purchaser, holder of a security interest, or judgment lien creditor until notice of the lien has been filed in the appropriate office within the State (or county or other governmental subdivision), as designated by State law,

in which the real property subject to the lien is physically located. If the State has not by law designated one office for the receipt of such notices of liens, the notice shall be filed in the office of the clerk of the United States district court for the district in which the real property is physically located. For purposes of this subsection, the terms "purchaser" and "security interest" shall have the definitions provided in 26 U.S.C. §6323(h). This paragraph does not apply with respect to any person who has or reasonably should have actual notice or knowledge that the United States has incurred costs giving rise to a lien under paragraph (1) of this subsection.

(4) The costs constituting the lien may be recovered in an action in rem in the United States district court for the district in which the removal or remedial action is occurring or has occurred. Nothing in this subsection shall affect the right of the United States to bring an action against any person to recover all costs and damages for which such person is liable under subsection (a) of this section.".

PENALTIES

Sec. 211.(a). Section 103(d)(2) is amended by striking $20,000" and inserting "$25,000" in lieu thereof.

(b) Section 106(b) is amended by striking "$5,000" and inserting "$10,000" in lieu thereof.

FEDERAL AGENCY SETTLEMENTS

Section 212(a). Section 107(g) is amended by inserting "(1)" after "(g)" and by adding the following new paragraph at the end thereof:

34

"(2) The head of each such department, agency, or instrumentality or his designee may consider, compromise, and settle any claim or demand under this Act arising out of activities of his agency, in accordance with regulations prescribed by the Attorney General: _Provided_, that any award, compromise, or settlement in excess of $2,500 shall be made only with the prior written approval of the Attorney General or his designee. Any such award, compromise, or settlement shall be paid by the agency concerned out of appropriations available to that agency. The acceptance of any payment under this paragraph shall be final and conclusive, and shall constitute a complete release of any claim against the United States and against the employees of the United States whose acts or omissions gave rise to the claim or demand, by reason of the same subject matter.

FOREIGN VESSELS

Section 213. Section 107(a)(1) is amended by striking "(otherwise subject to the jurisdiction of the United States).".

35

TITLE III--ADMENDMENTS TO THE INTERNAL REVENUE CODE OF 1954

Section 301. SHORT TITLE

This title may be cited as the "Superfund Revenue Act of 1985".

Section 302. TAX ON PETROLEUM AND CERTAIN CHEMICALS

(a) TERMINATION OF TAX.--

(1) Subsection (d) of section 4611 of such Code is amended to read as follows:

(d) TERMINATION.-- The tax imposed by this section shall not apply after September 30, 1990, except that if on September 30, 1988 or September 30, 1989 --

(1) The unobligated balance in the Hazardous Substance Superfund as of such date exceeds $1.5 billion and

(2) the secretary, after consultation with the Administrator of the Environmental Protection Agency, determines that such unobligated balance will exceed $1.5 billion on September 30 of the following year if no tax is imposed under sections 4611, 4661, and 4681 during the calendar year following the date referred to above, then no tax shall be imposed by this section during the first calendar year beginning after the date referred to in paragraph (1).

(b) EFFECTIVE DATE.-- The amendments made by this section shall take effect on October 1, 1985.

Section 303. TAX ON HAZARDOUS WASTE AND REPEAL OF POST-CLOSURE
   TAX.

(a)   In general-- Sections 4681 and 4682 of the Internal
Revenue Code of 1954 (relating to a tax on hazardous wastes) are
amended to read as follows:

"Section 4681.   IMPOSITION OF TAX.

(a) GENERAL RULE.-- There is hereby imposed a tax on--

   (1) the receipt of hazardous waste at a qualified
hazardous waste management unit,

   (2) the receipt of hazardous waste for transport from
the United States for the purpose of ocean disposal, and

   (3) the exportation of hazardous waste from the United
States.

(b) AMOUNT OF TAX.-- The amount of the tax imposed by
subsection (a) shall be equal to the following:

   (1)   For each ton of hazardous waste received in a
landfill, surface impoundment, waste pile, or land treatment
unit that is a qualified hazardous waste management unit, the
amount of tax shall be equal to:

      (A) $9.80 for the period beginning October 1, 1985
      and ending September 30, 1986 (hereinafter in this
      section referred to as the "1986 fiscal year of the
      reauthorization period");

      (B) $10.09 for the period beginning October 1,
      1986 and ending September 30, 1987 (hereinafter in this

section referred to as the "1987 fiscal year of the
reauthorization period");

(C) $11.13 for the period beginning October 1, 1987
and ending September 30, 1988 (hereinafter in this
section referred to as the "1988 fiscal year of the
reauthorization period");

(D) $13.48 for the period beginning October 1,
1988 and ending September 30, 1989 (hereinafter in this
section referred to as the "1989 fiscal year of the
reauthorization period");

(E) $16.32 for the period beginning October 1,
1989 and ending September 30, 1990 (hereinafter in this
section referred to as the "1990 fiscal year of the
reauthorization period");

(F) $16.32 for the period beginning October 1,
1990 and ending September 30, 1991 (hereinafter in this
section referred to as the "1991 extension period").

(2) For each ton of hazardous waste exported from the
United States, received for transport from the United States
for the purpose of ocean disposal, or received at a qualified
hazardous waste management unit other than specified in
paragraph (1), the amount of tax shall be equal to:

(A) $2.61 for the 1986 fiscal year of the
reauthorization period;

(B) $2.68 for the 1987 fiscal year of the
reauthorization period;

(C) $2.96 for the 1988 fiscal year of the

reauthorization period;

    (D) $3.59 for the 1989 fiscal year of the reauthorization period;

    (E) $4.37 for the 1990 fiscal year of the reauthorization period;

    (F) $4.37 for the 1991 extension period.

(c) EXCLUSION FOR CERTAIN WASTE. -- The tax imposed by subsection (a) shall not apply to the following:

    (1) The treatment, storage, or disposal of any hazardous waste by any person pursuant to any removal or remedial action under the Comprehensive Environmental Response, Compensation, and Liability Act of 1980, as amended, provided:

    (A) the response action has been selected or approved by the Administrator of the Environmental Protection Agency; and

    (B) the release, or threatened release, of the hazardous substances which caused the response action occurred prior to October 1, 1985.

    (2) Any hazardous waste which has been generated at a Federal facility and is subsequently received at a qualified hazardous waste management unit or exported from the United States.

(d) PERSON ON WHOM TAX IMPOSED.--

    (1) Owner or Operator.-- The tax imposed by subsection (a)(1) of this section shall be paid by the owner or operator

of the qualified hazardous waste management unit.

(2) Owner or Operator.-- The tax imposed by subsection (a)(2) of this section shall be paid by the owner or operator of the vessel or aircraft that disposes of hazardous waste in or over the ocean.

(3) Exporter.-- The tax imposed by subsection (a)(3) of this section shall be paid by the exporter of the hazardous waste.

(e) TERMINATION.--The tax imposed by this section shall not apply after September 30, 1990, unless the Secretary determines that receipts (taking into account subsequent adjustments) appropriated or credited to the Superfund during the period beginning October 1, 1985 and ending September 30, 1990 total less than $5.2 billion, provided, however, that in no event shall the tax imposed by this section apply after March 31, 1991.

"Section 4682. ADJUSTMENT OF TAX RATES.--

(a) IN GENERAL. -- Not later than October 1, 1987 and October 1 of each subsequent fiscal year of the reauthorization period, the amount of tax imposed by subsection (b)(1) and (b)(2) of section 4681 shall be adjusted as provided in subsection (b) of this paragraph.

(b) METHOD OF ADJUSTING RATES.--

(1) Determination by the Secretary. -- For each fiscal year of the reauthorization period, the Secretary shall

determine:

    (A) the aggregate net revenue collected with respect to section 4611;

    (B) the aggregate net revenue collected with respect to section 4661;

    (C) the aggregate net revenue collected at the rate specified in subsection (b)(1) of section 4681;

    (D) the aggregate net revenue collected at the rate specified in subsection (b)(2) of section 4681;

    (E) amounts recovered on behalf of the Hazardous Substance Superfund under the Comprehensive Environmental Response, Compensation and Liability Act of 1980 (hereinafter in this section referred to as 'CERCLA') and on behalf of the Hazardous Substance Superfund under CERCLA, as amended;

    (F) moneys recovered or collected under section 311(b)(6)(B) of the Clean Water Act;

    (G) penalties assessed under title I of CERCLA;

    (H) punitive damages under section 107(c)(3) of CERCLA;

    (I) amounts credited to the Hazardous Substance Superfund as provided in section 9602(b); and

    (J) amounts credited to the Hazardous Substance Superfund attributable to intrafund transactions.

Such determinations (hereinafter collectively referred to in this section as the "revenue amount") for each fiscal year shall be made on the basis of actual revenues collected as of

41

the end of each fiscal year, taking into account subsequent adjustments.

(2) Projected revenue amounts. -- The following amounts are the projected revenue amounts for each fiscal year of the reauthorization period:

(A) for fiscal year 1986, the projected revenue amount is $978 million;

(B) for fiscal year 1987, the projected revenue amount is $989 million;

(C) for fiscal year 1988, the projected revenue amount is $1035 million,

(D) for fiscal year 1989, the projected revenue amount is $1093 million, and

(E) for fiscal year 1990, the projected revenue amount is $1205 million.

(3) Adjustments. --

(A) Adjustment of 1988 Fiscal Year Tax Rates.-- If--

(i) $978 million minus the revenue amount determined by the Secretary under paragraph (1) for the 1986 fiscal year of the reauthorization period (the "1986 difference") is greater than zero, and

(ii) the sum of:

(I) the 1986 difference, plus

(II) the difference between $591 million and the estimated net revenue from the tax imposed at the rates specified by subsections (b)(1) and (b)(2) of section 4681 for the 1988 fiscal year of the reauthorization period (the "estimated 1988 waste tax difference") is greater than zero,

the tax rates imposed by subsections (b)(1) and (b)(2) of section 4681 for the 1988 fiscal year of the reauthorization period shall be adjusted by multiplying each such rate by a factor determined by dividing the sum of the 1986 difference plus $591 million, by the difference between $591 million and the estimated 1988 waste tax difference.

(B) Adjustment of 1989 Fiscal Year Tax Rates.-- If--

(i) $989 million minus the revenue amount determined by the Secretary under paragraph (1) for the 1987 fiscal year of the reauthorization period (the "1987 difference") is greater than zero, and

(ii) the sum of:

(I) the 1987 difference, plus

(II) the difference between $610 million and the estimated net revenue from the tax imposed at the rates specified by subsections (b)(1) and (b)(2) of section 4681 for 1989 fiscal year of the reauthorization period (the "estimated 1989 waste tax difference")

is greater than zero, the tax rates imposed by subsections (b)(1) and (b)(2) of section 4681 for the

1989 fiscal year of the reauthorization period shall be
adjusted by multiplying each such rate by a factor
determined by dividing the sum of the 1987 difference
plus $610 million, by the difference between $610
million and the estimated 1989 waste tax difference.

    (C) Adjustment of 1990 Fiscal Year Tax Rates.--

        (i) If --

            (I) the 1986 difference is greater than
zero, and

            (II) the difference between the sum of
$1,035 million plus the 1986 difference and
the revenue amount determined by the Secretary
under paragraph (1) for the 1988 fiscal year
of the reauthorization period (the "1988
difference") is greater than zero, and

            (III) the sum of the 1988 difference plus
the difference between $634 million and the
estimated net revenue from the tax imposed at
the rates specified by subsections (b)(1) and
(b)(2) of section 4681 for the 1990 fiscal
year of the reauthorization period (the
"estimated 1990 waste tax difference") is
greater than zero,

the tax rates imposed by subsections (b)(1) and
(b)(2) of section 4681 for the 1990 fiscal year of
the reauthorization period shall be adjusted by
multiplying each such rate by a factor determined

by dividing the sum of the 1988 difference plus
$634 million, by the difference between $634
million and the estimated 1990 waste tax
difference.

    (ii) If --

        (I) the 1986 difference is not greater
than zero, and

        (II) the 1988 difference is greater than
zero, and

        (III) the estimated 1990 waste tax
difference is greater than zero,
the tax rates imposed by subsections (b)(1) and
(b)(2) of section 4681 for the 1990 fiscal year of
the reauthorization period shall be adjusted by
multiplying each such rate by a factor determined
by dividing the sum of the 1988 difference plus
$634 million, by the difference between $634
million and the estimated 1990 waste tax
difference.

(D) Adjustment of 1991 Extension Period Tax
Rates.--

    (i) If --

        (I) the 1987 difference is greater than
zero, and

        (II) the difference between the sum of
$1093 million plus the 1987 difference and the
revenue amount determined by the Secretary

45

under paragraph (1) for the 1989 fiscal year
of the reauthorization period (the "1989
difference") is greater than zero, and

(III) the sum of the 1989 difference plus
the difference between $1205 billion and the
projected revenue amount for the 1990 fiscal
year of the reauthorization period (the "1990
difference") is greater than zero,

the tax rates imposed by subsections (b)(1) and
(b)(2) of section 4681 for the 1991 extension
period shall be multiplied by a factor determined
by dividing the sum of the 1989 difference plus the
1990 difference by the expected net revenue from
the tax imposed by section 4681 at the 1991
extension period tax rates for the period beginning
October 1, 1990 and ending March 31, 1991.

(ii) If --

(I) the 1987 difference is not greater
than zero, and

(II) the 1989 difference is greater than
zero, and

(III) the 1990 difference is greater than
zero,

the tax rates imposed by subsections (b)(1) and
(b)(2) of section 4681 for the 1991 extension
period shall be multiplied by a factor determined
by dividing the sum of the 1989 difference plus the

1990 difference by the expected net revenue from the tax imposed by section 4681 at the 1991 extension period tax rates for the period beginning October 1, 1990 and ending March 31, 1991.

(b) Subchapter C of chapter 38 (relating to environmental taxes) is amended by inserting after section 4682 the following new section:

"Section 4683. DEFINITIONS AND SPECIAL RULES.

(a) DEFINITIONS.-- For purposes of this subchapter--

(1) HAZARDOUS WASTE.-- The term 'hazardous waste' means any waste which is listed or identified under section 3001 of the Solid Waste Disposal Act, as amended. The Secretary, in consultation with the Administrator of the Environmental Protection Agency, will prescribe rules relating to the imposition of tax, if any, on wastes listed under the Solid Waste Disposal Act, as amended, after the date of enactment of this Act.

(2) QUALIFIED HAZARDOUS WASTE MANAGEMENT FACILITY.-- The term 'qualified hazardous waste management facility' means any facility, as defined under subtitle C of the Solid Waste Disposal Act, as amended, which has received a permit or is accorded interim status under --

(A) section 3005 of the Solid Waste Disposal Act, or

(B) a State program authorized under section 3006 of such Act.

(3) QUALIFIED HAZARDOUS WASTE MANAGEMENT UNIT.-- The

term 'qualified hazardous waste management unit' means either
the smallest area of land on or in which hazardous waste is
placed, or a structure on or in which hazardous waste is
placed, that isolates hazardous wastes within a qualified
hazardous waste management facility and which is subject to
requirements to obtain interim status or a final permit under
subtitle C of the Solid Waste Disposal Act, as amended.

(4) TON.-- The term 'ton' means 2000 pounds.

(5) FRACTIONAL PART OF TON.-- In the case of a fraction
of a ton, the tax imposed by section 4681 shall be the same
fraction of the amount of such tax imposed on a whole ton.

(6) OCEAN DISPOSAL. -- The term 'ocean disposal' means
the incineration or dumping of hazardous waste over or into
ocean waters or the waters described in section 101(b) of the
Marine Protection Research, and Sanctuaries Act of 1972,
pursuant to section 102 of such Act.

(7) The terms 'treatment', 'storage', and 'disposal'
mean treatment, storage, and disposal as defined in section
1004 of the Solid Waste Disposal Act, as amended.

(8) The terms 'landfill', 'surface impoundment', 'waste
pile', and 'land treatment unit' mean a landfill, surface
impoundment, waste pile, and land treatment unit as defined
under regulations promulgated by the Administrator of the
Environmental Protection Agency pursuant to sections 3004 and
3005 of the Solid Waste Disposal Act, as amended.

(b) CREDIT FOR TAX PAID.-- Under regulations prescribed by

the Secretary, if --

(1) a tax under section 4681 is paid by a person with respect to hazardous waste, and

(2) such waste is subsequently received at another qualified hazardous waste management unit, received for transport for ocean disposal, or exported from the United States, an amount equal to the product of:

    (A) the lesser of

        (i) the quantity of hazardous waste subsequently transferred, or

        (ii) the quantity of hazardous waste on which the tax was previously paid under section 4681, multiplied by

    (B) the lesser of

        (i) the rate of tax specified in subsection (b) of section 4681 payable by the owner, operator, or exporter receiving the hazardous waste so transferred, or

        (ii) the rate of tax specified in subsection (b) of section 4681 previously paid,

shall be allowed as a credit or refund (without interest) to such person in the same manner as if it were an overpayment of tax imposed by such section.

    (c) Information Reporting Requirement.--

        (1) In general.-- Subpart A of part III of subchapter A of chapter 61 is amended by inserting after section 6039D the

following new section:

"Sec. 6039E.   Information with Respect to Tax on Hazardous Waste.

Each person on whom a tax is imposed under section 4681(a) shall submit to the Secretary such information as the Secretary may by regulation require, including information which such person is required to provide the Administrator of the Environmental Protection Agency under the Solid Waste Disposal Act."

(2) Penalty.-- Subchapter B of chapter 68 (relating to assessable penalties) is amended by redesignating section 6708 (relating to mortgage credit certificates) as section 6709 and by adding at the end thereof the following new section:

"Sec. 6710.   Failure to Provide Information with Respect to Tax
              on Hazardous Waste.

(a)   In General.-- Any person who fails to meet any requirement imposed by section 6039E shall pay a penalty of $25 for each day during which such failure continues, unless it is shown that such failure is due to reasonable cause and not due to willful neglect.   The maximum penalty imposed under this subsection shall not exceed $25,000.

(b)   Penalty In Addition to Other Penalties.-- The penalty imposed by this section shall be in addition to any other penalty provided by law.

(d) Conforming amendments.--

(1) The table of sections for subchapter C of chapter 38 of the Internal Revenue Code of 1954 is amended by redesignating the item relating to definitions and special rules as section 4683 and by adding after the item relating to section 4681 the following new item:

"4682. ADJUSTMENT OF TAX RATES."

(2) The table of sections for subpart A of Part III of subchapter A of chapter 61 of the Internal Revenue Code of 1954 is amended by inserting after the item relating to section 6039E the following new item:

"6039F. Information with Respect to Tax on Hazardous Waste."

(3) The table of sections for subchapter B of chapter 68 is amended by redesignating the item relating to mortgage credit certificates as section 6709 and by adding to the end thereof the following new item:

"Sec. 6710. Failure to provide information with respect to tax
        on hazardous waste disposal."

(e) Effective Date.-- The amendments made by this section shall apply to hazardous waste received, or exported after September 30, 1985.

51

REPEAL OF THE POST-CLOSURE TRUST FUND

Section 304.

(a) Repeal of Trust Fund. -- Section 232 of the Hazardous Substance Response Revenue Act of 1980 is hereby repealed.

(b) Technical Amendment. -- Sections 107(k) and 111(j) of the Comprehensive Environmental Response, Compensation, and Liability Act of 1980 are hereby repealed.

(c) Effective Date. -- The amendments made by this section shall take effect on October 1, 1985. .

CREATION OF HAZARDOUS SUBSTANCE SUPERFUND

Section 305. HAZARDOUS SUBSTANCE SUPERFUND.

(a) In general.-- Subchapter A of chapter 98 of the Internal Revenue Code of 1954 (relating to establishment of trust funds) is amended by adding at the end thereof the following new section:

"Section 9505. HAZARDOUS SUBSTANCE SUPERFUND.

(a) CREATION OF TRUST FUND.-- There is established in the Treasury of the United States a trust fund to be known as the 'Hazardous Substance Superfund' (hereinafter in this section referred to as the 'Superfund'), consisting of such amounts as may be appropriated or credited to the Superfund.

(b) TRANSFERS OF CERTAIN TAXES TO THE SUPERFUND.-- There are hereby appropriated to the Superfund amounts equivalent to--

(1) the taxes received in the Treasury under section 4611 (relating to tax on petroleum), section 4661 (relating to tax on certain chemicals), and section 4681 (relating to tax on hazardous wastes),

(2) amounts recovered on behalf of the Superfund under the Comprehensive Environmental Response, Compensation and Liability Act of 1980 (hereinafter in this section referred to as 'CERCLA') and on behalf of the Superfund under CERCLA, as amended

(3) all moneys recovered or collected under section

311(b)(6)(B) of the Clean Water Act,

(4) penalties assessed under title I of CERCLA,

(5) punitive damages under section 107(c)(3) of CERCLA, and

(6) the balance, as of September 30, 1985, in the "Post-Closure Liability Trust Fund", established under section 232 of CERCLA.

(c) EXPENDITURES FROM SUPERFUND.-- Amounts in the Superfund are authorized to be appropriated only for purposes of making expenditures which are described in section 111 of CERCLA as in effect on the date of enactment of this title for releases or threatened releases into the environment, including--

(1) response costs,

(2) claims asserted and compensable, but unsatisfied under section 311 of the Clean Water Act, and

(3) related costs described in section 111(c) of CERCLA.

(d) AUTHORITY TO BORROW.--

(1) In general.-- There are authorized to be appropriated to the Superfund, as repayable advances, such sums as may be necessary to carry out the purposes of Superfund.

(2) LIMITATIONS ON ADVANCES TO SUPERFUND.--

(A) AGGREGATE ADVANCES.-- The maximum aggregate amount of repayable advances to the Superfund which is outstanding at any one time shall not exceed an amount

. **54**

which the Secretary estimates will be equal to the sum
of the amounts described in paragraph (1) of subsection
(b) which will be transferred to the Superfund during
the following 12 months.

  (B) FINAL REPAYMENT.-- No advance shall be made to
the Superfund after September 30, 1990 and all advances
to such Fund shall be repaid on or before such date.
(3) REPAYMENT OF ADVANCES.--

  (A) In general.-- Advances made pursuant to this
subsection shall be repaid, and interest on such
advances shall be paid, to the general fund of the
Treasury when the Secretary determines that moneys are
available for such purposes in the Superfund (or when
required by paragraph (2)(B)).

  (B) RATE OF INTEREST.-- Interest on advances made
pursuant to this subsection shall be at a rate
determined by the Secretary of the Treasury (as of the
close of the calendar month preceding the month in which
the advance is made) to be equal to the current average
market yield on outstanding marketable obligations of
the United States with remaining periods to maturity
comparable to the anticipated period during which the
advance will be outstanding and shall be compounded
annually.

  (e) LIABILITY OF THE UNITED STATES LIMITED TO AMOUNT IN
TRUST FUND.--

55

(1) GENERAL RULE.-- Any claim filed against the Superfund may be paid only out of the Superfund.

(2) COORDINATION WITH OTHER PROVISIONS.-- Nothing in CERCLA or the Comprehensive Environmental Response, Compensation, and Liability Act Amendments of 1985 (or in any amendment made by either of such Acts) shall authorize the payment by the United States Government of any amount with respect to any such claim out of any source other than the Superfund.

(3) ORDER IN WHICH UNPAID CLAIMS ARE TO BE PAID.-- If at any time the Superfund is unable (by reason of paragraph (1)) to pay all of the claims payable out of the Superfund at such time, such claims shall, to the extent permitted under paragraph (1), be paid in full in the order in which they were finally determined.

(f) Unless reauthorized by the Congress, the authority to collect taxes conferred by this Act shall terminate when the sum of the amounts appropriated or credited to the Superfund during the reauthorization period pursuant to the provisions of this Act total $5.3 billion. The Secretary of the Treasury shall estimate when this level or will be reached and shall prescribe rules providing procedures for the termination of the tax authorized by this Act and imposed under sections 4611, 4661, and 4681 of the Internal Revenue Code of 1954.

56

(b) CONFORMING AMENDMENTS.--

(1) Subtitle B of the Hazardous Substance Response Revenue Act of 1980 (relating to establishment of Hazardous Substance Trust Fund) is hereby repealed.

(2) Paragraph (11) of section 101 of the Comprehensive Environment Response, Compensation and Liability Act of 1980 is amended to read as follows:

"(11) 'Fund' or 'Trust Fund' means the Hazardous Substance Superfund established by section 9505 of the Internal Revenue Code of 1954."

(3) Section 303 of the Comprehensive Environmental Response, Compensation, and Liability Act of 1980 is repealed.

(c) CLERICAL AMENDMENT.-- The table of sections for subchapter A of chapter 98 of such Code is amended by adding at the end thereof the following new item:

"Sec. 9505. Hazardous Substance Superfund."

(d) EFFECTIVE DATE.--

(1) In general. The amendments made by this section shall take effect on October 1, 1985.

(2) SUPERFUND TREATED AS CONTINUATION OF OLD TRUST FUND.-- The Hazardous Substance Superfund established by the amendment made by this section shall be treated for all purposes of law as a continuation of the Hazardous Substance Response Trust Fund established by section 221 of the Hazardous Substance Response Revenue Act of 1980. Any

reference in any law to the Hazardous Substance Response
Trust Fund established by such section 221 shall be deemed to
include (wherever appropriate) a reference to the Hazardous
Substance Superfund established by the amendments made by
this section.

5501

58

TITLE IV--MISCELLANEOUS PROVISIONS

APPLICABILITY OF AMENDMENTS

Sec. 401. The amendments made by this Act to section 104(a) and (b) of the Comprehensive Environmental Response, Compensation, and Liability Act of 1980 shall not apply to releases listed as of January 1, 1985, in the national hazardous substance response plan published pursuant to section 105(8)(B) of that Act.

59

SECTION-BY-SECTION ANALYSIS

EPA'S PROPOSED AMENDMENTS TO CERCLA

SECTION 1

Short Title

The short title of the legislation is the "Comprehensive Environmental Response, Compensation, and Liability Act Amendments of 1985" (CERCLA Amendments).

SECTION 2

Amendment to CERCLA

This legislation, which reauthorizes the Superfund program from FY 1986 to FY 1990, amends the Comprehensive Environmental Response, Compensation, and Liability Act of 1980 (CERCLA or "Superfund").

SECTION 3

Statement of Findings and Purposes

This section sets forth the findings and purposes of CERCLA. The major findings are that --

o Releases and threats of releases of hazardous substances continue to pose serious threats to public
   health and the environment;

o A major source of the hazardous substance release
   problem results from releases from uncontrolled
   hazardous waste facilities; and

o To protect human health and the environment, a
   comprehensive Federal program is needed. The program
   must include strengthened enforcement authority, a
   Federal-State partnership and expanded citizen participation for effective response to hazardous waste
   sites and releases or threatened releases of hazardous
   substances.

The objective of this section is to clarify Congressional intent that the focus of the Superfund program should be on responding to releases or threatened releases of hazardous substances from uncontrolled hazardous waste sites.

SECTION 4

Definitions

Section 101(14) lists those substances which are hazardous under CERCLA by reference to substances listed under five other environmental laws. Section 101(14)(C) includes as hazardous under CERCLA "any hazardous waste having the characteristics identified under or listed pursuant to section 3001 of the Solid Waste Disposal Act ....".

This amendment would clarify that a substance need not be a "waste" to be considered a CERCLA hazardous substance under this subsection, so long as the substance meets the criteria of section 3001 of the Solid Waste Disposal Act.

SECTION 101

Authority to Respond

CERCLA section 104(a)(1) currently authorizes response action "unless the President determines that such removal or remedial action will be done properly by the owner or operator of the facility...or by any other responsible party." The amendment would clarify and confirm that the President has the discretion to decide when responsible parties are authorized to conduct cleanup in lieu of Fund-financed response.

This amendment is not intended to preclude or discourage responsible parties from conducting cleanup actions without the formal permission of the Federal government. The current requirements of section 105 of CERCLA (National Contingency Plan) contemplate a significant role for private parties in response actions.

The amendment is intended to clarify that the Federal government would not be precluded from conducting a response action, merely because responsible parties have indicated some willingness to take some form of response action. This amendment would confirm that if the Federal government determines that Federal response is needed, the President would have the discretion to determine the appropriate response and to take action; responsible parties would not be authorized to forestall Federal response.

Scope of Program

The language in the statute authorizes response to the release into the environment of any designated hazardous substance, or pollutant or contaminant which may present a threat to public health, welfare, or the environment.

61

The amendment would focus Superfund response authority
on the problems associated with releases of hazardous substances
from uncontrolled hazardous waste sites. Specifically, the
amendment would --

* delete "pollutant or contaminant" from the Act;

* delete "welfare" from the phrase "public health,
welfare, and the environment" in the Act;

* authorize response whenever there is a release or
substantial threat of a release into the environment
which may present a "risk" to public health or the
environment; and

* prohibit Superfund response from certain categories
of releases, unless the President determines that a
major public health or environmental emergency exists
and that no other person has the authority or capability to respond in a timely manner --

-- from mining activities covered by SMCRA;

-- from the lawful application of pesticides
registered under FIFRA;

-- affecting residential, business, or community
structures when contamination is not caused
by a release from a hazardous substance
treatment, storage, or disposal facility;

-- affecting public or private domestic water
supply wells when contamination is not caused
by a release from a hazardous substance treatment, storage, or disposal facility;

-- from naturally occurring substances in their
unaltered form; and

-- covered by and in compliance with a permit,
issued under other federal environmental laws.

The effect of the amendment would be to ensure that
Superfund responses are focused on those releases of hazardous
substances which present the greatest threat to public health
and the environment, and to enhance EPA's ability to effectively
manage the program.

SECTION 102

Statutory Limits on Removals

Section 104(c)(1) of CERCLA limits removal actions to six months in duration and $1 million in cost unless certain waiver criteria are met. These criteria incude: a finding that continued action is necessary to prevent or mitigate the emergency and to protect public health and the environment, and that assistance would not otherwise be provided on a timely basis. Because of the limits established in this provision, some removals have been scaled-down below the level needed to achieve a cost-effective response.

This amendment would provide an additional and independent criterion for waiving the statutory limits on removal actions and increase the six month duration limitation to one year. The new criterion would permit removals to exceed the $1 million cost and one year duration limitations if the response action is "appropriate and consistent with a permanent remedy." The amendment would ensure that removals accomplish a more complete response, if such response is appropriate in that situation.

The primary effect of the amendment would be to enhance the President's ability to choose the most effective response in removal situations. Generally, the amendment would allow, where appropriate, the first operable units of remedial actions to be considered removals. This would provide the Agency with increased flexibility to quickly initiate the appropriate removal. This ability to implement a response quickly would enhance efforts to contain the migration of hazardous substances. In turn, this would result in increased public health and environmental protection and may be less costly since hazardous substances could be contained before they migrate to a much larger area requiring greater response.

SECTION 103

Permanent Remedies

Section 104(c)(4) of CERCLA requires the selection of an appropriate remedial action that is consistent with the National Contingency Plan (NCP) and is cost-effective in light of concerns about protecting public health and the environment, considerations of Fund-balancing, and the need for immediate action. There is no explicit requirement that the selection of a remedial action take into consideration permanent solutions or alternative treatment technologies.

EPA currently considers the long-term effectiveness and the permanence of alternatives in its selection of the appropriate remedial action. This amendment would provide explicit Congressional approval of EPA's position and would allow revision of the NCP to implement this approach to permanent remedies.

SECTION 104

Offsite Remedial Action

Section 101(24) of CERCLA, which defines "remedy or remedial action", provides that additional threshold criteria must be met before the President may undertake off-site disposal of hazardous substances. This creates a bias against off-site disposal and reflects past Congressional and EPA emphasis on on-site land disposal as the preferred remedial action.

The objective of the amendment is to eliminate the statutory bias for on-site remedies by making the statute neutral with regard to on-site or off-site remedies.

Congress, as reflected in the 1984 amendments to the Resource Conservation and Recovery Act, and EPA have come to recognize the value of treatment and other alternative technologies.

The primary effect of this amendment would be to reduce the proliferation of sites requiring monitoring in perpetuity (by consolidating wastes from many sites into one larger and closely monitored facility), by recognizing the value of permanent off-site remedies, such as treatment.

SECTION 105

National Contingency Plan (NCP)

This amendment would (1) eliminate the requirement that the NCP include at least 400 facilities, and (2) clarify that States are allowed only one highest priority designation for the life of the list.

The deletion of the phrase "at least 400 facilities" would allow the Agency to select and place on the National Priorities List, only those facilities which present "the greatest danger to public health or welfare or the environment."

The second part of the amendment would be a Congressional ratification of EPA's present policy which is to permit the States to make only one highest priority designation. This policy is reflected in the most recent proposed revisions to the NCP.

These amendments allow the President to effectively limit the NPL to only those facilities which pose significant problems to public health or the environment as determined through Agency regulation.

SECTION 106

Cooperative Agreements

The amendment would explicitly permit contracts and cooperative agreements to cover more than one facility, as is current EPA policy, and clarifies and confirms that response includes enforcement activities associated with a remedial or removal action. The objective of the amendment is to facilitate State response activities by permitting States to enter into agreements covering more than one site, and by providing Fund money for response actions, including enforcement activities.

The primary effect of the amendment would be to increase State participation in response and enforcement activities. This would increase the overall pace and effectiveness of the Superfund program.

SECTION 107

Publicly Operated Facilities

Section 104(c)(3) of CERCLA requires States to pay at least 50 percent of response costs for hazardous substance releases from facilities <u>owned</u> by the State or political subdivision thereof at the time the release occurred.

The amendment would change the 50 percent State cost share to 75 percent and impose the 75 percent or greater cost-share only at those facilities <u>operated</u> directly or indirectly by the State or political subdivision. The test for imposing the 75 percent or greater cost-share would be related to operation rather than ownership of the facility at the time of disposal of hazardous substances. The cost-share under this amendment would apply to sites owned and operated by the State; sites owned by the State and operated by a private party under a contract or lease with the State; and sites

owned by a private party but operated by the State. The
objective of the amendment is to impose the cost-share on
States only in those cases where the State is involved in
the operation of the facility, either directly or indirectly.

This amendment would also clarify that for purposes of
this amendment only that the term facility will not include
navigable waters or the beds underlying those waters, and thus
a 75 percent cost share would not be imposed on States for
response actions at such facilities.

SECTION 108

Siting of Hazardous Waste Facilities

Section 104(c)(3) of CERCLA requires that States assure
the availability of hazardous waste disposal facilities for
off-site remedial actions that are in compliance with subtitle
C of RCRA. States are not, however, required to nor provided
incentives for creating or expanding existing capacity for
managing wastes, or otherwise provide for future treatment
and disposal of hazardous wastes. In order to maintain an
aggressive Superfund program, it is essential to ensure that
States have adequate waste disposal capabilities.

This amendment would provide initiatives to States to
create and expand capacity for managing wastes within the
State by prohibiting the use of Fund money for response
actions in those States that do not assure the availability
of hazardous waste disposal capacity sufficient to handle
that State's needs during a period of time to be specified
by regulation. The amendment would be effective two years
after enactment.

There would be limited exceptions to this prohibition.
First, the amendment would permit Fund expenditures for
alternative drinking water or for temporary relocation of
affected individuals from their homes for up to one year.
Second, Fund money could be used to finance a response action
in a State that does not provide the above assurance if the
President determines that a major public health or environmental
emergency exists.

Any response action taken where the State fails to
assure the availability of sufficient offsite capacity would
be subject to a higher cost share.

The amendment would also require States to pay any additional
costs associated with transporting wastes outside the State's
boundaries (or outside the region, if the State has entered
into a regional agreement for hazardous waste treatment and
disposal) in addition to the cost of the remedy. This clause
would be effective upon enactment.

The objective of the amendment is to create an economic incentive for States to expand existing or create new long-term in-state capacity to manage hazardous wastes.

SECTION 109

Community Involvement

CERCLA does not presently address the role of community involvement in response actions. Existing federal policy does, however, provide for an active community role as expressed in existing program guidance and the proposed revisions to the National Contingency Plan.

This amendment would require public notification and an opportunity for public comment on the proposed action. The primary objective of the amendment is to ensure community involvement in remedial actions taken pursuant to this Act, including Fund-financed and enforcement actions.

Because the President has already incorporated the requirements set forth in this amendment in operating guidance, the amendment itself would not impose new responsibilities on the federal government.

The amendment confirms the President's commitment to community involvement in the Superfund program.

SECTION 110

Health Related Authorities

Section 104(i) of CERCLA establishes the Agency for Toxic Substances and Disease Registry (ATSDR). ATSDR, in cooperation with EPA and other Federal agencies, is authorized to implement the health related authorities of the Act. These authorities include the establishment and maintenance of: a national registry of diseases and illnesses associated with and persons exposed to hazardous substances, and a data base on the health effects of hazardous substances. CERCLA does not clearly define specific roles and responsibilities of ATSDR and EPA in implementing these and other health related authorities.

The amendment would clarify that the primary purpose of health related activities is to support response actions through health assessments, consultations, and other technical assistance relating to the health effects of exposure to hazardous substances, and to improve the ability to render future public health recommendations through expanding the existing body of scientific knowledge.

In addition, the amendment would clarify existing roles and responsibilities of ATSDR and EPA in conducting various health related activities. Specifically, the amendment would authorize EPA as well as State and local officials to request that ATSDR provide health consultations, assessments, and other assistance to determine the health effects of exposure to hazardous substances. ATSDR may provide such assistance. The President would also be authorized to conduct exposure and risk assessments at sites where a release has occurred.

The amendment would not significantly affect current health related activities but it merely provides a statutory basis for current roles and responsibilities undertaken by ATSDR and EPA.

SECTION 111

Compliance with Other Environmental Laws

This amendment would authorize the President to specify in the National Contingency Plan (NCP) the extent to which remedial and removal actions selected under section 104 or selected under section 106 should comply with applicable or relevant standards and criteria established under other Federal, State or local environmental and public health laws. The amendment would specify the factors the President must consider in making this determination; these include: the level of health or environmental protection provided by the standard; the technical feasibility of achieving the standard; the interim or permanent nature of the response; the need for expedient action; and the need to preserve funds to respond to other respond to other releases.

The objective of the amendment is to clarify and confirm the President's authority to determine when response actions should comply with other Federal, State, or local laws, which is set forth in existing EPA policy. This amendment confirms that because of the unique statutory provisions of CERCLA, and requirements for response action that strict compliance with other statutory provisions is often not appropriate or necessary.

SECTION 112

Actions Under the National Contingency Plan

Section 107(d) of CERCLA exempts persons from liability for damages resulting from actions taken or omitted in responding to hazardous substance releases.

This amendment would add that persons (e.g., EPA contractors and others) conducting response actions in accordance with the NCP or at the direction of an on-scene coordinator are also exempt from liability for future response costs. This means that, for example, contractors would not be held liable for additional response costs at a site if another response action is taken at a site where the contractor already conducted a previous action (if a second response action was taken because the first response was not sufficient to address the problem), unless the original action was negligent or intentionally misconducted.

The primary effect of the amendment would be to limit contractor liability for future response costs. The amendment would not affect third party liability claims. Nor would the amendment affect the liability of persons liable or potentially liable under section 107(a) who undertake a response action under this act.

Section 113

Natural Resource Damage Claims

The amendment would clarify existing language about the responsibilities of Federal and State natural resources trustees. In general, the Federal or State trustee would perform assessments of damage to resources under its jurisdiction, except that Federal trustees may perform assessments on behalf of States and may be reimbursed by States for performing the assessments. Neither Federal nor State trustees would be required to use the damage assessment regulations being prepared by the Department of the Interior, but if they used the Department of the Interior regulation the assessment would be entitled to a presumption of validity.

The amendment would also eliminate use of the Fund to pay trustees for damage to natural resources. Accordingly, all references to natural resource damage claims against the Fund would be deleted from the Act. The ability of Federal and State trustees to recover damages from responsible parties under section 107 would not diminished.

Finally, Federal agencies with custody and accountability for specific Federal facilities would be the sole trustee of natural resources on, under, or above such facilities for purposes of CERCLA.

SECTION 114

Response Claims

Section 111 of CERCLA authorizes parties who conduct response actions to assert claims against the Fund to recover necessary response costs incurred in carrying out the National Contingency Plan. The procedures to be followed in presenting and processing these claims against the Fund are set forth in section 112. This amendment would clarify and streamline the process for response claims.

The amendment would make the following changes:

o Clarify authority to preauthorize response claims;

* Eliminate provisions for negotiations with responsible parties;

* Substitute an administrative hearing process for claims adjustments and arbitration; and

o Clarify time frames for review of claims.

The availability of response claims can expedite private party cleanup. Following preauthorization for all or portions of the cleanup, private parties can promptly conduct cleanup action, and bring claims to the Fund when the response action is completed.

CERCLA currently prescribes five steps at a minimum in the process from initial presentation of the claim to the responsible party to final payment of an award. Where administrative review and judicial appeal are involved the process may take as many as eight steps before the claimant receives final payment of an award.

The amendments to this section would streamline the claims procedure. First, section 111 would be amended to clarify the authority of the Agency to preauthorize response claims. Preauthorization can be used to assure that response actions are conducted properly, and that they are limited to available funds.

Second, the provisions for negotiations with responsible parties prior to payment of claims would be eliminated. Such negotiations as are needed would be conducted prior to preauthorization.

Third, an administrative hearing process would be substituted for the arbitration procedure presently provided for in the statute. The arbitration procedure is a vestige of certain economic damage claims which were not enacted in 1980. In that the claims procedures will involve only reimbursement of costs, there is no reason for claims to be arbitrated.

Response costs, are not particularly appropriate for consideration by a panel of arbitrators.

Fourth, certain ambiguities in the timeframes for Presidential action would be clarified.

SECTION 115

Indian Tribes

CERCLA is presently silent regarding the status of tribal governments and Indian lands. Current CERCLA policy, however, recognizes tribal governments as independent sovereigns with authority and responsibility over reservations roughly analogous to that of State governments. This means that tribal governments are subject to various notification, consultation, health related activity, and financial and disposal capacity assurance requirements.

The proposed amendment would clarify the role of States, Indian tribes, and the Federal government for facilities on Indian lands. It defines Indian lands to include only those where there is some type of trust responsibility or restriction against alienation.

Subsection (a) would add two new definitions, "Indian tribe" and "Indian lands." Both definitions are tied to the United States trust responsibility. Not all Federally recognized Indian tribes would be included in the CERCLA definition; only those tribes for which land is held in trust.

Section (b) would set forth the procedure for remedial actions on Indian lands. Indian tribes would be required to provide the assurances specified in section 104(c)(3) for sites on Indian lands. If the Secretary of the Interior finds that a tribe cannot provide these assurances, the Department of the Interior may provide them on behalf of the tribe. States would not be required to provide assurance for sites wholly on Indian lands.

The amendment authorizes the President to enter into
agreements with Indian tribes to carry out response actions
under section 104 and the National Contingency Plan and to
enforce these agreements. Indian tribes would be reimbursed
from the Fund for reasonable response costs.

Also, Indian tribes would be notified by the National Response
Center of releases that affect Indian lands.

SECTION 116

Preemption

Section 114(c) of CERCLA preempts States from requiring
persons to contribute to any fund designed to provide compensation
for claims for response costs or damages which may be compen-
sated under CERCLA. The provision is not clear and it has been
argued that the intent of this provision is to preempt States
from imposing State taxes to finance certain CERCLA and
non-CERCLA action.

The amendment would delete the section which preempts
States from imposing taxes for purposes already covered by
CERCLA. The objective of the amendment is to ensure that
States may impose taxes to meet Superfund cost-share require-
ments, and to foster State cleanup at sites not covered by
CERCLA.

The primary effect of the amendment would be to remove a
potential barrier to the creation of State superfund programs.
The amendment may result in an increase in the number and
pace of hazardous substance response actions undertaken or
partially funded by States since States would be able to
raise funds to assist such hazardous substance response.

SECTION 117

State Cost-Share

Section 104(c)(3)(C)(i) of CERCLA requires States to pay
ten percent of costs for remedial actions at privately owned
facilities.

This amendment would alter the existing Federal-State
cost-share to require States to pay 20 percent of the remedial
action costs at privately owned sites. The cost-share for
State or political subdivision sites would be 75 percent
(see section 106 of this Act).

The objective of this amendment is to reduce the existing
burden on the Federal government for financing remedial
response actions by requiring the States to pay a larger
share of costs at privately owned sites. The amendment is
consistent with an overall goal of these amendments in
increasing the role of the States in conducting response
actions.

TITLE II -- PROVISIONS RELATING PRIMARILY TO ENFORCEMENT

SECTION 201

Civil Penalties for Non-Reporting

Section 103(a) of CERCLA requires any person in charge of a vessel or facility to notify the National Response Center as soon as the person in charge has knowledge of any release of a hazardous substance in an amount that equals or exceeds the reportable quantity established under section 102. These notifications serve as one basis for the Federal government to determine whether response action is appropriate for the release.

The existing statute provides only criminal penalties for failure to report. This amendment would increase the criminal penalty to $25,000 and provide additional enforcement flexibility by allowing the imposition of a civil penalty of up to $10,000 per violation.

The amendment would enable the Administrator to assess civil penalties aggregating less than $25,000 for such violations; penalties aggregating more than $25,000 may be recovered by the Attorney General through a civil action.

Civil penalties for violations of notification requirements have several advantages:

First, civil penalties may be imposed in situations where the violations do not merit the sanctions associated with criminal violations.

Second, when the Federal government takes an enforcement action to compel private party cleanup action for such a release, the Federal government may now also seek penalties for violations of the notification provision in the cleanup enforcement action.

SECTION 202

Contribution and Parties to Litigation

This amendment would change section 107 of CERCLA
to provide a greater degree of finality to settlements reached
with responsible parties, and to expedite private party
cleanup by simplifying the litigation process in imminent
hazard and cost recovery actions.

This amendment would clarify and confirm existing law
governing liability of potentially responsible parties in
three respects:

- parties found liable under section 106 or 107
  would have a right of contribution, allowing them to
  sue other liable or potentially liable parties to
  recover a portion of the costs paid;

- parties who reach a judicially approved good faith
  settlement with the government would not liable for
  the contribution claims of other liable parties; and

- where a civil or administrative action is underway,
  contribution actions could be brought only after a
  judgment is entered or a settlement in good faith is
  reached.

The first provision should help to encourage private
party settlements and cleanups. Parties who settle or who
pay judgments as a result of litigation, could attempt to
recover some portion of their loss in subsequent contribution
litigation from parties who were not sued in the enforcement
action. Private parties may be more willing to assume the
financial responsibility for cleanup if they are assured that
they can seek contribution from others.

The second provision would help bring an increased measure
of finality to settlements. Responsible parties who have entered
into a judicially approved good faith settlement under the Act
would be protected from paying any additional portion of
costs to other responsible parties in a contribution action.

The third provision would allow more expeditious management
of litigation. Hazardous waste sites often involve dozens or
even hundreds of potentially responsible parties with differing
types and degrees of involvement in the facility. While
the government may sue all potentially responsible parties,
it need not sue all these parties. It may instead sue a
limited number of parties to secure complete cleanup or all
costs of cleanup under the theory of joint and several liability.
In some instances these parties have in turn sued other
potentially responsible parties in the same judicial action.
In several cases this has resulted in massive and potentially
unmanageable litigation.

The amendment would clarify that if an enforcement action is underway, claims for contribution or indemnification could not be brought until a judgment or settlement is reached. This change would allow the government to limit the number of parties in its actions, so that litigation could be conducted in a more efficient and expeditious fashion.

SECTION 203

Access and Information Gathering

Section 104(e) of CERCLA clearly authorizes the Agency to request information concerning the treatment, storage, disposal or handling of hazardous substances, and to enter premises where hazardous substances were generated, stored, treated, disposed, or transported. This amendment would clarify and confirm the President's right to access and information concerning the release or threatened release of hazardous substances by making explicit the original intent of Congress when CERCLA was enacted in 1980.

Currently, there is no explicit authority to enforce information requests under CERCLA. In addition, there is no explicit language to compel parties to provide access to the site or adjacent areas. Access to the site is obviously needed to conduct a response action. The President may also need access to adjacent areas to conduct sampling or move equipment.

While landowners generally will provide access voluntarily, explicit statutory authority would encourage private parties to consent to access and information requests, and would provide explicit mechanisms for the President to obtain access and information when such requests are reasonable but refused.

This amendment would also establish procedures for the President to issue orders for access and information. The President would notify potential recipients of orders and provide an opportunity for consultation. The President could also seek to have the Federal courts enjoin interference with access and direct private parties to comply with orders. This provision would enable the government to seek judicial relief so that necessary response actions would not be unduly delayed.

SECTION 204

Administrative Orders for Section 104(b) Actions

CERCLA section 104(b) currently authorizes the President to conduct a variety of investigations, studies, and information gathering activities. Under this section, remedial investigations and feasibility studies (RI/FSs) are performed to serve as the basis for choosing the appropriate extent of remedy.

In some circumstances, it may be appropriate to allow potentially responsible parties to conduct RI/FSs or other investigations or studies. This approach would free up government resources to address other sites, and would increase the likelihood that private parties would assume responsibilities for cleanup of the site. Such private-party RI/FSs are most effective when they are performed pursuant to an administrative order that clearly sets out the responsibilities of the private parties.

This amendment to CERCLA would provide for administrative orders on consent without the need for any findings by the President with regard to potential hazard at the facility, to allow the planning and investigative stages of response actions to proceed more expeditiously. The order would be enforceable in district court, and the court could issue a civil penalty for noncompliance.

It should be noted that EPA retains the authority to choose the appropriate remedy, based on a Record of Decision developed by EPA. This amendment would not authorize orders on consent for actual cleanup activities under section 104.

This section would also include a technical amendment to section 107 of CERCLA. Section 107 currently provides for treble damages from any person who is liable for a release or threat of release and who fails without sufficient cause to comply with an order under section 104. The penalties established for violations of administrative orders for access under section 203 of this Act, and orders on consent for private party studies and investigations, are sufficient incentives to assure compliance. Accordingly, the reference to treble damages for violations of section 104 orders would be removed. This would not change the President's authority to seek treble damages for violations of orders under section 106.

SECTION 205

Non-Trust Fund and Pre-Trust Fund Expenditures

This amendment would clarify and confirm that CERCLA establishes liability for costs incurred by the United States in response to a release or threatened release of a hazardous substance from a treatment, storage or disposal facility where the response was after passage of the Resource Conservation and Recovery Act of 1976 and the party knew or should have known of the response action. Such costs must not have been inconsistent with remedial or removal actions under CERCLA.

The United States has incurred substantial response costs in connection with responses at hazardous waste facilities occurring after enactment of RCRA that are wholly consistent with CERCLA's goals and authorities. Where the person knew or should have known of the Federal response action, but did not act to clean up the release, it is entirely appropriate and consistent with CERCLA to clarify and confirm that responsible parties are liable for such response costs.

SECTION 206

Statute of Limitations

CERCLA currently includes no explicit statute of limitations for the filing of cost recovery actions under section 107. Nevertheless, the Federal government recognizes the need for filing of cost recovery actions in a timely fashion, to assure that evidence concerning liability and response costs is fresh, to help replenish the Fund, and to provide some measure of finality to affected responsible parties. The absence of an explicit statute of limitations has also led to some uncertainty concerning whether the existence of such a statute of limitations should be assumed under Federal law.

This amendment would eliminate this uncertainty by establishing a six-year statute of limitations for the filing of cost recovery actions. The six-year statute of limitations is the same as the period established by a clear line of cases involving the parallel provisions in section 311 of the Clean Water Act. Because response actions may extend for a number of years, the government is not precluded from commencing an action for recovery of costs at any time after such costs have been incurred.

For purposes of this section, the response action is regarded as completed upon completion of any operation and maintenance activities funded by the Federal government.

In addition, this amendment would provide a three-year statute of limitations: for damage actions, running from the date of discovery of the loss; for contribution actions, running from entry of judgment or the date of settlement; and for rights subrogated pursuant to a claim paid from the Fund, from the date of payment of such claim.

SECTION 207

Pre-Enforcement Review

The purpose of this amendment is to clarify the process for judicial review of government decisions on the appropriate extent of remedy and liability of responsible parties. This section establishes that:

o   review of all Presidential decisions concerning remedy is on the administrative record;

o   there is no pre-enforcement review of section 106 administrative orders; and

o   administrative orders are subject to judicial review once response action is completed.

(a)   Record Review:

While CERCLA does not explicitly state how decisions on remedies will be judicially reviewed, the Federal government has taken the position and certain courts have suggested that review of decisions concerning remedy, like most administrative decisions, are on the basis of the administrative record. This amendment would clarify and confirm that judicial review of the response action is limited to the administrative record and that the action shall be upheld unless it is arbitrary, capricious, or otherwise not in accordance with law. Reliance on an administrative record helps assure that the basis for the response decision is clearly articulated and open to the scrutiny by the public and responsible parties.

Limiting judicial review of response actions to the administrative record also expedites the process of review and ensures that the reviewing court's attention is focused on the information and criteria used in selecting the remedy.

(b)   Pre-Enforcement Review:

Section 106 orders may be subject to judicial review at the time the government acts to enforce the order and collect penalties for non-compliance. This amendment would clarify and confirm that orders are not subject to judicial review prior to that time.

The clarification reflects the fact that pre-enforcement review would be a significant obstacle to the use of administrative orders. It is likely that pre-enforcement review would lead to considerable delay in providing cleanups, increase response costs and discourage settlements and voluntary cleanups.

(c)   Review of Orders:

The changes discussed above clarify and confirm the existing process. Section 208(c) would amend section 106 to establish new procedures for reimbursement of certain response costs and to provide for judicial review of administrative orders once the response action required by the order is completed.

Under the amendment, responsible parties can request reimbursement from the Fund for costs incurred in responding to an order. If the President refuses to grant all or part of a petition for reimbursement, responsible parties may file an action in district court seeking reimbursement. Responsible parties can obtain reimbursement if they can show that:

o   they are not liable, and that the costs which they incurred in responding to the order were reasonable; or

o   the response action ordered by the President was arbirtrary and capricious or otherwise not in accordance with law.

This provision is intended to foster compliance with orders and expeditious cleanup, allowing potentially responsible parties to preserve their positions concerning liability and the appropriateness of the response action, in circumstances where they agree to undertake the cleanup. Under the record review provisions discussed above, responsible parties would also have opportunities for input into the decision making process for choosing the appropriate response action.

SECTION 208

Nationwide Service of Process

Rule 4(f) of the Federal Rules of Civil Procedure limits effective service of process to the territorial limits of the State in which the district court is held, unless a Federal statute provides otherwise. Difficulties have arisen in obtaining personal jurisdiction over certain defendants in actions by the United States under CERCLA. This amendment would remove these difficulties by providing that the United States may serve a defendant in any district where he resides, transacts business, or may otherwise be found.

SECTION 209

Abatement Action

This amendment would delete the references to "welfare" in section 106 of CERCLA. Consequently, enforcement or abatement action could only be taken when the President determines that there may be an imminent and substantial endangerment

to the public health or the environment because of an actual
or threatened release of a hazardous substance from a facility.
This amendment focuses CERCLA enforcement efforts on public
health and the environment.

SECTION 210

Federal Lien

This amendment would enable the United States to recover
at least some of its response costs through an in rem action
against the real property that is the subject of the response
action. Such protection for the United States would also
enable it to recover the increase in land value resulting
from the response action, thus preventing unjust enrichment
of the property owner.

The amendment would provide that all costs and damages
for which a person is liable to the United States under
section 107(a) shall be a lien on all real property affected
by the response action. The lien would arise at the time the
United States first incurs response costs, but would not be
perfected as against purchasers, security interest holders,
and judgment lien creditors (all as defined in the tax lien
statute, 26 U.S.C. §6321 et seq.) until notice of the lien
has been recorded or filed. The notice provision would not apply
with respect to any person who knew or should have known that
the United States had incurred response costs.

SECTION 211

Penalties

This amendment would increase criminal penalties in
section 103(d)(2) of CERCLA for destruction of records from
$20,000 to $25,000. Civil penalties under section 106(b) of
CERCLA for violation of a 106 order would be increased from
$5,000 to $10,000 per day. These increases in penalties are
intended to significantly strengthen existing incentives for
compliance with CERCLA provisions.

SECTION 212

Federal Agency Settlement

The existing section 107(g) of CERCLA makes Federal
agencies liable for response costs and natural resource
damages from releases of hazardous substances in the same
manner as a private entity. This may be the basis for
legitimate claims which should be paid by the United States
without resort to litigation. However, CERCLA currently
neither confers authority nor specifies procedures for
administrative payment of such claims.

This amendment provides procedures for administrative settlement of CERCLA claims. The language is modeled closely after a similar provision in the Federal Tort Claims Act, 10 U.S.C. § 2672. Under the amendment, Federal agencies are authorized to settle claims for $25,000 or less in accordance with Justice Department procedures, and to arrive at tentative settlements for Justice Department approval for amounts over $25,000.

SECTION 213

Foreign Vessel Liability

This amendment would delete from CERCLA a clause that had the unintended effect of excluding from liability under section 107 all foreign vessels not under United States jurisdiction, even when such vessels release hazardous substances in areas otherwise subject to United States jurisdiction.

TITLE III -- AMENDMENTS TO THE INTERNAL REVENUE CODE OF 1954

Title II of CERCLA amended the Internal Revenue Code of 1954, establishing the Hazardous Substance Response Trust Fund (Fund). The Fund is comprised primarily of revenue derived from excise taxes on certain petrochemicals and inorganic raw materials, as well as on domestic crude oil and imported petroleum products (87%) and appropriations from the General Fund (12%). Revenues in the Fund are used to finance Superfund response and support activities.

The present CERCLA tax scheme is referred to as a "feedstock tax" because it imposes a tax on the basic chemical building blocks of chemical products. The hazardous substances and wastes associated with the problems addressed by CERCLA are byproducts of production processes that use these raw materials.

The Fund was designed to contain approximately $1.6 billion from FY 1981 through FY 1985. Current authorization to impose taxes to finance the program expires September 30, 1985. This amendment is needed to authorize the imposition of taxes to finance Superfund response actions over the next five years.

The tax structure set forth in these amendments has been designed to meet the following objectives:

* to provide a stable and predictable source of revenue;

* to broaden the tax base from which contributions are received;

* to minimize adverse economic impacts on taxed industries; and

* to focus the tax on the type of industries and practices that have caused the problems that are addressed by Superfund.

The amendment would authorize a Fund of approximately $1 billion per year, or roughly $5.3 billion from FY 1986 through FY 1990. This represents the level of funding that can be effectively managed over the next five years and raised without significant adverse affects on tax paying firms.

The amendment would establish a Fund with revenue derived primarily from three sources.

The first source of revenue would be derived from a feedstock tax. This tax would be imposed on crude oil and petroleum products as well as the 42 chemical feedstocks taxed under the present statute. The tax rates imposed on these feedstocks would remain the same as the rates established in 1980: approximately $4.87 per ton for petrochemical feedstocks, approximately $4.45 per ton for inorganic raw materials (with adjustments for elemental equivalency), and 0.79 cents per barrel for crude oil and petroleum products. This feedstock tax would maintain the current CERCLA exemptions on methane or butane used as fuel, substances used in the production of fertilizers, sulfuric acid produced as a by-product of air pollution control, substances derived from coal, and taxable chemicals made from previously taxed taxable chemicals. The feedstock tax has been designed to raise approximately $300 million per year.

The second source of revenue would be derived from a waste-management tax. This tax would be imposed on the receipt of hazardous wastes at a qualified treatment, storage, or disposal unit (i.e. a unit permitted under the Resource Conservation and Recovery Act (RCRA)), as well as on hazardous wastes disposed of in the ocean or exported from the United States. The tax liability would be imposed on the owner or operator of a qualified hazardous waste management facility, the owner or operator of a vessel that disposes of wastes into or over the ocean, and the exporter of hazardous wastes.

The tax rates imposed under the waste-management tax would increase each year of the tax, and would be higher for landfills, surface impoundments, waste piles, and land treatment units. The following amount per wet-weight ton would be imposed:

Year	Rate *
FY 86	$ 9.80 per ton
FY 87	$10.09
FY 88	$11.13
FY 89	$13.48
FY 90	$16.32

For waste exported from the U.S., disposed into or over the ocean, or received at a qualified hazardous waste manage-ment unit other than specified above, the following amount per wet-weight ton would be imposed:

Year	Rate *
FY 86	$ 2.61 per ton
FY 87	$ 2.68
FY 88	$ 2.96
FY 89	$ 3.59
FY 90	$ 4.37

* Beginning in 1987, the tax rates would be adjusted annually to compensate for any shortfalls in projected revenues. If necessary to meet revenue targets, the tax may be extended from October 1, 1990, through March 31, 1985, at the same rates applicable in Fiscal Year 1990.

Wastes managed in units not subject to permits under
subtitle C of RCRA (e.g. wastes stored in tanks and containers
for less than 90 days), wastes from CERCLA response actions, and
wastes generated by Federal facilities would not be subject to
the waste-management tax. Additionally, a credit would be
given for taxes already paid on wastes that are transferred
from one taxable unit to another. If the units involved in
the transfer have different applicable tax rates, the credit
would be based on the lower rate.

The waste-management tax has been designed to raise approximately $600 million per year.

The third source of revenue would be derived from interest
on Superfund investments, fines, costs recovered from parties
responsible for response actions financed from the Fund, and
intra-fund transfers. This portion of the Fund would raise
approximately $100 million per year.

TITLE IV -- MISCELLANEOUS PROVISIONS

SECTION 401

Applicability of Amendments

This amendment would add a new section to CERCLA providing
that the amendments relating to section 104(a) and (b), which
limit response authority under CERCLA, would not affect sites
listed on the NPL prior to January 1, 1985.

The effect of the amendment would be that sites listed as
final on the NPL prior to January 1, 1985 would not be affected
by the amendments to sections 104(a) and (b). Sites which
remain proposed for inclusion on the NPL may be affected by
the amendments. In other words, sites which remain proposed
that do not pertain to releases from uncontrolled hazardous
waste sites or are specifically excluded from Superfund
response (e.g., mining wastes covered by SMCRA or sites
contaminated solely as a result of the lawful application of
pesticides) would not be eligible for Superfund response,
because they did not become final NPL sites by January 1,
1985.

99TH CONGRESS
1ST SESSION

H. R. 1940

To clarify certain responsibilities of the Department of Defense under the Comprehensive Environmental Response, Compensation, and Liability Act of 1980, and for other purposes.

IN THE HOUSE OF REPRESENTATIVES

APRIL 3, 1985

Mr. FAZIO (for himself, Mr. FLORIO, Mr. MOODY, Mr. GUNDERSON, Mr. MORRISON of Connecticut, Mr. DURBIN, Mr. STUDDS, Mrs. BOXER, Mr. MARTINEZ, Mr. OWENS, Mrs. BURTON of California, Mr. RODINO, Mr. BOLAND, Mr. STOKES, Mr. LEVINE of California, Mr. HUGHES Mr. MICHEL. Mr. FRANK, Mr. BEILENSON, Mr. HOWARD, Mr. TOWNS, Mr. BARNES, Mr. SAVAGE, Mr. RANGEL, Mr. FAUNTROY, Mr. SEIBERLING, Mr. HEFTEL of Hawaii, Mr. TORRES, Mr. DICKS, Mr. HERTEL of Michigan, Mr. BIAGGI, Mr. ROE, and Mr. SABO) introduced the following bill; which was referred jointly to the Committees on Energy and Commerce, Public Works and Transportation, and Armed Services

---

A BILL

To clarify certain responsibilities of the Department of Defense under the Comprehensive Environmental Response, Compensation, and Liability Act of 1980, and for other purposes.

1   *Be it enacted by the Senate and House of Representa-*

2 *tives of the United States of America in Congress assembled,*

2

1 SECTION 1. SHORT TITLE AND TABLE OF CONTENTS.

2   (a) SHORT TITLE.—This Act may be cited as the "De-

3 fense Environmental Restoration Act of 1985".

4   (b) TABLE OF CONTENTS.—

5 SEC. 2. COMPLIANCE BY DEFENSE DEPARTMENT WITH

6   CERCLA.

7   (a) CERCLA RULES, ETC., APPLICABLE TO DOD.—

8 Except as provided in subsection (b), all Federal guidelines,

9 rules, regulations, procedures, and criteria other than internal

10 operating procedures which are applicable to—

11   (1) preliminary assessments carried out under the

12   Comprehensive Environmental Response, Compensa-

13   tion, and Liability Act of 1980 (hereinafter in this Act

14   referred to as CERCLA) for facilities at which any

15   hazardous substance has been released,

16   (2) evaluations of such facilities under the Nation-

17   al Contingency Plan,

18   (3) inclusion on the National Priorities List, or

19   (4) response actions at such facilities

1 shall be applicable to facilities under the administrative juris-

2 diction of the Secretary of Defense in the same manner and

3 to the same extent as such guidelines, rules, regulations, pro-

4 cedures, and criteria are applicable to facilities which are

5 owned and operated by a nongovernmental entity. Such

6 guidelines, rules, regulations, procedures, and criteria shall

7 also be applicable to response actions carried out by the Sec-

8 retary of Defense at facilities which were, but are no longer,

9 under the administrative jurisdiction of the Secretary.

10   (b) EXCEPTION OF FINANCIAL RESPONSIBILITY RE-

11 QUIREMENTS.—No requirement in effect under CERCLA or

12 other laws regarding bonding, insurance, or financial respon-

13 sibility for hazardous substances shall be applicable to the

14 Secretary of Defense.

15   (c) COMPLIANCE WITH NATIONAL ENVIRONMENTAL

16 POLICY ACT.—Removal or remedial actions selected or

17 taken pursuant to this section or secured under section 106 of

18 CERCLA constitute fulfillment of the requirements of section

19 102 of the National Environmental Policy Act of 1969

20 (Public Law 91-190, 83 Stat. 852).

21 SEC. 3. DOD ENVIRONMENTAL RESTORATION PROGRAM.

22   (a) AUTHORITIES UNDER CERCLA.—

23   (1) DELEGATION.—Except as provided in para-

24   graphs (2), (3), and (4) of this subsection, no authority

25   for response action vested in the President, or in the

4

1 Administrator of the Environmental Protection

2 Agency, under the Comprehensive Environmental Re-

3 sponse, Compensation, and Liability Act of 1980 may

4 be delegated or transferred, by Executive order of the

5 President or otherwise, to the Secretary of Defense or

6 to any officer or employee of the Department of De-

7 fense. All such response authority shall be delegated to

8 the Administrator of the Environmental Protection

9 Agency.

10 (2) NATURAL RESOURCE TRUSTEES.—The Sec-

11 retary and other officials and employees of the Depart-

12 ment of Defense may be designated trustees of natural

13 resources, with the same authority as other Federal

14 trustees of natural resources.

15 (3) EPA DELEGATION TO DOD.—

16 (A) IN GENERAL.—Except for those authori-

17 ties specifically prohibited from being transferred,

18 the Administrator may delegate authority vested

19 in the Administrator or delegated to the Adminis-

20 trator under CERCLA to the Secretary of

21 Defense or another officer or employee of the De-

22 partment of Defense where the Administrator de-

23 termines this to be a cost-effective method to

24 more expeditiously and effectively implement his

responsibilities and retains ultimate oversight and

2 review of the functions delegated.

3 (B) PROHIBTIONS ON DELEGATION.—The

4 Administrator shall retain, and may not delegate

5 to the Secretary (or any other officer or employee

6 of the Department of Defense) the authority to

7 approve remedial action implemented at a site for

8 which the Secretary of Defense has responsibility

9 under subsection (c) of this section and which is

10 listed on the National Priorities List, unless such

11 action is an emergency removal.

12 (4) NATIONAL SECURITY.—The President may

13 issue such orders regarding response action at any spe-

14 cific site or facility of the Department of Defense as

15 may be necessary to protect the national security inter-

16 ests of the United States at that site or facility. Such

17 orders may include, where necessary to protect such

18 interests, an exemption from any prohibition on delega-

19 tion of authority to the Secretary contained in this sub-

20 section with respect to the site or facility concerned.

21 (b) ENVIRONMENTAL RESTORATION PROGRAM.—The

22 Secretary of Defense shall establish an office within the

23 Office of the Secretary of Defense which shall have the re-

24 sponsibility for carrying out the Defense Environmental Res-

25 toration Program, including authorities delegated under sub-

6

1 section (a)(3), in consultation with the Environmental Protec-

2 tion Agency. Goals of the program shall include, but not be

3 limited to:

4   (1) the identification, investigation, and cleanup of

5 contamination from hazardous substances and wastes;

6   (2) correction of other environmental damage,

7 such as unexploded ordinance detection and disposal

8 which creates an imminent and substantial endanger-

9 ment to the public health, welfare or environment; and

10   (3) demolition and removal of unsafe and unsound

11 buildings and structures.

12 (c) RESPONSIBILITY FOR RESPONSE ACTIONS.—

13   (1) BASIC RESPONSIBILITY.—The Secretary of

14 Defense shall carry out (in accordance with the provi-

15 sions of section 2 and section 3(a)(3)) all response ac-

16 tions with respect to releases of hazardous sub-

17 stances—

18   (A) from each facility or site owned by,

19 leased to, or otherwise possessed by the United

20 States and under the administrative jurisdiction of

21 the Secretary; and

22   (B) from each facility or site which was

23 under the administrative jurisdiction of the Secre-

24 tary and owned by, leased to, or otherwise pos-

1   sessed by, the United States at the time of actions

2   leading to contamination by hazardous substances;

3   (C) from each vessel of the Department of

4   Defense, including vessels owned or bareboat

5   chartered and operated.

6   (2) APPLICATION OF CHAPTER 169 OF TITLE

7   10.—Response actions, or portions of response actions,

8   pursuant to this section which do not result in a new

9   facility designed for on-going operations are not mili-

10   tary construction for purposes of title 10, chapter 169,

11   of the United States Code or this Act.

12   (3) OTHER RESPONSIBLE PARTIES.—Paragraph

13   (1) shall not apply to removal and remedial action if a

14   determination has been made under section 104(a) of

15   CERCLA that such removal and remedial action will

16   be done properly and expeditiously by another respon-

17   sible party. Nothing in this Act shall be construed to

18   affect the liability of any person or entity under sec-

19   tions 106 and 107 of CERCLA.

20   (4) STATE AND LOCAL FEES AND CHARGES.—

21   The Secretary of Defense shall pay, in the same

22   manner as any private person, all fees and charges im-

23   posed by State and local authorities for the storage

24   and/or disposal of hazardous substances on lands

25   which are under the administrative jurisdiction of the

1   Secretary, unless the payment is the responsibility of a

2   lessee, contractor, or other private person.

3   (5) IMMINENT HAZARD AUTHORITIES.—Where

4   there may be an imminent and substantial endanger-

5   ment to public health or the environment at a facility

6   or site at which the Secretary is authorized to respond,

7   the Secretary may implement the administrative abate-

8   ment authorities of section 106 of CERCLA, in consul-

9   tation with the Administrator, and petition the Attor-

10 ney General of the United States to implement the

11 abatement authorities of section 106 of CERCLA.

12 (d) AUTHORIZATION OF APPROPRIATIONS FOR ENVI-

13 RONMENTAL RESTORATION PROGRAM.—

14   (1) 5 YEAR AUTHORIZATION.—There are author-

15 ized to be appropriated to the Secretary of Defense for

16 the first 5 fiscal years commencing after September 30,

17 1985, such sums as may be necessary to carry out the

18 responsibilities of the Secretary described in this sec-

19 tion. Such sums shall remain available until expended

20 and may not be reprogrammed for any other use.

21 Funds authorized to be appropriated under this para-

22 graph may not be used for emergency removal action

23 for which funds are appropriated pursuant to subsection

24 (e).

1   (2) AMOUNTS RECOVERED UNDER CERCLA.—

2 Amounts recovered under section 107 of CERCLA for

3 response actions of the Secretary shall also be avail-

4 able, as appropriated by the Congress, for purposes of

5 carrying out the responsibilities of the Secretary under

6 this section. The Secretary may administratively con-

7 sider, compromise, and settle any claim or demand

8 under CERCLA arising out of activities of the Depart-

9 ment of Defense, from amounts appropriated under this

10 subsection, in accordance with regulations promulgated

11 by the Attorney General. Any award, compromise, or

12 settlement in excess of $25,000 shall be made only

13 with the prior approval of the Attorney General or his

14 designee.

15   (e) AUTHORIZATION OF APPROPRIATIONS FOR EMER-

16 GENCY REMOVAL.—

17   (1) SEPARATE EMERGENCY CLEAN UP AC-

18 COUNT.—There is authorized to be appropriated to the

19 Secretary of Defense for the first 5 fiscal years com-

20 mencing after September 30, 1985, such sums as may

21 be necessary to establish a separate emergency clean-

22 up account. Sums appropriated under this subsection

23 shall remain available until expended. The separate ac-

24 count shall be maintained by the Secretary of the

25 Treasury and shall be available to the Secretary of De-

1 fense for carrying out removal actions with respect to

2 releases or threatened releases of any hazardous sub-

3 stance which may present an imminent and substantial

4 endangerment to the public health or the environment.

5 (2) SINGLE SITE OR FACILITY LIMITATION.—Not

6 more than $1,000,000 may be expended from sums au-

7 thorized to be appropriated under this subsection with

8 respect to a single site or facility unless the Secretary

9 finds, in consultation with the Administrator, that—

10 (A) continued response actions are immedi-

11 ately required to prevent, limit, or mitigate an

12 emergency,

13 (B) there is an immediate risk to public

14 health or welfare or the environment, and

15 (C) such assistance will not otherwise be pro-

16 vided on a timely basis.

17 (3) COMPLETION DEADLINES.—Each removal

18 action carried out with the use of funds authorized to

19 be appropriated under this subsection shall to the maxi-

20 mum extent practicable, be completed within 6 months

21 from the date on which such removal action is com-

22 menced, and in no event later than 18 months from

23 such date on which such removal action is commenced.

24 (4) NOTIFICATION OF CONGRESS.—Within 15

25 days of expending or obligating funds authorized to be

11

appropriated under this subsection for purposes of any
2 site or facility, the Secretary shall notify the Commit-
3 tees on Appropriations and on Armed Services of the
4 United States Congress.

5 (f) USE OF OPERATION AND MAINTENANCE FUNDS
6 FOR RESPONSE ACTIONS.—Notwithstanding subsections (d)
7 and (e), the Secretary of Defense may expend or obligate any
8 funds which are available for operation and maintenance of
9 facilities under his authority to carry out response actions
10 (including emergency actions) authorized under this Act
11 whenever, at his discretion, he deems the use of such funds to
12 be necessary and appropriate.

13 (g) SERVICES OF OTHER AGENCIES.—The Secretary of
14 Defense may obtain the services of any Federal, State or
15 local agency of government, on a reimbursable basis, to assist
16 him in carrying out any of his responsibilities under this sec-
17 tion, including but not limited to the identification, investiga-
18 tion and cleanup of any off-site contamination possibly result-
19 ing from the release of any hazardous substance or waste at
20 any facility under his administrative jurisdiction.

21 SEC. 4. RESEARCH, DEVELOPMENT, AND DEMONSTRATION
22 PROGRAM.

23 (a) PROGRAM.—The Secretary of Defense shall estab-
24 lish a program to carry out research, development, and dem-
25 onstration with respect to—

1   (1) means of reducing the quantities of hazardous

2   waste generated by activities and facilities under the

3   jurisdiction of the Secretary;

4   (2) methods of treating, including recycling and

5   detoxifying, hazardous waste of the types and quanti-

6   ties generated by current and former activities of the

7   Secretary and facilities currently and formerly under

8   the jurisdiction of the Secretary;

9   (3) identifying more cost-effective hazardous sub-

10   stance cleanup technologies; and

11   (4) toxicological data collection and methodology

12   on risk of exposure to hazardous waste generated by

13   the Department of Defense.

14 (b) AUTHORIZATION OF APPROPRIATIONS.—There are

15 authorized to be appropriated to the Secretary of Defense for

16 the first 5 fiscal years commencing after September 30,

17 1985, such sums as may be necessary to carry out the re-

18 search and development program established under this sec-

19 tion. Such sums shall remain available until expended and

20 may not be reprogammed for any other use.

21 **SEC. 5. WIDELY USED HAZARDOUS SUBSTANCES.**

22 (a) NOTICE TO ATSDR.—The Secretary of Defense

23 shall notify the Administrator of the Agency of Toxic Sub-

24 stances and Disease Registry established under section 104(i)

25 of CERCLA of 25 hazardous substances which the Secretary

1 of Defense determines to be the most widely used hazardous

2 substances at facilities under his jurisdiction for which no

3 standard is in effect under the Toxic Substances Control Act,

4 the Safe Drinking Water Act, the Clean Air Act, or the

5 Clean.Water Act and for which no water quality criteria are

6 in effect under any provision of the Clean Water Act.

7   (b) TOXICOLOGICAL PROFILES.—The Agency for

8 Toxic Substances and Disease Registry established under

9 section 104(i) of CERCLA shall prepare toxicological profiles

10 of each of the 25 substances referred to in subsection (a). The

11 Secretary of Defense shall transfer to such Agency such toxi-

12 cological data and such sums as may be necessary for the

13 Agency to prepare the profiles of such 25 substances.

14   (c) AUTHORIZATION OF APPROPRIATIONS.—There are

15 authorized to be appropriated to the Secretary of Defense

16 such sums as may be necessary for the fiscal years commenc-

17 ing after September 30, 1985 for purposes of this section.

18 Such sums shall remain available until expended, and may

19 not be reprogrammed for any other use.

20   (d) DEADLINES.—The notice required under subsection

21 (a) shall be submitted not later than 1 year after the date of

22 the enactment of this Act. The profiles required under sub-

23 section (b) shall be completed not later than 1 year after the

24 date on which funds are transferred to the Agency for Toxic

1 Substances and Disease Registry by the Secretary of De-
2 fense.

3 **SEC. 6. NOTICE OF ENVIRONMENTAL RESTORATION ACTIVI-**
4 **TIES.**

5   (a) EXPEDITED NOTICE.—The Secretary of Defense
6 shall take such actions as necessary to insure that the region-
7 al offices of the Environmental Protection Agency and appro-
8 priate State and local authorities for the State in which a
9 facility under his administrative jurisdiction is located receive
10 prompt notice of—

11   (1) the discovery of releases or threatened releases
12   of hazardous substances at installations;

13   (2) the extent of the threat to public health and
14   the environment which may be associated with any
15   such release or threatened release;

16   (3) proposals made by the Secretary to carry out
17   response actions with respect to any such release or
18   threatened release;

19   (4) the initiation of any response action with re-
20   spect to such release or threatened release and the
21   commencement of each distinct phase of such activities.

22   (b) COMMENT BY EPA AND STATE AND LOCAL AU-
23 THORITIES.—The Secretary of Defense shall require that an
24 adequate opportunity for timely review and comment be af-
25 forded to the Administrator of the Environmental Protection

1 Agency and to appropriate State and local officials after

2 making any proposal referred to in paragraph (1), (2), or (3)

3 of subsection (a) and prior to undertaking any activities or

4 action referred to in subsection (a)(4). The preceding sentence

5 shall not apply if the action is an emergency removal taken

6 because of imminent and substantial endangerment to human

7 health or the environment and consultation would be imprac-

8 tical.

9   (c) TECHNICAL REVIEW COMMITTEE.—Whenever pos-

10 sible and practical, the Secretary of Defense shall establish a

11 Technical Review Committee to review and comment on De-

12 partment of Defense proposals outlined in subsection (b) in a

13 timely manner. Members of the Technical Review Committee

14 shall include but not be limited to at least one representative

15 of Secretary of Defense, the Environmental Protection

16 Agency, and appropriate State and local authorities.

17 SEC. 7. PUBLIC PARTICIPATION.

18   (a) NOTICE AND COMMENT.—Before adoption of any

19 plan for remedial action to be undertaken by the Secretary of

20 Defense at any site on the National Priorities List, the Secre-

21 tary shall—

22   (1) publish a notice and brief analysis of the pro-

23   posed plan and make such plan available to the public,

1   (2) provide a reasonable opportunity for submis-

2   sion of written and oral comments regarding the pro-

3   posed plan.

4 The notice and analysis published under paragraph (1) shall

5 include sufficient information as may be necessary to provide

6 a reasonable explanation of the proposed plan.

7   (b) FINAL PLAN.—Notice of the final remedial action

8 plan adopted shall be published and the plan shall be made

9 available to the public before commencement of any remedial

10 action. Such final plan shall be accompanied by a discussion

11 of any significant changes (and the reasons for such changes)

12 in the proposed plan and a response to each of the significant

13 comments, criticisms, and new data submitted in written or

14 oral presentations under subsection (a).

15   (c) PUBLICATION.—For the purposes of this section,

16 publication shall include, at a minimum, publication in a

17 major local newspaper of general circulation.

18 **SEC. 8. ANNUAL REPORT TO CONGRESS.**

19   (a) REPORT ON PROGRESS IN IMPLEMENTATION.—

20 The Secretary of Defense shall furnish an annual report to

21 the Congress for each fiscal year which commences after the

22 date of the enactment of this Act. The report shall describe

23 the progress made by the Secretary during the fiscal year in

24 implementing the requirements of this Act and the Compre-

1 hensive Environmental Response, Compensation, and Liabil-
2 ity Act of 1980.

3 (b) ITEMS INCLUDED.—The report under this section
4 shall include, but shall not be limited to—

5   (1) a statement for each facility under the admin-
6   istrative jurisdiction of the Secretary of the number of
7   individual sites at such installation at which any haz-
8   ardous substance has been identified;

9   (2) the status of response actions contemplated or
10   undertaken at each such site; and

11   (3) the specific cost estimates and budgetary pro-
12   posals involving response actions contemplated or un-
13   dertaken at each such site.

14 **SEC. 9. IDENTIFICATION OF MILITARY CONSTRUCTION FUNDS**
15 **   FOR   ENVIRONMENTAL   RESTORATION**
16 **   PROJECTS.**

17 (a) IDENTIFICATION OF FUNDS IN BUDGET.—(1) The
18 Secretary of Defense shall provide to Congress detailed infor-
19 mation on military construction projects requested in the
20 Budget that are attributable to environmental restoration
21 programs. Such information shall include—

22   (A) the total amount requested for such projects
23   and the amount requested for such projects by each
24   military department; and

25   (B) a listing of each such project.

1   (2) Such information shall be provided in budget docu-
2 ments submitted to Congress in connection with the annual
3 budget request for military construction activities of the De-
4 partment of Defense.

5   (b) SEPARATE LEGISLATIVE AUTHORIZATION FOR
6 ENVIRONMENTAL RESTORATION MILITARY CONSTRUC-
7 TION PROJECTS.—Any proposed legislation submitted to
8 Congress by the Secretary of Defense for the annual military
9 construction authorization Act shall set forth any amount re-
10 quested for military construction projects for environmental
11 restoration as a separate amount for each military depart-
12 ment and for the defense agencies.

13 SEC. 10. EMERGENCY CONSTRUCTION FOR RESPONSE AC-
14   TIONS.

15   (a) AUTHORITY.—Subject to subsections (b) and (c), the
16 Secretary may carry out a military construction project not
17 otherwise authorized by law if the Secretary, in consultation
18 with the Administrator, determines that—

19   (1) the project is vital to protect the public health
20   or environment from an imminent and substantial en-
21   dangerment resulting from a release or threatened re-
22   lease of any hazardous substance, and

23   (2) that the requirement for the project is so
24   urgent that the deferral of the project for inclusion in
25   the next Military Construction Authorization Act

would be inconsistent with protecting the public health

2 or environment from an imminent and substantial en-

3 dangerment.

4 (b) REPORT TO CONGRESS.—When a decision is made

to carry out a military construction project under this section,

the Secretary shall submit a report in writing to the appropri-

5 ate committees of Congress on that decision. Each such

8 report shall include—

9 (1) the justification for the project and the current

10 estimate of the cost of the project,

11 (2) the justification for carrying out the project

12 under this section, and

13 (3) a statement of the source of the funds to be

14 used to carry out the project. The project may then be

15 carried out only after the end of the 21-day period be-

16 ginning on the date the notification is received by such

17 committees, or after each such committee has approved

18 the project, if the committees approved the project

19 before the end of that period.

20 (c) LIMITATIONS.—

21 (1) MAXIMUM AMOUNT OBLIGATED.—The maxi-

22 mum amount that the Secretary may obligate in any

23 fiscal year under this section is $30,000,000.

24 (2) TOTAL UNOBLIGATED FUNDS.—A project car-

25 ried out under this section shall be carried out within

1   the total amount of funds appropriated for military con-

2   struction that have not been obligated. `

3   **SEC. 11. DEFINITIONS.**

4   As used in this Act—

5   (1) CERCLA.—The term "CERCLA" means the

6   Comprehensive Environmental Response, Compensa-

7   tion, and Liability Act of 1980.

8   (2) CERCLA TERMS.—The terms "Administra-

9   tor", "facility", "hazardous substance", "response",

10   "release", "remedial action", "National Contingency

11   Plan", and "National Priorities List" have the same

12   meanings as when used in CERCLA.

13   (3) ADMINISTRATIVE JURISDICTION OF THE SEC-

14   RETARY.—The term "administrative jurisdiction of the

15   Secretary" includes administrative jurisdiction of the

16   Secretary of Defense and the Secretaries of the Mili-

17   tary departments.

18   (4) SECRETARY.—The term "Secretary" means

19   the Secretary of Defense, or his designee.

O

99TH CONGRESS
1ST SESSION

H. R. 3065

To amend the Comprehensive Environmental Response, Compensation, and Liability Act of 1980 to authorize a program of research, development and demonstration for innovative or experimental treatment technologies for use in remedial actions.

IN THE HOUSE OF REPRESENTATIVES

JULY 24, 1985

Mr. TORRICELLI (for himself, Mr. VOLKMER, Mr. SCHEUER, Mr. FUQUA, Mr. LUJAN, and Mrs. SCHNEIDER) introduced the following bill; which was referred jointly to the Committees on Energy and Commerce, Public Works and Transportation, and Science and Technology

SEPTEMBER 20, 1985

Additional sponsors: Mr. McCURDY, Mr. RITTER, and Mr. SMITH of New Hampshire

---

A BILL

To amend the Comprehensive Environmental Response, Compensation, and Liability Act of 1980 to authorize a program of research, development and demonstration for innovative or experimental treatment technologies for use in remedial actions.

1   *Be it enacted by the Senate and House of Representa-*

2 *tives of the United States of America in Congress assembled,*

1 **SECTION 1. SHORT TITLE.**

2 This Act may be cited as "The Superfund Clean-up

3 Technology Research and Demonstration Act".

4 **SEC. 2. FINDINGS AND PURPOSE.**

5 (a) FINDINGS.—The Congress finds that—

6 (1) the number of hazardous substances facilities

7 which will require a response pursuant to the Compre-

8 hensive Environmental Response, Compensation, and

9 Liability Act of 1980 is expected to increase substan-

10 tially in the near future;

11 (2) the Environmental Protection Agency's prac-

12 tice of relying on removal and containment measures to

13 clean up uncontrolled hazardous waste sites under the

14 Superfund program does not permanently reduce the

15 risk of release of hazardous substances into the envi-

16 ronment;

17 (3) the use of treatment technologies which per-

18 manently alter the composition of hazardous waste so

19 as to reduce the toxicity, volume, or mobility of haz-

20 ardous wastes can provide significantly greater protec-

21 tion to the environment and to public health, at lower

22 long-term costs, than can short-term measures such as

23 removal and containment;

24 (4) various regulatory factors often limited the

25 ability of alternative and innovative treatment technol-

1　those technologies in cleaning up uncontrolled hazard-
2　ous waste sites;

3　　　(5) a sustained program of research and develop-
4　ment is essential for the development of alternative and
5　innovative treatment technologies which can be used to
6　permanently and signficantly reduce the environmental
7　and public health risks posed by uncontrolled hazard-
8　ous waste sites.

9　(b) PURPOSE.—The purpose of this Act is to establish
10　within the Environmental Protection Agency a program of
11　research and demonstration for alternative and innovative
12　treatment technologies that can be used in remedial actions
13　under the Superfund program, and to provide incentives for
14　the development and use of such technologies.

15　**SEC. 3. ALTERNATIVE OR INNOVATIVE TREATMENT TECH-**
16　　　　　　**NOLOGY RESEARCH AND DEMONSTRATION**
17　　　　　　**PROGRAM.**

18　Title I of the Comprehensive Environmental Response,
19　Compensation, and Liability Act of 1980 is amended by
20　adding the following new section immediately after section
21　115:

1 "SEC. 116. ALTERNATIVE OR INNOVATIVE TREATMENT TECH-

2 NOLOGY RESEARCH, EVALUATION AND DEM-

3 ONSTRATION PROGRAM.

4 "(a) ESTABLISHMENT OF PROGRAM.—The Administrator is authorized and directed to carry out a program of
research, evaluation, testing, development, and demonstra-
5 tion of alternative or innovative treatment technologies which
8 may be utilized in remedial actions to achieve more perma-
9 nent protection of the public health and welfare and the
10 environment.

11 "(b) TECHNOLOGY TRANSFER.—In carrying out the
12 program established in subsection (a), the Administrator shall
13 conduct a technology transfer program, including the devel-
14 opment, collection, evaluation, coordination and dissemina-
15 tion of information relating to the utilization of alternative or
16 innovative treatment technologies for remedial actions. The
17 Administrator shall establish and maintain a central reference
18 library for such information. The information maintained by
19 the Administrator shall be made available to the public, sub-
20 ject to the provisions of section 552 of title 5 of the United
21 States Code and section 1905 of title 18 of the United States
22 Code, and to other Government agencies in a manner that
23 will facilitate its dissemination: *Provided*, That upon a show-
24 ing satisfactory to the Administrator by any person that any
25 information, or portion thereof, obtained under this section by

1 the Administrator directly or indirectly from such person,

2 would, if made public, divulge—

3   "(1) trade secrets; or

4   "(2) other proprietary information of such person,

5 the Administrator shall not disclose such information and dis-

6 closure thereof shall be punishable under section 1905 of title

7 18 of the United States Code. This subsection is not author-

8 ity to withhold information from Congress or any committee

9 of Congress upon request of the Chairman.

10   "(c) CONTRACTS AND GRANTS.—In carrying out ac-

11 tivities under subsection (a), the Administrator is authorized

12 to enter into contracts and cooperative agreements with, and

13 make grants to, persons, public entities, and nonprofit private

14 entities (as defined by section 501(c)(3) of the Internal Reve-

15 nue Code of 1954, 26 U.S.C. 501(c)(3)). The Administrator

16 shall, to the maximum extent possible, enter into appropriate

17 cost-sharing arrangements under this section.

18   "(d) RESEARCH ASSISTANCE.—

19   "(1) ASSISTANCE AND INFORMATION.—The Ad-

20   ministrator shall, as he deems appropriate, provide as-

21   sistance or information to persons, public entities, and

22   nonprofit private entities who wish to have alternative

23   and innovative treatment technologies tested or evalu-

24   ated for utilization in remedial activities.

1   "(2) USE OF SITES.—The Administrator may ar-

2   range for the use of sites listed as national priority

3   sites under section 105(8)(B) for the purposes of re-

4   search, testing, evaluation, development, and demon-

5   stration, under such terms and conditions as the Ad-

6   ministrator shall require to assure the protection of

7   human health and the environment.

8   "(3) SAVING PROVISION.—Nothing in this Act

9   shall be construed to affect the provisions of the Solid

10   Waste Disposal Act.

11   "(e) DESIGNATION OF DEMONSTRATION SITES.—In

12 carrying out the program authorized by this section, the Ad-

13 ministrator shall, within 2 years after the date of enactment

14 of this section, and after notice and an opportunity for public

15 comment, designate at least 10 sites listed under section

16 105(8)(B) as appropriate for field demonstrations of alterna-

17 tive or innovative treatment technologies. If the Administra-

18 tor determines that 10 sites cannot be designated consistent

19 with the criteria of this subsection, he shall within the 2-year

20 period report to the appropriate committees of Congress ex-

21 plaining the reasons for his inability to designate such sites.

22 Within 12 months after designation of a site, the Administra-

23 tor shall begin or cause to begin a demonstration of alterna-

24 tive or innovative treatment technologies at such site. In des-

25 ignating such sites, the Administrator shall, consistent with

1 the protection of human health and the environment, consider

2 each of the following criteria:

3   "(1) The potential for contributing to solutions to

4   those waste problems which pose the greatest threat to

5   human health, which cannot be adequately controlled

6   under present technologies, or which otherwise pose

7   significant management difficulties.

8   "(2) The availability of technologies which have

9   been sufficiently developed for field demonstration and

10   which are likely to be cost-effective and reliable.

11   "(3) The suitability of the sites for demonstrating

12   such technologies, taking into account the physical, bi-

13   ological, chemical, and geological characteristics of the

14   sites, the extent and type of contamination found at the

15   sites, and the capability to conduct demonstrations in

16   such a manner as to assure the protection of human

17   health and the environment.

18   "(4) The likelihood that the data to be generated

19   from the demonstration at the site will be applicable to

20   other sites.

21   "(f) DEFINITION.—For the purposes of this section, the

22 term 'alternative or innovative treatment technologies' means

23 those technologies which permanently alter the composition

24 of hazardous waste through chemical, biological, or physical

25 means so as to significantly reduce the toxicity, mobility, or

1 volume (or any combination thereof) of the hazardous waste

2 or contaminated materials being treated.".

3 SEC. 4. REPORTS TO CONGRESS.

4 (a) ANNUAL REPORT.—At the time of the submission of

the annual budget request to Congress, the Administrator

shall submit a report to the appropriate Committees of the

5 House of Representatives and the Senate on the progress of

8 the research, development, and demonstration program au-

9 thorized by this Act, including an evaluation of the demon-

10 stration projects undertaken, findings with respect to the effi-

11 cacy of such demonstrated technologies in achieving perma-

12 nent and significant reductions in risk from hazardous wastes,

13 the costs of such demonstrations, and the potential applicabil-

14 ity of, and projected costs for, such technologies at other un-

15 controlled sites.

16 (b) CONGRESSIONAL REVIEW.—If the total estimated

17 Federal contribution to the cost of any field demonstration

18 project under section 3 exceeds $5,000,000, the Administra-

19 tor shall provide a full and comprehensive report on the pro-

20 posed demonstration project to the appropriate Committees

21 of the House of Representatives and the Senate and no funds

22 may be expended for such project under the authority granted

23 by this section prior to the expiration of 60 calendar days (not

24 including any day on which either House of Congress is not

25 in session because of an adjournment of more than 3 calendar

1 days to a day certain) from the date on which the Adminis-

trator's report on the proposed project is received by the

Congress.

2
4 SEC. 5. TESTING PROCEDURES AND STANDARDS.

5 (a) REVISION OF NATIONAL CONTINGENCY PLAN.—

6 The Administrator of the Environmental Protection Agency

7 shall revise and republish the National Contingency Plan re-

8 quired by section 105 of the Comprehensive Environmental

9 Response, Compensation, and Liability Act of 1980. The re-

10 visions shall include standards and testing procedures by

11 which alternative or innovative treatment technologies can be

12 determined to be appropriate for use in remedial actions

13 under title I of the Comprehensive Environmental Response,

14 Compensation, and Liability Act of 1980. The revision shall

15 be made within one year after the date of enactment of this

16 Act, and after notice and an opportunity for public comment.

17 (b) ELEMENTS OF NATIONAL CONTINGENCY PLAN.—

18 Section 105 of the Comprehensive Environmental Response,

19 Compensation, and Liability Act of 1980 is amended as

20 follows:

21 (1) Strike out "and" at the end of paragraph

22 (8)(B).

23 (2) Strike out the period at the end of paragraph

24 (9) and substitute "; and".

1   (3) Add the following new paragraph at the end

2 thereof:

3   "(10) standards and testing procedures by which

4 alternative or innovative treatment technologies can be

5 determined to be appropriate for utilization in remedial

6 actions authorized by this Act.".

7   (c) SAVINGS PROVISION.—Nothing in this section is in-

8 tended to alter the authority of the President under section

9 104 of the Comprehensive Environmental Response, Com-

10 pensation, and Liability Act of 1980.

11 **SEC. 6. RESPONSE AUTHORITIES.**

12   Section 104(c)(4) of the Comprehensive Environmental

13 Response, Compensation, and Liability Act of 1980 is

14 amended by adding the following at the end thereof: "In

15 evaluating the cost-effectiveness of a remedial action, the Ad-

16 ministrator shall select permanent solutions, including alter-

17 native or innovative treatment technologies as defined in sec-

18 tion 116(c) to the extent that such solutions are achievable

19 and feasible."

20 **SEC. 7. FUNDING FOR RESEARCH, DEVELOPMENT, AND DEM-**

21   **ONSTRATION PROGRAM.**

22   (a) AUTHORITY TO USE SUPERFUND MONEYS.—Sec-

23 tion 111 of the Comprehensive Environmental Response,

24 Compensation, and Liability Act of 1980 is amended by

25 adding the following new subsection after subsection (l):

11

1   "(m) Research, Development, and Demonstra-

2 tion Program.—There is authorized to be appropriated for

3 each of the fiscal years 1986, 1987, 1988, 1989, and 1990,

4 from sums appropriated or transferred to the Hazardous Sub-

5 stance Response Trust Fund established under section 221,

6 not more than $25,000,000 to be used for purposes of carry-

7 ing out the research, development, and demonstration pro-

8 gram for alternative or innovative technologies authorized

9 under section 116. Amounts made available under this sub-

10 section shall remain available until expended.".

11   (b) Amendment of Funding Provisions.—

12   (1) Section 221.—(A) Section 221(c)(1) of the

13   Comprehensive Environmental Response, Compensa-

14   tion, and Liability Act of 1980 is amended as follows:

15   (i) strike out "as in effect on the date of the

16   enactment of this Act,".

17   (ii) strike out "and" at the end of subpara-

18   graph (C).

19   (iii) Strike out the period at the end of sub-

20   paragraph (D) and substitute ", and".

21   (iv) Add the following at the end thereof:

22   "(E) the cost of carrying out section 116 (relating

23   to research, development, and demonstration of alter-

24   native and innovative treatment technologies).".

12

1 (B) Section 221(c)(2) of such Act is amended by

2 inserting after "shall be reserved" the following: "for

3 the purposes specified in section 116 and".

4 (2) SECTION 111.—(A) Section 111(a) of such

5 Act is amended as follows:

6   (i) Strike out "and" at the end of paragraph

7 (3).

8   (ii) Strike out the period at the end of para-

9 graph (4) and substitute ", and".

10   (iii) Add the following at the end thereof:

11 "(5) the cost of carrying out section 116 (relating

12 to research, development, and demonstration of alter-

13 native and innovative treatment technologies).".

14 (B) Section 111(e)(2) of such Act is amended to

15 read as follows:

16 "(2) For reservation of certain amounts appropriated to

17 the Fund established under title II for specific purposes, see

18 section 221(c)(2).".

19 **SEC. 8. LIABILITY OF PERSONS ENGAGED IN FIELD DEMON-**

20   **STRATIONS OF ALTERNATIVE AND INNOVATIVE**

21   **TREATMENT TECHNOLOGIES.**

22 Title I of the Comprehensive Environmental Response,

23 Compensation, and Liability Act of 1980 is amended by

24 adding the following new section after section 116:

1 "SEC. 117. LIABILITY FOR FIELD DEMONSTRATIONS.

2   "(a) LIABILITY OF PERSONS CONDUCTING FIELD

3 DEMONSTRATIONS.—

4   "(1) IN GENERAL.—Notwithstanding the provi-

5   sions of section 114, no person, public entity, or non-

6   profit private entity, in the course of conducting field

7   demonstrations pursuant to section 116 of this title,

8   shall be liable under this title, under any other Federal

9   law, under the law of any State or political subdivision,

10   or under common law to any person for injuries, costs,

11   damages, expenses, or other liability (including but not

12   limited to claims for indemnification or contribution and

13   claims by third parties for death, personal injury, ill-

14   ness or loss of or damage to property or economic loss)

15   which results from a release or threatened release from

16   a facility as a result of such field demonstration.

17   "(2) NEGLIGENCE, ETC.—Paragraph (1) shall not

18   apply in the case of a release that was caused by con-

19   duct of the person, public entity, or nonprofit private

20   entity conducting field demonstrations which was negli-

21   gent, reckless, or intentional misconduct.

22   "(3) PERSONS RETAINED OR HIRED.—Any

23   person retained or hired, by a person, public entity, or

24   nonprofit private entity conducting field demonstrations

25   pursuant to section 116, to provide any services relat-

14

1 emption from liability provided to the person, public

2 entity, or nonprofit private entity conducting said field

3 demonstration.

4 "(b) SAVINGS PROVISIONS.—

5   "(1) LIABILITY OF OTHER PERSONS.—Nothing in

6 this subsection shall affect the liability under this Act

7 or under any other authority of Federal or State law of

8 any person other than a person, public entity, or non-

9 profit private entity conducting a field demonstration

10 pursuant to section 116 of this title.

11   "(2) BURDEN OF PLAINTIFF.—Nothing in this

12 section shall affect the plaintiff's burden of establishing

13 the liability under this title.

14 "(c) EXCEPTION TO EXEMPTION.—The exemption

15 provided under subsection (a) shall not apply to any person

16 covered by the provisions of paragraph (1), (2), (3), or (4) of

17 section 107(a) with respect to the release or threatened re-

18 lease concerned if such persons would be covered by such

19 provisions even if he had not carried out any actions referred

20 to in subsection (d) of this section.

21 "(d) DEFINITION.—For the purpose of this section, a

22 person, public entity, or nonprofit private entity is 'conduct-

23 ing a field demonstration pursuant to section 116 of this title'

24 if such entity or person is carrying out a written contract or

25 agreement with—

15

1   "(1) the Administrator;

2   "(2) any other Federal agency;

3   "(3) a State; or

4   "(4) any responsible party;

5 to conduct demonstrations at sites listed under section

6 105(8)(B) of alternative or innovative treatment technologies

7 as defined in section 116(c).

8   "(e) STUDY.—Within one year from the date of the en-

9 actment of this section, the Administrator shall transmit to

10 Congress a study of the effects of the standards of liability

11 and financial responsibility requirements imposed by the

12 Comprehensive Environmental Response, Compensation, and

13 Liability Act of 1980 on the cost of, and incentives for, devel-

14 oping and demonstrating alternative and innovative treat-

15 ment technologies.".

O

THE SUPERFUND CLEAN-UP TECHNOLOGY RESEARCH AND DEMONSTRATION ACT

SEPTEMBER 4, 1985.—Ordered to be printed

Mr. FUQUA, from the Committee on Science and Technology, submitted the following

REPORT

together with

ADDITIONAL VIEWS

[To accompany H.R. 3065 which on July 24, 1985, was referred jointly to the Committee on Energy and Commerce, the Committee on Public Works and Transportation, and the Committee on Science and Technology]

[Including cost estimate of the Congressional Budget Office]

The Committee on Science and Technology, to whom was referred the bill (H.R. 3065) to amend the Comprehensive Environmental Response, Compensation, and Liability Act of 1980 to authrize a program of research, development and demonstration for innovative or experimental treatment technologies for use in remedial actions, having considered the same, reports favorably thereon with amendments and recommends that the bill as amended do pass.

The amendments (stated in terms of the page and line numbers of the introduced bill) are as follows:

1. On page 5, line 14, strike the words, "shall, as he deems appropriate" and insert, "may, consistent with the provisions of this section".

2. On page 8, lines 7 and 8, strike the word "uncontrolled" and insert "hazardous waste".

3. On page 8, line 16, strike "60" and insert "30".

4. Page 10, beginning in line 6, strike the sentence beginning with "In evaluating the cost-effectiveness" and insert in lieu thereof the following:

2

Any remedial action selected under section 104 for a facility at which a release or threatened release occurs shall require that level or standard of control of each hazardous substance or pollutant or contaminant at that facility which is necessary to protect human health and environment. In selecting a remedial action under section 104, the Administrator shall evaluate alternatives which achieve the requirements of the preceding sentence and shall assess the cost-effectiveness of such alternatives. In making such assessment, the Administrator shall specifically assess the long-term effectiveness of various alternatives, including an assessment of permanent solutions and alternative or innovative treatment technologies or resource recovery technologies that, in whole or in part, will result in a permanent and significant decrease in the toxicity, mobility, or volume of the hazardous substance, pollutant, or contaminant, taking into account each of the following:

(A) The long-term uncertainties associated with land disposal.

(B) The goals, objectives, and requirements of the Solid Waste Disposal Act.

(C) The persistence, degradability in nature, toxicity, mobility, and propensity to bioaccumulate of such hazardous substances and their constituents.

(D) The potential threat to human health and the environment associated with excavation, transportation, and redisposal.

(E) Short- and long-term potential for adverse health effects from human exposure.

(F) Long-term maintenance costs.

Following an evaluation under this subsection, the Administrator shall select that cost-effective remedial action which, to the maximum extent practicable, utilizes such permanent solutions and alternative or innovative treatment technologies or resource recovery technologies.

5. Page 15, after line 8, insert:

SEC. 9. SMALL BUSINESS PARTICIPATION.

The Administrator shall, to the maximum extent practicable, provide adequate opportunity for small business participation in the activities authorized under this Act.

CONTENTS

I. PURPOSE OF THE BILL

The purpose of the bill is to amend the Comprehensive Environmental Response, Compensation and Liability Act of 1980 ("CERCLA", or "Superfund") to establish within the Environmental Protection Agency (EPA) a program of research, development and demonstration of alternative or innovative treatment technologies for use in remedial actions under the Superfund program.

II. COMMITTEE ACTIONS

HEARINGS

The Committee on Science and Technology has conducted an extensive review of currently available and potential treatment technologies and their use under the Superfund program through hearings held by both the Subcommittee on Natural Resources, Agriculture Research and Environment and the Subcommittee on Investigations and Oversight.

On May 2, 1985, the Subcommittee on Natural Resources, Agriculture Research and Environment held a hearing on innovative hazardous waste treatment technologies. At the hearing, the Congressional Office of Technology Assessment (OTA) released a report on "Superfund Strategies" which addressed the potential for alternative or innovative treatment technologies to improve significantly remedial actions taken under the Superfund program. The OTA "Superfund Strategies" Report (hereinafter referred to as the OTA Report) indicated that technologies were available, or were under development, which could provide permanent protection from releases of hazardous wastes at Superfund sites by destroying or detoxifying hazardous wastes. At the same time, the OTA Report noted numerous difficulties facing the development and use of such technologies, including the administration of the EPA's Superfund clean-up program.

As a result of the testimony received at the hearing conducted by the Subcommittee on Natural Resources, Agriculture Research and Environment, Congressman Torricelli introduced H.R. 2802, the "Superfund Clean-up Technology Research and Demonstration Act of 1985" on June 18, 1985, with six cosponsors.

On April 23 and May 18, 1985, the Subcommittee on Investigations and Oversight held hearings on innovative technologies for the permanent clean-up of hazardous waste, in Washington, D.C., and Union, Missouri respectively. The first hearing focused on inadequacies both in research opportunities and in health effects information, while the second hearing concentrated on public participation in the Superfund decisionmaking process.

Testimony by witnesses at both hearings underscored the need both for additional research into permanent clean-up technologies and for opportunities to demonstrate and prove the viability of such new technologies. As a result of the testimony received at the hearings, Congressman Volkmer introduced H.R. 2865 on June 25, 1985.

The Subcommittee on Natural Resources, Agriculture Research and Environment held a hearing on H.R. 2802 on June 26, 1985. Testimony was received from Congressman James J. Florio, Congressman Harold M. Volkmer, EPA witnesses, environmental group representatives, and industry group representatives.

COMMITTEE CONSIDERATION

On July 23, 1985 the Subcommittee on Natural Resources, Agriculture Research and Environment considered H.R. 2802, and, a quorum being present, adopted an amendment in the nature of a substitute offered by Congressman Torricelli to incorporate a number of improvements reflecting comments received from EPA, from industry representatives and environmental group representatives. The amendment also reflects comments and suggestions offered by Mr. Florio, Mr. Lujan, Mrs. Schneider, Mr. Ritter, and Mr. Henry, as well as language suggested by Congressman Volkmer incorporating some provisions of H.R. 2865. By unanimous voice vote, the Subcommittee ordered a clean bill passed and reported to the full Committee.

On July 24, 1985, a clean bill incorporating the amendment in the nature of a substitute adopted by the Subcommittee was introduced as H.R. 3065, the "Superfund Clean-up Technology Research and Demonstration Act" by Mr. Torricelli for himself, Mr. Volkmer, Mr. Scheuer, Mr. Fuqua, Mr. Lujan, and Mrs. Schneider. The bill was retained in full Committee, and acted on July 25, 1985, when the Committee adopted several amendments and ordered the bill, as amended, reported.

EXPLANATION OF AMENDMENTS

The Committee adopted several amendments to H.R. 3065, as set out above. The first amendment includes three clarifying changes, considered and adopted en bloc. The first one clarifies the language of the proposed new section 16(d) so that the subsection is tied in with the rest of the section and cannot be used as an independent authority. The second change substitutes words that have been defined, "hazardous waste," for a word that has not been defined, "uncontrolled." The third change reduces the layover time before the Administrator can begin projects over $5 million from 60 to 30 days.

The second amendment substitutes new text for Section 6 of the bill. The substitute language is intended to clarify what is intended by cost-effective action and provides that the Administrator shall specifically assess, in selecting various remedial alternatives, the long-term effectiveness of various alternatives, including permanent solutions and alternative and innovative treatment technologies. Under the amendment as adopted, the Administrator is required to select that cost-effective remedial action which, to the maximum extent practicable, utilizes permanent solutions and alternative or innovative treatment technologies. The language of the substitute is very similar to Sec. 121(c) of H.R. 2817, the "Superfund Amendments of 1985", as amended and reported by the

House Energy and Commerce Committee on August 1, 1985. (H. Rep. 99–253, Part I).

The third amendment requires the Administrator of the EPA, to the maximum extent practicable, to provide adequate opportunity for small business participation in the research and demonstration program created by the bill.

III. BACKGROUND AND NEED FOR LEGISLATION

A. Hearings and Testimony

1. CLEAN-UPS UNDER THE SUPERFUND PROGRAM

In 1980, Congress enacted the Comprehensive Environmental Response, Compensation, and Liability Act of 1980, ("CERCLA" or "Superfund"), which established federal authority to clean up abandoned hazardous waste dump sites and to respond to emergencies caused by releases of hazardous substances. The Act also created a Hazardous Substances Response Trust Fund to pay for clean-up between 1981 and 1985.

A number of recent studies, including the OTA Report and the Government Accounting Office (GAO) report, "EPA's Inventory of Potential Hazardous Waste Sites is Incomplete", indicate that the number of hazardous substances facilities which will require clean-up actions under the Superfund program will substantially increase in the near future. While EPA estimates the there are a total of 2,000 sites that are likely to be placed on the National Priority List, the OTA Report estimates the total number of such sites to be closer to 10,000.

An examination of the EPA's efforts to clean up Superfund sites indicates that, for the most part, EPA relies heavily on a combination of removal of contaminated materials to disposal facilities permitted under the Resource Conservation and Recovery Act ("RCRA") and construction of physical barriers to prevent the migration of remaining hazardous wastes into the groundwater and surrounding environment. While such methods are likely to reduce the risk of release of hazardous substances in the short term, serious questions have been raised about the safety, efficacy, and cost of such measures over the long-term.

The OTA Report, for example, noted a number of serious problems with such approaches. First, moving the waste from one site to another simply shifts the risk from one community to another. For example, risks of accidents during transportation expose a potentially wide area to toxic waste spills. Further, the fact that the receiving site may be operating under a RCRA permit is no assurance that there will be no further risks from the waste. Recent reports have indicated that a number of RCRA sites which have received Superfund wastes are themselves leaking and contaminating groundwater. In addition, about half of the 1300 RCRA land disposal sites with interim permits are not in compliance with groundwater monitoring requirements and may face closing when their interim permit status ends in November, 1985. The OTA Report extimated that up to half of the present RCRA disposal sites will themselves become Superfund sites.

The OTA Report also questioned the adequacy of reliance on containment barriers to prevent the migration of wastes from the site, indicating that the techniques have been developed out of the construction industry and have not been tested for long-term efficacy for containing hazardous wastes. According to the OTA Report, there is a significant risk that containment barriers will fail at some point, leading to migration of hazardous substances into the groundwater and into the environment. The problems of attempting to contain wastes is compounded by the lack of knowledge concerning groundwater behavior and the difficulty of assessing any of the hydrogeological characteristics of a given site. Some of the case studies included in the OTA Report, particularly the Stringfellow site, provide examples of some of the difficulties in assessing sites.

2. ALTERNATIVE AND INNOVATIVE TREATMENT TECHNOLOGIES

Witnesses at the hearing before the Subcommittee on Natural Resources, Agriculture Research and Environment testified that a number of technologies are available, or are in an advanced stage of development, which can treat hazardous wastes through physical, chemical, or biological means to reduce the toxicity, mobility or volume of the wastes. Such permanent treatment of hazardous wastes clearly offers a long-term protection not afforded by conventional removal, storage, and containment methodologies. In addition, many of the technologies can be applied on-site, reducing the risk of release during transportation or the necessity for temporary storage. The OTA Report identified 26 promising new technologies with a wide variety of applications.

Despite the promise of such permanent treatment technologies, industry witnesses at the hearing before the Subcommittee on Natural Resources, Agriculture Research and Environment confirmed the findings of the OTA report that EPA was not considering such technologies in Superfund clean-ups and was not promoting the development of such technologies. A number of factors appear to explain this situation.

Several of the witnesses identified certain provisions within CERCLA which have the effect of discouraging the selection of permanent treatment technologies in Superfund clean-ups. Section 104(c)(4) of CERCLA requires the Administrator to choose a "cost-effective" remedial response which balances the need for protection of the public health and environment against the availability of amounts from the Trust Fund. This emphasis on "cost-effectiveness", together with the fund-balancing test, frequently leads to the choice of the lowest cost remedial measures, with the effect of excluding permanent treatment technologies which usually have higher initial capital costs than conventional removal and containment measures.

Similarly, the cost-sharing provisions of CERCLA also favor the choice of conventional removal and containment techniques. CERLA permits EPA to pay up to 90 percent of the initial cost of clean-up, while States are required to pay all of the future maintenance and operation costs. This cost-sharing provision creates an

initial capital costs but higher long-term maintenance and operation costs.

Other witnesses noted that the lack of clear-cut clean-up standards in CERCLA also discouraged the use of permanent treatment
technologies.

Witnesses from the industry also testified that EPA had no program which could assist them in determining whether their technologies could be useful in Superfund remedial actions. While EPA
requires new technologies to demonstrate their effectiveness before
it will determine whether the technology is appropriate for use in
Superfund clean-ups, the agency gives no guidance as to what data
it would require to demonstrate such effectiveness. Some developers have been faced with the frustrating dilemma of having EPA
reject proposals to field test new technologies precisely because the
developer did not have the supporting data which could only be obtained by field testing.

Developers also testified about frustrating encounters with bureaucratic delays. Applications of new technologies for necessary
permits, approval of testing protocols, and assistance in obtaining
samples of, or access to, wastes at Superfund sites, have frequently
snarled developers in time-consuming regulatory red tape, significantly raising the costs and risks of new technology development.

3. EPA TESTIMONY

While EPA indicated its general agreement with the goal of increased use of permanent clean-up technologies, and cited recent
policy announcements to that effect, EPA testified before the Subcommittee on Natural Resources, Agriculture Research and Environment that it did not support H.R. 2802. EPA contended that
new authority was not needed since it already had the ability to
conduct research and development activities under existing RCRA
authority. EPA also stated that it was opposed to the use of Superfund to support fundamental, as opposed to applied, research. Further, EPA criticized the provision in H.R. 2802 requiring the Administrator to designate one site in each EPA region as a demonstration site on the ground that it did not grant the EPA sufficient
flexibility to choose the most appropriate number and location of
demonstration sites. EPA also raised concerns about the liability
that would be faced by those conducting field demonstrations and
research on Superfund sites for damages that could stem from the
failure of an experiment or demonstration. Finally, EPA expressed
concerns that demonstrations on Superfund sites could result in
higher clean-up costs to be borne by responsible parties.

As discussed below in the Explanation of the Bill, the Committee
believes that the legislation as reported responds directly to the
concerns raised by EPA.

B. EXISTING EPA RESEARCH AND DEMONSTRATION PROGRAM

EPA's present research and demonstration program for Superfund clean-up technologies is limited. By statute, the Trust Fund

such as site assessment and sampling. The Superfund research program applies completed research and expertise obtained from other programs to the clean-up of Superfund sites. While this program has provided some funding for in-house research of incineration technologies for Superfund clean-ups, it is not a source of funding for permanent clean-up technology research by universitities or the private sector.

EPA also conducts some research relevant to Superfund under the authority of RCRA. The environmental engineering and technology research program has recently examined incineration and other treatment technologies, in-situ methods for the destruction of dioxins, and the operational characteristics of treatment and disposal of hazardous wastes. The monitoring research program involves developing procedures for characterizing wastes and techniques for field monitoring of hazardous waste sites. Under this program, EPA's Hazardous Waste Engineering Research Laboratory in Cincinatti has examined 21 thermal treatment processes.

The RCRA research program, however, does not provide funding for unsolicited proposals from the private sector for research or demonstrations of Superfund clean-up technologies. Further, the focus of the RCRA program is on disposal, containment, and storage technologies, and treatment of industrial hazardous waste streams. While some of the research is relevant to Superfund clean-ups, problems of particular importance to Superfund, such as the difficulty of characterizing and treating complex mixtures of hazardous wastes found in abandoned waste dumps, the difficulties of site characterization and assessment, and the need to develop technologies which can be safely used in Superfund sites, are not adequately addressed in EPA's RCRA hazardous waste research program.

EPA's academic research centers program are sources of funding for university research. EPA funds several university research centers which conduct multidisciplinary research in hazardous waste, including a research center for Advance Control Technology at the University of Illinois at Urbana, a Waste Elimination research center at the Illinois Institute of Technology and the University of Notre Dame, and a hazardous waste research center at Tufts University. EPA presently supports each of the Centers with approximately $500,000 in funding every year, but the Administration's fiscal year 1986 budget request proposed cutting the research centers program by 35 percent.

Finally, EPA's competitive peer-reviewed grant program and its Small Business Innovation Research program are, according to the OTA Report, viewed by industry as one of the few sources of funding for private sector research for treatment technologies. However, limited funding and other restrictions have hampered the utility of these programs. Along with the research centers program, the competitive grants program was slated for a 35 percent reduction in the Administration's fiscal year 1986 budget request. Further, only non-profit entities are eligible for funding under the

C. NEED FOR LEGISLATION

1. BUILDING ON THE EPA SUPERFUND RESEARCH PROGRAM

The EPA already has in place a substantial in-house research program with respect to hazardous waste, including a substantial engineering and environmental technology component with the potential capability of conducting high-quality research on Superfund clean-up technologies. EPA's existing extramural research program has developed productive relationships with the nation's leading universities on hazardous waste research, and with waste management firms and other private sector entities involved with treatment research. While research conducted under these programs has been of a high quality, it has had only limited application to Superfund clean-up problems.

The bill builds upon EPA's existing research capabilities to ensure the development and use of permanent solutions to the problems of hazardous waste sites. The bill supplements EPA's present expertise in hazardous waste research by establishing a research program specifically designed to develop, test and evaluate permanant Superfund clean-up technologies. Further, the bill directs a solution-oriented approach to EPA's research. By focusing on the need to apply the results of research to Superfund clean-up problems, the bill furthers cooperation and coordination between EPA's research office and its regulatory office, which ultimately has the legal responsibility to choose the methods for cleaning up Superfund sites.

The bill would expand EPA's research program to make better use of the expertise existing in universities and in the private sector. The Committee believes that the participation of the private sector, which is a major source of innovation and technology development, is particularly critical for a successful research program in this particular area.

The Committee believes that a sustained program of research and demonstration of alternative and innovative treatment technologies is most appropriately located at the EPA. Putting the program at EPA takes advantage of EPA's existing expertise and established contract and grant procedures, with minimal additional burden and cost. EPA is the agency charged by Congress with the duty to clean up the nation's hazardous waste sites. The Administrator of the EPA alone has the legal responsibility to choose the remedial measures to be taken to clean up a Superfund site. A research program designed to provide solutions for those problems properly belongs at the EPA and can be undertaken without undue delay.

2. ADDITIONAL FUNDING FOR EXTRAMURAL RESEARCH BY THE PRIVATE SECTOR

The market for Superfund site clean-up technologies is unique, in part because the market is largely dependent upon the EPA's actions. Since the EPA has the legal responsibility to choose the technology for cleaning up Superfund sites, only those technologies which are likely to receive EPA's approval are likely to be the sub-

10

industry witnesses testified concerning their perception that EPA's regulatory program is biased against permanent treatment technologies in favor of removal, storage and containment technologies. In addition, in the few cases where the private sector has developed promising technologies, EPA's failure to evaluate them for use in Superfund cleanups has added to the perception that the EPA is not interested in permanent treatment solutions.

The Committee believes that public funds are needed to supplement, but not duplicate, the research and development of new treatment technologies occuring in the private sector. Given the present regulatory factors hindering EPA acceptance of permanent treatment technologies, the private sector is not likely to provide sufficient funding for the development and demonstration of new treatment technologies.

While some firms have sufficient financial resources to conduct their own demonstration projects without government funding, such firms lack an incentive to invest in expensive demonstration projects in the face of EPA bureaucratic obstacles and an uncertain market created by EPA's implementation of the Superfund program. A successful state program in Missouri suggests that some firms may be willing to fund demonstration projects when agencies are willing to cooperate and provide access to hazardous waste sites for research purposes.

Other firms, however, perceive that it is growing more difficult to raise capital from the private sector for demonstration purposes. The lack of private capital creates a particular hardship for smaller firms and entrepreneurs who have developed a new technology to the point where it is ready for demonstration, typically the most costly phase of research. Yet without such demonstrations, EPA will not consider the technology to be sufficiently proven for the purposes of use in Superfund clean-up programs.

IV. EXPLANATION OF THE BILL

SECTION 2—FINDINGS AND PURPOSE

This section sets out the Congress' findings that the EPA's practice of relying upon removal and containment measures does not provide permanent protection, and that alternative or innovative treatment technologies which permanently alter the composition of hazardous waste to reduce the toxicity, mobility of volume of wastes can provide significantly greater long-term protection. Congress also finds that various regulatory factors have often inhibited the use and development of new technologies, and that a sustained program of research, development and demonstrations of alternative or innovative treatment technologies for use in Superfund clean-ups is needed.

SECTION 3—ALTERNATIVE OR INNOVATIVE TREATMENT TECHNOLOGY RESEARCH AND DEMONSTRATION PROGRAM

Section 3 authorizes and directs the Administrator of EPA to carry out a program of research, evaluation, testing, development

In addition to authorizing the conduct of such research and demonstration activities within the EPA, section 3(c) authorizes the Administrator, in carrying out the research and demonstration program, to enter into contracts and cooperative agreements with, and make grants to, persons, public entities, and nonprofit private entities.

While the bill specifies certain components to be included in the program, such as the technology transfer activities and field demonstrations, the bill largely grants the Administrator discretion in the direction and development of the research and demonstration program. To ensure a sound scientific basis as well as the application of the research results to actual clean-up activities, it is anticipated that both the Office of Research and Development and the Office of Emergency and Remedial Response would be involved with the program.

While the primary purpose of the program is to foster the development of alternative and innovative treatment technologies that can be used in remedial actions under Superfund, ancillary research needed to design, implement, or evaluate demonstrations of such technologies, such as site characterization, monitoring, and ecosystem damage assessment, would be appropriate activities under this section.

Under section 3(b), the Administrator is required to carry out, as a part of the overall program, technology transfer activities. Several witnesses indicated the importance of collecting information about alternative and innovative technologies in a central reference facility that would be readily accessible to the public and to interested persons. This section requires the Administrator to collect, evaluate, coordinate, and disseminate information relating to the use of alternative or innovative treatment technologies. As part of the information collection, the Administrator should collect and maintain data obtained from field demonstrations required under section 3(e) relating to the cost, efficacy, and safety of the alternative or innovative treatment technologies that were demonstrated. These technology transfer activities play an integral role in the development of new technologies by the private sector.

Information collected and maintained by the Administrator pursuant to this section is required to be made available to the public under the provisions of the Freedom of Information Act. The bill protects trade secrets and other proprietary information from public disclosure by providing for a process of petitioning the Administrator. This procedure is intended to balance public disclosure against a firm's interest in protecting commercially valuable trade secrets. In the same manner, the bill makes no distinction between technologies which are proprietary and those which are not.

Section 3(c) states that the Administrator is authorized to enter into contracts and agreements with, and make grants to, persons, public entities, and nonprofit private entities as defined in section 501(c)(3) of the Internal Revenue Code of 1954. By expanding on the definition of "person" contained in section 101(21) of CERCLA, which includes private for-profit firms, the Committee intends to make clear that universities, research centers, State and local governments, and other private nonprofit groups would be eligible to receive funding. Further, the Administrator would be able to support through contracts, agreements, or grants, a program or center to evaluate, test, or certify new technologies. Such a program, which could bring together experts from industry and academia, could also provide direct assistance to the Administrator in carrying out his responsibilities under the bill.

Section 3(c) states that the Administrator shall enter into appropriate cost-sharing arrangements to the maximum extent possible. Given the limited amount of funding available, and the relative expense of field demonstrations, cost-sharing becomes even more critical in funding field demonstrations. While the primary emphasis of the program should be on funding technologies which appear to hold the greatest promise, the agency should not ordinarily fund field demonstrations where the developers would appear to be able to otherwise conduct the project without EPA funding.

Section 3(d) directs the Administrator to provide research assistance in carrying out the provisions of the bill. A number of industry representatives testified as to the difficulty of obtaining information and assistance from the EPA in attempting to have new treatment technologies tested or evaluated by the EPA. The OTA Report reached similar conclusions and noted that EPA had no procedures for evaluating technologies other than conventional incineration. Section 3(d)(1) is intended to require the Administrator to establish procedures by which persons, public entities, or non-profit private entities can be assured of obtaining information and assistance concerning the evaluation or testing of their technologies. This section does not require that EPA itself do the testing, or that EPA is required to test all technologies proffered. Rather, it simply requires the Administrator to provide information or assistance so that developers will know what procedures or protocols might be applicable. For example, the Administrator might refer the applicant to procedures for receiving grants, or to the protocols published under section 5 of the Act, or to testing, evaluation or certification services known to the Administrator.

Section (3)(d)(2) authorizes the Administrator to arrange for the use of Superfund sites for research and demonstration purposes, subject to such terms and conditions as the Administrator shall require for the protection of human health and the environment. Under this provision, the Administrator could make Superfund sites available for private research and testing. Section 3(d) is not intended, however, to affect the permit requirements or authority of the Solid Waste Disposal Act. Consequently, in some circumstances it might be necessary to obtain a research and development permit under section 3005 of that Act.

Section 3(e) requires the Administrator, as part of the overall research and demonstration program, to designate at least ten sites on the national priority list as appropriate for field demonstrations of alternative or innovative treatment technologies. If the Administrator cannot designate all ten sites in accordance with the selection criteria specified in the bill within a two year period, the Administrator is required to report to Congress on the reasons for his inability to designate the sites. Within twelve months after the designation of a site, a field demonstration shall begin, or cause to begin, a demonstration of alternative or innovative treatment tech-

13

The purpose of the requirement to designate sites is to encourage appropriate field demonstration activity. If new technologies are to be used in the Superfund program, field demonstrations are necessary to provide the data on efficacy, cost and safety in actual field conditions that will be required. Given the OTA Report's listing of twenty-six technologies in various stages of testing, and the need to develop such technologies as rapidly as possible, the Committee feels that the goal of ten sites is reasonable. Further, a demonstration program of ten sites will be adequate to signal to the private sector EPA's commitment to evaluating and using permanent treatment technologies, and help to stimulate private sector investment and research.

In designating any appropriate site, the Administrator is required to consider certain criteria contained in the bill. In essence, those criteria include the potential of a field demonstration for contributing to a solution of the most serious hazardous waste threats, the availability of promising technologies ready for field demonstration, the suitability of the sites for such demonstrations, and the likelihood that such demonstrations will generate information which will be applicable to other sites. These criteria were added by the Committee in response to EPA's concern that a requirement to designate one site in each EPA region, contained in H.R. 2802 as introduced, would not give the Administrator sufficient flexibility to choose appropriate sites. The sites shall be designated by the Administrator only after notice and an opportunity for public comment.

The Administrator need not designate all ten sites at once. However, if at the end of two years, ten sites have not been designated, subsection (e) requires the Administrator to submit a report to the appropriate Committees of Congress, setting forth the reasons for the failure to designate the ten sites.

In carrying out demonstration projects at the designated sites, the EPA is not required to conduct all of the demonstrations itself. Indeed, it is expected that the majority of the demonstrations will be conducted by researchers outside of the Agency. Further, some sites may be appropriate for more than one field demonstration, and for testing of more than one type of technology. Such determinations have been left largely to the Administrator's discretion.

Since such demonstrations are, by their nature, experimental, it is expected that other remedial response actions will be necessary to clean up the sites designated as demonstration sites under this section. In some cases, the demonstration may be part of a clean up strategy, while in other cases, a demonstration may precede clean up efforts. In this regard, it is not the Committee's intent that sites which are designated for field demonstrations should be reserved exclusively for research purposes and not cleaned up. Research and demonstration liability concerns are addressed by section 6 and are discussed below.

Section 3(f) defines the term "alternative or innovative treatment technologies" as technologies which permanently alter the composi-

SECTION 4—REPORTS TO CONGRESS

To assist the Congress in its oversight of the research and demonstration program established by the bill, Section 4 requires the Administrator to submit an annual report to Congress on the progress of the program. The report will include an evaluation of the demonstration projects undertaken, findings with respect to the efficacy of such demonstrated technologies in achieving permanant and significant reductions in risk from hazardous waste, and the potential applicability of, and project costs for, such technologies at other hazardous waste sites. In discussing the potential applicability of, and costs for, such technologies at other sites, the Administrator is required only to indicate to what extent the technology may be applicable to similar problems existing at other comparable sites, and would not be required to discuss applicability to different types of hazardous wastes.

In addition, if the total estimated Federal contribution to the cost of any field demonstration exceeds $5 million, the Administrator is required to provide a report on the project to Congress and to wait for 30 days before expending funds on the project. This provision will help ensure that the limited funds in the program are spent prudently.

SECTION 5—TESTING PROCEDURES AND STANDARDS

Both the OTA Report and testimony from industry representatives underscored the failure of EPA to provide guidance for the evaluation of technologies other than incineration. Firms which would be willing to underwrite the costs of testing and demonstration cannot do so without assurances from the EPA that such tests will provide the data that EPA needs to evaluate the technology. While the Committee understands the difficulty involved in developing test protocols and standards that have general application for alternative or innovative treatment processes, the bill encourages EPA to give higher priority to developing such protocols and standards by requiring such protocols and standards to be included as part of the National Contingency Plan.

SECTION 6—RESPONSE AUTHORITIES

As previously discussed, the present CERCLA provisions relating to the choice of remedial actions create incentives for EPA to choose removal and containment strategies over permanent treatment technologies. Section 6 of the bill addresses this concern directly by amending CERCLA to require the Administrator to choose such permanent treatment solutions to the "maximum extent practicable." Under this section, the Administrator would be required to assess a number of specified factors in determining the appropriate cost-effective remedial response, including long term maintenance costs and the long term uncertainties associated with land disposal. The emphasis on the consideration of long-term costs, which is consistent with EPA's recent policy statement on off-site response actions (May 6, 1985), should serve to make treat-

15

The assessment required by Section 6 is identical to the provisions in Sec. 121(c) of H.R. 2817, the "Superfund Amendments Act of 1985", as amended and reported by the House Energy and Commerce Committee on August 1, 1985. (H. Rep. 99–253, Part 1). While your Committee has adopted the language accepted by the Energy and Commerce Committee, it sees no significant difference between the "maximum extent practicable" standard adopted and the "feasible and achievable" standard contained in H.R. 3065 as introduced. The Administrator is required to favor permanent treatment solutions over short-term removal and containment options if the permanent treatment technology is cost-effective, over the long-term. This factor is important since, in any single year, new technology to destroy hazardous waste would not succeed with the cost of storage, therefore, the cost competitiveness of destruction is when it is evaluated over time.

SECTION 7—FUNDING

Section 7 of the bill authorizes to be appropriated, for the five fiscal years beginning in 1986, no more than $25 million per year from the Trust Fund for the research and demonstration program established by the Act. The figure of $25 million was deemed appropriate by a number of witnesses testifying before the Subcommittee on Natural Resources, Agriculture Research and Environment. While the Committee agrees that the Trust Fund should be reserved for uses which are directly related to cleaning up abandoned hazardous waste sites, the Committee believes that the research and demonstration program authorized by the bill will be of direct benefit to Superfund clean-ups. Permanent clean-up technologies will enable EPA to clean up Superfund sites at lower long-term total costs than the use of temporary removal and containment measures.

SECTION 8—LIABILITY OF PERSONS ENGAGED IN FIELD DEMONSTRATIONS

Representatives of industry testified at the Subcommittee hearing that the spectre of joint, several, and strict liability under the Superfund law was inhibiting the use and development of innovative technologies at Superfund sites. Demonstrations of innovative technologies involve a risk that such technologies might fail to clean up a site, or might even contribute to a worsening of conditions at the site. EPA also expressed concern over the liability faced by researchers conducting demonstrations at Superfund sites under this program. Researchers might be reluctant to conduct field demonstrations if they are likely to face joint, several and strict liability for Superfund clean-up costs as a result of the demonstration failing.

To respond to EPA's concern and to encourage the use of innovative treatment technologies and field demonstrations, the bill exempts persons, public entities, and nonprofit private entities conducting field demonstrations from the strict, several, and joint lifor "response action contractors" under H.R. 2817, the "Superfund Amendments of 1985", as amended, which was reported by the House Energy and Commerce Committee on August 1, 1985. To the extent that response action contractors choose an innovative technology to clean up a site, the limited liability provision of H.R. 2817 should apply.

SECTION 9—SMALL BUSINESS PARTICIPATION

The Committee recognizes that many promising innovative and alternative hazardous waste treatment technologies have been, and will continue to be, developed by small, entrepreneurial business firms. Several new technologies developed by small business firms have been identified as showing great promise for future remedial actions.

However, according to testimony received during hearings on this legislation, several of these technologies face significant technical barriers before they can be successfully utilized in Superfund remedial activities. Thus this legislation specifies that the Administrator shall, to the maximum extent practicable, provide for adequate small business participation in the programs authorized under this section.

V. SECTIONAL SUMMARY OF THE BILL

Section 1. Short Title.

Section 2. Findings and Purpose. This section states that Congress finds that the EPA's practice of relying upon removal and containment measures does not provide permanent protection, and that containment measures does not provide permanent protection, and that new technologies which alter hazardous wastes to reduce toxicity, mobility, or volume can provide significantly greater permanent protection. This section also finds that various regulatory factors have often inhibited the use and development of new technologies, and that a sustained research, development and demonstration program is needed.

Section 3. Section 3 amends the Comprehensive Environmental Response, Compensation, and Liability Act (CERCLA) to establish a research, development and demonstration program at EPA for alternative or innovative treatment technologies to be used in Superfund clean-ups.

The program would include a technology transfer program. Information collected under the program will be publicly available, subject to the provisions of the Freedom of Information Act. Provisions to protect against the disclosure of trade secrets has been included.

The Act authorizes the Administrator to enter into contracts and to make grants with persons, public entities, and private nonprofit entities. The Administrator is directed to enter into appropriate cost-sharing arrangements.

Section 3 also directs the Administrator to provide research assistance and information, and to make sites available for research. Nothing under the act is intended to affect permit provisions required by the Resource Conservation and Recovery Act.

The Administrator is directed to designate, within two years, ten Superfund sites for field demonstrations of alternative or innova-

17

tive treatment technologies, according to specified criteria. If the Administrator cannot designate such sites, he is required to report back to Congress within the two year period on the reasons for the inability to do so. Field demonstrations at the designated sites are required to begin within a year of the designation of a site.

Section 4. This section requires the Administrator to provide an annual report to Congress on the progress of the research, development and demonstration program. It also requires Congressional review of any field demonstration estimated to cost more than $5 million in federal funds.

Section 5. This section amends CERCLA to require EPA to publish in its National Contingency Plan test procedures and standards by which alternative or innovative treatment technologies can be determined to be appropriate for use in Superfund clean-ups.

Section 6. This section amends CERCLA by requiring the EPA Administrator to assess a number of factors when selecting remedial measures, and requires the Administrator to select permanent measures, and alternative or innovative treatment technologies, to the maximum extent practicable.

Section 7. This section amends CERCLA to permit the use of Superfund Trust Fund monies for the research and demonstration program established by the Act. The bill provides for funding of no more than $25 million for the five fiscal years 1986–1990.

Section 8. This section provides for an exemption from the strict, several and joint liability of the Superfund law for field demonstrations of alternative and innovative technologies under this research program. Researchers would share the same liability for negligence that would be shared by other response action contractors under H.R. 2817, as amended and reported by the Energy and Commerce Committee.

Section 8 also requires EPA to provide a report to Congress on the impact of liability and other requirements imposed by CERCLA on the development and use of alternative or innovative treatment technologies.

Section 9. This section requires the Administrator, to the maximum extent practicable, to afford an adequate opportunity for participation by small businesses in the program established by the bill.

VI. CONGRESSIONAL BUDGET ACT INFORMATION

The bill provides for new authorization rather than new budget authority and consequently the provisions of section 308(a) of the Congressional Budget Act are not applicable.

VII. CONGRESSIONAL BUDGET OFFICE COST ESTIMATE

U.S. CONGRESS,
CONGRESSIONAL BUDGET OFFICE,
Washington, DC, July 31, 1985.

Hon. DON FUQUA,
.Chairman on Science and Technology, House of Representatives,
Rayburn House Office Building, Washington, DC.

DEAR MR. CHAIRMAN: The Congressional Budget Office has prepared the attached cost estimate for H.,R. 3065, The Superfund Clean-up Technology Research and Demonstration Act.

If you wish further details on this estimate, we will be pleased to provide them.

With best wishes,
Sincerely,

RUDOLPH G. PENNER.

CONGRESSIONAL BUDGET OFFICE—COST ESTIMATE

1. Bill number: H.R. 3065.
2. Bill title: The Superfund Clean-up Technology Research and Demonstration Act.
3. Bill status: As ordered reported by the House Committee on Science and Technology, July 25, 1985.
4. Bill purpose: This bill establishes a research and demonstration program within the Environmental Protection Agency (EPA) for alternative treatment technologies for hazardous wastes subject to actions under the Superfund program. The EPA Administrator is authorized to enter into contracts and cooperative agreements and make grants to carry out the purposes of this bill. The bill authorizes appropriations of up to $25 million from the Hazardous Substance Response Trust Fund in each of the fiscal years 1986 through 1990.

The Administrator is authorized to set up a program for technology transfer and is required, over two years, to designate ten sites for field demonstrations of new technologies. The EPA is required to publish standards and procedures by which alternative treatment technologies will be determined to be appropriate for use of Superfund monies.

5. Estimated cost to the Federal Government:

[By fiscal years, in millions of dollars]

	1986	1987	1988	1989	1990
Authorization level	25	25	25	25	25
Estimated outlays	7	25	25	25	25

The costs of this bill fall within budget function 300.

Basis of estimate: For the purpose of this estimate, it is assumed that all funds authorized are appropriated prior to the beginning of the fiscal year and that funds are obligated and disbursed in the same manner as similar programs currently in place.

6. Estimated cost to state and local governments: None.

19

7. Estimate comparison: None.
8. Previous CBO estimate: None.
9. Estimate prepared by: Paul M. DiNardo.
10. Estimate approved by: James L. Blum, Assistant Director for Budget Analysis.

VIII. OVERSIGHT FINDINGS AND RECOMMENDATIONS, COMMITTEE ON GOVERNMENT OPERATIONS

No findings and recommendations on oversight activity pursuant to Rule X, Clause (2)(b), and Rule XI, Clause 2(l)(3), of the Rules of the House of Representatives, have been submitted by the Committee on Government Operations for inclusion in this report.

IX. OVERSIGHT FINDINGS AND RECOMMENDATIONS, COMMITTEE ON SCIENCE AND TECHNOLOGY

Pursuant to Rule XI, Clause 2(l)(3) of the Rules of the House of Representatives, and under the authority of Rule X, Clause 2(b)(1) and Clause 3(f), the results and findings of oversight activities considered by the Committee on Science and Technology are incorporated in the recommendations found in the present bill and report.

X. EFFECT OF LEGISLATION ON INFLATION

In accordance with Rule XI, Clause 2(l)(4), of the Rules of the House of Representatives, this legislation is assessed to have no adverse inflationary or prices and costs in the operation of the national economy.

XI. CHANGES IN EXISTING LAW MADE BY THE BILL, AS REPORTED

In compliance with Rule XIII, clause 3, of the Rules of the House of Representatives, changes in existing law made by the bill, as reported, are shown as follows (existing law proposed to be omitted is enclosed in black brackets, new matter is printed in italic, existing law in which no change is proposed is shown in roman, and large unchanged blocks of existing law is indicated by * * *):

COMPREHENSIVE ENVIRONMENTAL RESPONSE, COMPENSATION, AND LIABILITY ACT OF 1980

AN ACT To provide for liability, compensation, cleanup, and emergency response for hazardous substances released into the environment and the cleanup on inactive hazardous waste disposal sites

Be it enacted by the Senate and House of Representatives of the United States of America in Congress assembled, That this Act may be cited as the "Comprehensive Environmental Response, Compensation, and Liability Act of 1980".

TITLE I—HAZARDOUS SUBSTANCES RELEASES, LIABILITY, COMPENSATION

20

RESPONSE AUTHORITIES

Sec. 104. (a)(1) * * *

*   *

(c)(1) * '

*   *   *   *   *   *   *

(4) The President shall select appropriate remedial actions determined to be necessary to carry out this section which are to the extent practicable in accordance with the national contingency plan and which provide for that cost-effective response which provides a balance between the need for protection of public health and welfare and the environment at the facility under consideration, and the availability of amounts from the Fund established under title II of this Act to respond to other sites which present or may present a threat to public health or welfare or the environment, taking into consideration the need for immediate action. *Any remedial action selected under section 104 for a facility at which a release or threatened release occurs shall require that level or standard of control of each hazardous substance or pollutant or contaminant at that facility which is necessary to protect human health and environment. In selecting a remedial action under section 104, the Administrator shall evaluate alternatives which achieve the requirements of the preceding sentence and shall assess the cost-effectiveness of such alternatives. In making such assessment, the Administrator shall specifically assess the long-term effectiveness of various alternatives, including an assessment of permanent solutions and alternative or innovative treatment technologies or resource recovery technologies that, in whole or in part, will result in a permanent and significant decrease in the toxicity, mobility, or volume of the hazardous substance, pollutant, or contaminant, taking into account each of the following:*

(A) The long-term uncertainties associated with land disposal.

(B) The goals, objectives, and requirements of the Solid Waste Disposal Act.

(C) The persistence, degradability in nature, toxicity, mobility, and propensity to bioaccumlate of such hazardous substances and their constituents.

(D) The potential threat to human health and the environment associated with excavation, transportation, and redisposal.

(E) Short- and long-term potential for adverse health effects from human exposure.

(F) Long-term maintenance costs.

Following an evaluation under this subsection, the Administrator shall select that cost-effective remedial action which, to the maximum extent practicable, utilizes such permanent solutions and alternative or innovative treatment technologies or resource recovery technologies.

*   -   -

NATIONAL CONTINGENCY PLAN

for public comments, revise and republish the national contingency plan for the removal of oil and hazardous substances, originally prepared and published pursuant to section 311 of the Federal Water Pollution Control Act, to reflect and effectuate the responsibilities and powers created by this Act, in addition to those matters specified in section 311(c)(2). Such revision shall include a section of the plan to be known as the national hazardous substance response plan which shall establish procedures and standards for responding to releases of hazardous substances, pollutants, and contaminants, which shall include at a minimum.

(1) * * *

*

(8)(A) * * *

(B) based upon the criteria set forth in subparagraph (A) of this paragraph, the President shall list as part of the plan national priorities among the known releases or threatened releases throughout the United States and shall revise the list no less often than annually. Within one year after the date of enactment of this Act, and annually thereafter, each State shall establish and submit for consideration by the President priorities for remedial action among known releases and potential releases in that State based upon the criteria set forth in subparagraph (A) of this paragraph. In assembling or revising the national list, the President shall consider any priorities established by the States. To the extent practicable, at least four hundred of the highest priority facilities shall be designated individually and shall be referred to as the "top priority among known response targets", and, to the extent practicable, shall include among the one hundred highest priority facilities at least one such facility from each State which shall be the facility designated by the State as presenting the greatest danger to public health or welfare or the environment among the known facilities in such State. Other priority facilities or incidents may be listed singly or grouped for response priority purposes; [and]

(9) specified roles for private organizations and entities in preparation for response and in responding to release of hazardous substances, including identification of appropriate qualifications and capacity therefor[.] ; and

(10) standards and testing procedures by which alternative or innovative treatment technologies can be determined to be appropriate for utilization in remedial actions authorized by this Act.

*

USES OF FUND

SEC. 111. (a) The President shall use the money in the Fund for the following purposes:

(2) payment of any claim for necessary response costs incurred by any other person as a result of carrying out the national contingency plan established under section 311(c) of the Clean Water Act and amended by section 105 of this title: *Provided, however,* That such costs must be approved under said plan and certified by the responsible Federal official;

(3) payment of any claim authorized by subsection (b) of this section and finally decided pursuant to section 112 of this title, including those costs set out in subsection 112(c)(3) of this title; [and]

(4) payment of costs specified under subsection (c) of this section[.] *; and*

(5) the cost of carrying out section 116 (relating to research, development, and demonstration of alternative and innovative treatment technologies).

The President shall not pay for any administrative costs or expenses out of the Fund unless such costs and expenses are reasonably necessary for and incidental to the implementation of this title.

*

(e)(1) * * *

[(2) In any fiscal year, 85 percent of the money credited to the Fund under title II of this Act shall be available only for the purposes specified in paragraphs (1), (2), and (4) of subsection (a) of this section.]

(2) For reservation of certain amounts appropriated to the Fund established under title II for specific purposes, see section 221(c)(2).

*   *   *   *   *   *   *

(m) RESEARCH, DEVELOPMENT, AND DEMONSTRATION PROGRAM.— There is authorized to be appropriated for each of the fiscal years 1986, 1987, 1988, 1989, and 1990, from sums appropriated or transferred to the Hazardous Substance Response Trust Fund established under section 221, not more than $25,000,000 to be used for purposes of carrying out the research, development, and demonstration program for alternative or innovative technologies authorized under section 116. Amounts made available under this subsection shall remain available until expended.

*   *   *   *   *   *   *

SEC. 116. ALTERNATIVE OR INNOVATIVE TREAMENT TECHNOLOGY RESEARCH, EVALUATION AND DEMONSTRATION PROGRAM.

(a) ESTABLISHMENT OF PROGRAM.—The Administrator is authorized and directed to carry out a program of research, evaluation, testing, development, and demonstration of alternative or innovative treatment technologies which may be utilized in remedial actions to achieve more permament protection of the public health and welfare and the environment.

(b) TECHNOLOGY TRANSFER.—In carrying out the program established in subsection (a) the Administrator shall conduct a technology transfer program, including the development, collection, evaluation, coordination and dissemination of information relating to the

central reference library for such information. The information maintained by the Administrator shall be made available to the public, subject to the provisions of section 552 of title 5 of the United States Code and section 1905 of title 18 of the United States Code, and to other Government agencies in a manner that will facilitate its dissemination: Provided, That upon a showing satisfactory to the Administrator by any person that any information, or portion thereof, obtained under this section by the Administrator directly or indirectly from such person, would, if made public, divulge—

(1) trade secrets; or

(2) other proprietary information of such person, the Administrator shall not disclose such information and disclosure thereof shall be punishable under subsection 1905 of title 18 of the United States Code. This subsection is not authority to withhold information from Congress or any committee of Congress upon request of the Chairman.

(c) CONTRACTS AND GRANTS.—In carrying out activities under subsection (a), the Administrator is authorized to enter into contracts and cooperative agreements with, and make grants to, persons, public entities, and nonprofit private entities (as defined by section 501(c)(3) of the Internal Revenue Code of 1954, 26 U.S.C. 501(c)(3)). The Administrator shall, to the maximum extent possible, enter into appropriate cost-sharing arrangements under this section.

(d) RESEARCH ASSISTANCE.—

(1) ASSISTANCE AND INFORMATION.—The Administrator may, consistent with the provisions of this section, provide assistance or information to persons, public entities, and nonprofit private entities who wish to have alternative and innovative treatment technologies tested or evaluated for utilization in remedial activities.

(2) USE OF SITES.—The Administrator may arrange for the use of sites listed as national priority sites under section 105(8)(B) for the purposes of research, testing, evaluation, development, and demonstration, under such terms and conditions as the Administrator shall require to assure the protection of human health and the environment.

(3) SAVING PROVISION.—Nothing in this Act shall be construed to affect the provisions of the Solid Waste Disposal Act.

(e) DESIGNATION OF DEMONSTRATION SITES.—In carrying out the program authorized by this section, the Adminstrator shall, within 2 years after the date of enactment of this section, and after notice and an opportunity for public comment, designate at least 10 sites listed under section 105(8)(B) as appropriate for field demonstrations of alternative or innovative treatment technologies. If the Administrator determines that 10 sites cannot be designated consistent with the criteria of this subsection, he shall within the 2-year period report to the appropriate committees of Congress explaining the reasons for his inability to designate such sites. Within 12 months after designation of a site, the Administrator shall begin or cause to begin a demonstration of alternative or innovative treatment tech-

trator

24

(1) The potential for contributing to solutions to those waste problems which pose the greatest threat to human health, which cannot by adequately controlled under present technologies, or which otherwise pose significant management difficulties.

(2) The availability of technologies which have been sufficiently developed for field demonstration and which are likely to be cost-effective and reliable.

(3) The suitability of the sites for demonstrating such technologies, taking into account the physical, biological, chemical, and geological characteristics of the sites, the extent and type of contamination found at the sites, and the capability to conduct demonstrations in such a manner as to assure the protection of human health and the environment.

(4) The likelihood that the data to be generated from the demonstration at the site will be applicable to other sites.

(f) DEFINITION.—For the purposes of this section, the term "alternative or innovative treatment technologies" means those technologies which permanently alter the composition of hazardous waste through chemical, biological, or physical means so as to significantly reduce the toxicity, mobility, or volume (or any combination thereof) of the hazardous waste or contaminated materials being treated.

SEC. 117. LIABILITY FOR FIELD DEMONSTRATIONS.

(a) LIABILITY OF PERSONS CONDUCTING FIELD DEMONSTRATIONS.—

(1) IN GENERAL.—Notwithstanding the provisions of section 114, no person, public entity, or nonprofit private entity, in the course of conducting field demonstrations pursuant to section 116 of this title, shall be liable under this title, under any other Federal law, under the law of any State or political subdivision, or under common law to any person for injuries, costs, damages, expenses, or other liability (including but not limited to claims for indemnification or contribution and claims by third parties for death, personal injury, illness or loss of or damage to property or economic loss) which results from a release or threatened release from a facility as a result of such field demonstration.

(2) NEGLIGENCE, ETC.—Paragraph (1) shall not apply in the case of a release that was caused by conduct of the person, public entity, or nonprofit private entity conducting field demonstrations which was negligent, reckless, or intentional misconduct.

(3) PERSONS RETAINED OR HIRED.—Any person retained or hired, by a person, public entity, or nonprofit private entity conducting field demonstrations pursuant to section 116, to provide any services relating to such field demonstration shall have the same exemption from liability provided to the person, public entity, or nonprofit private entity conducting said field demonstration.

(b) SAVINGS PROVISIONS.—

(1) LIABILITY OF OTHER PERSONS.—Nothing in this subsection

person, public entity, or non-profit private entity conducting a field demonstration pursuant to section 116 of this title.

(2) BURDEN OF PLAINTIFF.—Nothing in this section shall affect the plaintiff's burden of establishing the liability under this title.

(c) EXCEPTION TO EXEMPTION.—The exemption provided under subsection (a) shall not apply to any person covered by the provisions of paragraph (1), (2), (3), or (4) of section 107(a) with respect to the release or threatened release concerned if such persons would be covered by such provisions even if he had not carried out any actions referred to in subsection (d) of this section.

(d) DEFINITION.—For the purpose of this section, a person, public entity, or nonprofit private entity is "conducting a field demonstration pursuant to section 116 of this title" if such entity or person is carrying out a written contract or agreement with—

(1) the Administrator;

(2) any other Federal agency;

(3) a State; or

(4) any responsible party;

to conduct demonstrations at sites listed under section 105(8)(B) of alternative or innovative treatment technologies as defined in section 116(c).

(e) STUDY.—Within one year from the date of the enactment of this section, the Administrator shall transmit to Congress a study of the effects of the standards of liability and financial responsibility requirements imposed by the Comprehensive Environmental Response, Compensation, and Liability Act of 1980 on the cost of, and incentives for, developing and demonstrating alternative and innovatve treatment technologies.

TITLE II—HAZARDOUS SUBSTANCE RESPONSE REVENUE ACT OF 1980

Subtitle B—Establishment of Hazardous Substance Response Trust Fund

SEC. 221. ESTABLISHMENT OF HAZARDOUS SUBSTANCE RESPONSE TRUST FUND.

(a) CREATION OF TRUST FUND.—There is established in the Treasury of the United States a trust fund to be known as the "Hazardous Substance Response Trust Fund" (hereinafter in this subtitle referred to as the "Response Trust Fund"), consisting of such amounts as may be appropriated or transferred to such Trust Fund as provided in this section.

(b) TRANSFERS TO RESPONSE TRUST FUND.—

(1) AMOUNTS EQUIVALENT TO CERTAIN TAXES, ETC.—There are hereby appropriated, out of any money in the Treasury not otherwise appropriated, to the Response Trust Fund amounts determined by the Secretary of the Treasury (hereinafter in

26

 (A) the amounts received in the Treasury under section 4611 or 4661 of the Internal Revenue Code of 1954,

 (B) the amounts recovered on behalf of the Response Trust Fund under this Act,

 (C) all moneys recovered or collected under section 311(b)(6)(B) of the Clean Water Act,

 (D) penalties assessed under title I of this Act, and

 (E) Punitive damages under section 107(c)(8) of this Act.

 (2) AUTHORIZATION FOR APPROPRIATIONS.—There is authorized to be appropriated to the Emergency Response Trust Fund for fiscal year—

 (A) 1981, $44,000,000,

 (B) 1982, $44,000,000,

 (C) 1983, $44,000,000,

 (D) 1984, $44,000,000, and

 (E) 1985, $44,000,000, plus an amount equal to so much of the aggregate amount authorized to be appropriated under subparagraphs (A), (B), (C), and (D) as has not been appropriated before October 1, 1984.

 (3) TRANSFER OF FUNDS.—There shall be transferred to the Response Trust Fund—

 (A) one-half of the unobligated balance remaining before the date of the enactment of this Act under the Fund in section 311 of the Clean Water Act, and

 (B) the amounts appropriated under section 504(b) of the Clean Water Act during any fiscal year.

(c) EXPENDITURES FROM RESPONSE TRUST FUND.—

 (1) IN GENERAL.—Amounts in the Response Trust Fund shall be available in connection with releases or threats of releases of hazardous substances into the environment only for purposes of making expenditures which are described in section 111 (other than section (j) thereof) of this Act, [as in effect on the date of the enactment of this Act,] including—

 (A) response costs,

 (B) claims asserted and compensable but unsatisfied under section 311 of the Clean Water Act,

 (C) claims for injury to, or destruction or loss of, natural resources, [and]

 (D) related costs described in section 111(c) of this Act[.], and

 (E) the cost of carrying out section 116 (relating to research, development, and demonstration of alternative and innovative treatment technologies).

 (2) LIMITATIONS ON EXPENDITURES.—At least 85 percent of the amounts appropriated to the Response Trust Fund under subsection (b)(1)(A) and (2) shall be reserved *for the purposes specified in section 116 and*—

 (A) for the purposes specified in paragraphs (1), (2), and (4) of section 111(a) of this Act, and

 (B) for the repayment of advances made under section 223(c), other than advances subject to the limitation of sec-

XII. ADDITIONAL VIEWS

ADDITIONAL VIEWS OF HON. F. JAMES SENSENBRENNER, JR.

The Superfund Clean-up Technology Research and Demonstration Act (H.R. 3065) provides incentives for the examination of a wide range of alternative and innovative technologies which would allow our nation to seek permanent solutions to the problems of hazardous waste.

Several new technologies developed by small business firms have been identified as showing great promise for future remedial actions. During full committee markup of H.R. 3065, I offered an amendment which would encourage the EPA Administrator to take a closer look at hazardous waste treatment technologies developed by small entrepreneurial business firms.

This amendment, which was adopted by a voice vote, adds a new Section 9 to the bill which simply requires the Administrator of EPA to the maximum extent practicable to provide adequate opportunity in other R&D authorizations that this committee has approved in the past. I think it is a valuable addition so small business can get a slice of the pie the Committee has authorized. In addition, my amendment was offered in order to encourage the Thomas Edisons of hazardous waste.

Although I feel my amendment has done the job of underscoring the need for the EPA to take a closer look at small business ventures, there are two major points relating to my amendment which should be considered by the EPA. First is that the contracts should not be so large as to be beyond the capacity of small business to bid. Second, information should be spread through the small business community so they will be fully aware of what types of opportunities there are to bid on contracts.

Finally, let me emphasize that this is not a mandatory set-aside. It does not impose any burdens on any agency aside from the EPA, thereby eliminating any jurisdictional problems or the necessity of obtaining a sequential referral of this bill once it is reported by this committee.

F. JAMES SENSENBRENNER, Jr.

ADDITIONAL VIEWS OF HON. ROBERT C. SMITH

I strongly support the Committee's decision to pass H.R. 3065, the Superfund Clean-up Technology Research and Demonstration Act of 1985 and commend Congressman Torricelli for his thoughtful approach to this legislation. Hazardous waste contamination is a critical priority as it is the most prevalent and serious environmental threat facing the United States. The demonstration program created by this legislation is of vital importance to address the clean up of hazardous waste sites in the State of New Hampshire and throughout the nation.

H.R. 3065 provides needed incentive for the examination of a wide range of alternative and innovative technologies that would allow our nation to seek permanent solutions to this critical environmental problem. H.R. 3065 would provide needed encouragement to help our nation shift from land disposal practices to alternative technologies which reduce the risk of further hazardous waste contamination.

Contrary to the belief of some, hazardous waste contamination is not just an urban, industrial problem. Hazardous waste contamination has created significant problems in rural areas of the Northeast. The towns of New Hampshire and other primarily rural states are deeply affected by hazardous waste groundwater contamination in particular. I have visited many of these rural hazardous waste sites, and in my meetings with local town citizens and officials, one of their top concerns is groundwater contamination resulting from hazardous waste sites in their areas. There are hundreds of citizens in rural areas who are the victims of hazardous waste contamination because of the way contaminated plumes spread underground to residential wells and municipal water supplies. I commend local officals in New Hampshire for making this issue a priority in their towns, and I certainly want the victims of hazardous waste contamination to know of my commitment and the Committee's commitment to see this grave matter addressed in Superfund's reauthorization through passage of H.R. 3065.

I perhaps feel as strongly about this issue as anyone else in Congress. The State of New Hampshire has thirteen sites on or proposed for addition to Superfund's National Priority List, and eleven of those sites are in the First District of New Hampshire which I represent. Given the known, expensive costs of groundwater treatment which will be needed at many sites in my district, it is in my state's best interest to encourage the development of permanent technologies to address this problem and reduce the cost of groundwater treatment wherever this procedure is to be used.

Without permanent solutions, I am sincerely afraid that our present hazardous waste management and clean-up methods are not nearly adequate to meet the challenge posed by this grave environmental problem. It makes no sense to clean up one waste site

(28)

and create another one in the process. Underestimating national clean-up needs could result in continued escalation of this environmental crisis when we have the technology to address the issue of permanent clean up now.

A recent OTA report on Superfund showed that EPA is heavily reliant on removal of contaminants to RCRA permitted facilities or containment barriers as methods to clean up hazardous waste sites. Repeated costs are inevitable with these types of actions and environmentally, risks could be transferred from one community to another, and to future generations. The OTA report argues that permanent clean up technologies would, in the long term, be more cost-effective and provide greater protection than currently existing approaches that might rely upon remedial disposal and containment.

This legislation authorizes $25 million out of the hazardous waste Trust Fund for establishing a program within EPA to promote the development and use of alternative and innovative clean up technologies at Superfund sites throughout the nation. This legislation is consistent with testimony received by the Committee and also a recent CBO report which recommends that accelerated research and development in advancing hazardous waste remedial measures is necessary to help achieve greater levels of environmental health and public safety. This legislation further recognizes that the current EPA practice of relying on storage and containment measures to clean up hazardous waste sites does not significantly and permanently reduce the risk of the release of hazardous substances into the environment.

According to testimony received by the Subcommittee on Natural Resources, Agriculture Research and Environment, EPA has earmarked relatively insignificant amounts of funding on clean-up technology research development and testing. To date, EPA has not demonstrated the major commitment to assist in development of innovative and alternative hazardous waste clean-up technology. Considering the large cost of the overall Superfund problem, advocating a fiscally prudent sum on development of alternative and innovative clean up technologies offers considerable economic advantages in the long-term.

In addition, this legislation may also help overcome some of the key institutional barriers to the successful use of these new technolgies. There are at least 26 alternative and innovative technologies eagerly waiting to be made available for testing and use in remedial clean-up of Superfund sites. This demonstration program more than pays for itself in terms of the incentive it provides for the use of these needed alternative and innovative clean up technologies and in responsibly addressing the problem of hazardous waste contamination in the United States. H.R. 3065 is a crucial step forward in any comprehensive Superfund reauthorization approach.

ROBERT C. SMITH.

APPENDIX   III

AMENDMENTS

This appendix contains amendments proposed to S. 51 and H.R. 2817 which do not appear in the debates. Where introductory statements were made by the sponsors, they are included. See the "Guide to Texts of Bills and Amendments" in Volume 1 for a complete listing of the documents and their location.

(5591)

AMENDMENTS   TO S. 51

(5593)

SUPERFUND LEGISLATION

STAFFORD AMENDMENTS NOS. 2 AND 3

(Referred to the Committee on Environment and Public Works).

Mr. STAFFORD submitted two amendments intended to be proposed by him to the bill (S. 51) to extend and amend the Comprehensive Environmental Response, Compensation, and Liability Act of 1980, and for other purposes; as follows:

AMENDMENT NO. 2

S. 51, the Superfund Improvement Act of 1985, is amended by adding a new title at the end thereof as follows:

TITLE II

SEC. 201. TAX ON PETROLEUM.

(a) INCREASE IN TAX.—Subsections (a) and (b) of section 4611 of the Internal Revenue Code of 1954 (relating to environmental tax on petroleum) are each amended by striking out "0.79 cent" and inserting in lieu thereof "4.5 cents".

(b) TERMINATION OF TAX.—

(1) Subsection (d) of section 4611 of such Code (relating to termination) is amended to read as follows:

"(d) TERMINATION.—The tax imposed by this section shall not apply after the earlier of—

"(1) September 30, 1990, or

"(2) the date on which the Secretary, in the manner prescribed by regulations, reasonably estimates that the sum of the amounts received in the Treasury of the United States by reason of the taxes imposed by this section and sections 4661, 4691, and 4696 will equal $6,470,000,000.".

(c) EFFECTIVE DATE.—The amendments made by this section shall take effect on January 1, 1985.

SEC. 202. INCREASE IN TAX ON CERTAIN CHEMICALS.

(a) INCREASE IN RATE OF TAX; ADDITIONAL CHEMICALS TAXED.—Subsection (b) of section 4661 of the Internal Revenue Code of 1954 (relating to amount of tax imposed on certain chemicals) is amended by striking out the table contained in such subsection and inserting in lieu thereof the following:

"In the case of	The tax (before any inflation adjustment) is the following amount per ton:	
	Sales during 1985	Sales after 1985
Organic Chemicals:		
Acetylene	8.83	10.23
Benzene	6.60	8.80
Butadiene	9.79	10.23
Butane	4.87	5.60
Butylene	5.15	6.87
Ethylene	6.89	9.19
Methane	3.44	3.44
Napthalene	6.89	9.19
Propylene	5.87	7.82
Toluene	5.19	6.92
Xylene	7.70	10.23
Inorganic Chemicals:		
Ammonia	2.64	3.52
Antimony	9.34	9.34
Antimony trioxide	7.87	7.88
Arsenic	9.34	9.34
Arsenic trioxide	7.16	7.16
Barium sulfide	4.83	4.83
Bromine	9.34	9.34
Cadmium	9.34	9.34
Chlorine	3.05	4.07
Chromite	1.52	1.52
Chromium	9.34	9.34
Cobalt	9.34	9.34
Cupric oxide	7.54	7.54
Cupric sulfate	3.93	3.93
Cuprous oxide	8.34	8.34
Hydrochloric acid	0.61	0.61
Hydrogen fluoride	8.88	8.88
Lead	8.27	11.03
Mercury	9.34	9.34
Nickel	9.34	9.34
Nitric acid	0.50	0.50
Phosphorus	9.34	9.34
Potassium dichromate	3.55	3.55
Potassium hydroxide	0.46	0.46
Sodium dichromate	3.93	3.93
Sodium hydroxide	0.59	0.59
Stannic chloride	4.45	4.45
Stannous chloride	5.98	5.98
Sulfuric acid	0.55	0.55
Zinc chloride	4.66	4.66
Zinc sulfate	3.99	3.99

"In the case of Other Organic or Inorganic Substances:	The tax is the following amount per ton:
Acetone	$8.64
Barium	.81
Bis (2-ethylhexyl) phthalate	8.64
Carbon tetrachloride	8.43
Chlorobenzene	27.66
Chloroform	25.93
1,2-Dichloroethane	4.54
Ethylbenzene	27.33
Methylene chloride	21.61
Methyl ethyl ketone	14.26
Pentachlorophenol	28.59
Phenol	44.95
1,1,2,2-Tetrachloroethane	6.05
1,1,2,2-Tetrachloroethene	21.18
Trichloroethylene	60.51
1,1,1-Trichloroethane	39.33
Vinylchloride	11.24

(b) INFLATION ADJUSTMENT IN AMOUNT OF TAX.—Section 4661 of such Code is amended by redesignating subsection (c) as subsection (d) and by inserting after subsection (b) the following new subsection:

"(c) INFLATION ADJUSTMENTS IN AMOUNT OF TAX.—

"(1) IN GENERAL.—In the case of any taxable chemical sold in a calendar year after 1985 the amount of the tax imposed by subsection (a) shall be the amount determined under subsection (b) increased by the applicable inflation adjustment for such calendar year.

"(2) APPLICABLE INFLATION ADJUSTMENT.—

"(A) IN GENERAL.—In the case of a taxable chemical, the applicable inflation adjustment for the calendar year is the percentage (if any) by which—

"(i) the applicable price index for the preceding calendar year, exceeds

"(ii) the applicable price index for 1984.

"(B) APPLICABLE PRICE INDEX.—For purposes of subparagraph (A), the applicable price index for any calendar year is the average for the months in the 12-month period ending on September 30 of such calendar year of—

"(i) in the case of organic substances, the producer price index for basic organic chemicals as published by the Secretary of Labor, or

"(ii) in the case of inorganic substances, the producer price index for basic inorganic chemicals as published by the Secretary of Labor.

"(3) ROUNDING.—If any increase determined under paragraph (1) is not a multiple of 1 cent, such increase shall be rounded to the nearest multiple of 1 cent (or if the increase determined under paragraph (1) is a multiple of ½ of 1 cent, such increase shall be increased to the next higher multiple of 1 cent).".

(c) EXEMPTION FOR EXPORTS OF TAXABLE CHEMICALS.—

(1) Section 4662 of such Code (relating to definitions and special rules) is amended by redesignating subsection (e) as subsection (f) and by inserting after subsection (d) the following new subsection:

"(e) EXEMPTION FOR EXPORTS OF TAXABLE CHEMICALS.—

"(1) TAX-FREE SALES.—

"(A) IN GENERAL.—No tax shall be imposed under section 4661 on the sale by the manufacturer or producer of any taxable chemical for export, or for resale by the purchaser to a second purchaser for export.

"(B) PROOF OF EXPORT REQUIRED.—Rules similar to the rules of section 4221(b) shall apply for purposes of subparagraph (A).

"(2) CREDIT OR REFUND WHERE TAX PAID.—

"(A) IN GENERAL.—Except as provided in subparagraph (B), if—

"(i) tax under section 4661 was paid with respect to any taxable chemical, and

"(ii) such chemical was exported by any person,

credit or refund (without interest) of such tax shall be allowed or made to the person who paid such tax.

"(B) CONDITION TO ALLOWANCE.—No credit or refund shall be allowed or made under ing to refunds and credits with respect to the tax on certain chemicals) is amended by adding at the end thereof the following new paragraph:

"(4) USE IN THE PRODUCTION OF ANIMAL FEED.—Under regulations prescribed by the Secretary, if—

"(A) a tax under section 4661 was paid with respect to nitric acid, sulfuric acid, phosphoric acid, ammonia, or methane used to produce ammonia, without regard to subsection (d)(7), and

"(B) any person uses such substance as a qualified animal feed substance,

then an amount equal to the excess of the tax so paid over the tax determined with regard to subsection (b)(7) shall be allowed as a credit or refund (without interest) to such person in the same manner as if it were an overpayment of tax imposed by this section.".

(e) EFFECTIVE DATES.—

(1) IN GENERAL.—The amendments made by this section shall take effect on January 1, 1985.

(2) The amendments made by subsection (d) shall take effect on the date of enactment * * *.

ENVIRONMENTAL TOXICS TAX

SEC. 203. Tax on Hazardous Pollutants.

(a) IN GENERAL.—Chapter 38 of the Internal Revenue Code of 1954 is amended by adding the following new subchapter:

"SUBCHAPTER D—TAX ON THE RELEASE OF HAZARDOUS SUBSTANCES AND DISPOSAL OF HAZARDOUS WASTES.

"Section 4691. Imposition of Tax.
"Section 4692. Definitions.
"Section 4693. Records, Statements and Returns.

"SEC. 4691. IMPOSITION OF TAX.

"(a) GENERAL RULE.—There is hereby imposed a tax on—

"(1) the release of any hazardous substance, and

"(2) the receipt of a hazardous waste for disposal at a hazardous waste disposal facility.

"(b) AMOUNT OF TAX.—The amount of the tax imposed by subsection (a) shall be equal to the following:

"(1) $150 for each ton of hazardous waste which is disposed of by landfill, surface impoundment or in waste piles;

"(2) $75 for each ton of a hazardous substance released in compliance with a federally permitted release;

"(3) $150 for each ton of a hazardous substance released in any other way.

"(c) ALTERNATIVE COMPUTATION OF TAX.—Under regulations provided by the Secretary, if the owner or operator of a hazardous waste disposal or hazardous substance handling facility can establish the amount of water of the hazardous waste or substance deposited or released, then such owner or operator may elect to pay, in lieu of the taxes which would otherwise be paid under this section, a tax reduced by the weight of water.

"(d) EXCLUSION FOR CERTAIN WASTES.—No tax shall be imposed under subsection (a) on any of the following:

"(1) The disposal of wastes which are, as of the date of enactment of this section, exempt from regulation as a hazardous waste under Section 3001 of the Solid Waste Disposal Act. In the event that any such waste is determined by the Administrator of the Environmental Protection Agency, following studies as required under section 8002 of such Act, to pose a potential danger to human health and environment, and the Administrator of the Environmental Protection Agency promulgates regulations for the disposal of such waste, then the Administrator shall transmit to both Houses of Congress, along with such regulations, his recommendation for imposing a tax, if any, on the disposal or long-term storage of such waste. A tax shall be imposed under subsection (a) on such waste only when authorized by Act of Congress.

"(2) The disposal of—

"(A) any waste by any person in the course of carrying out any removal or remedial action under the Comprehensive Environmental Response, Compensation, and Liability Act of 1980 if such disposal is carried out in accordance with a plan approved by the Administrator of the Environmental Protection Agency or the State, or

"(B) any waste removed from any facility listed on the National Priorities List (NPL).

"(e) LIABILITY FOR THE TAX.—The Tax imposed by this section shall be imposed on the owner or operator of the hazardous waste disposal facility or hazardous substance handling or treatment facility at which the hazardous waste is disposed of or released.

"(f) CREDIT FOR PRIOR TAX.—

"(1) IN GENERAL.—A credit shall be allowed in the computation of any tax due under this section on the disposal of a hazardous waste for any tax previously paid under this section by the disposer on the long term storage of such hazardous waste.

"(2) LONG-TERM STORAGE.—In the event that a person who has paid a tax under this section on the long-term storage of a hazardous waste causes such hazardous waste to be delivered to and received by another person who is the owner or operator of a qualified hazardous waste disposal facility, then such person who paid the tax on the long-term storage shall be allowed a credit for such tax in the computation of any tax subsequently due on the long-term storage or disposal of a hazardous waste.

"(3) SPECIAL RULE FOR FUNGIBLE WASTE.—For purposes of determining any credit allowances for fungible waste under the provisions of paragraphs (1) and (2), it shall be presumed that the last of such waste placed in a qualified hazardous waste storage facility shall be the first to be removed from such facility.

"(g) FRACTIONAL PART OF TON.—In the case of a fraction of a ton, the tax imposed by this section shall be the same fraction striking out "and" at the end of subparagraph (D), by striking out the period at the end of subparagraph (E) and inserting a comma and "and", and by adding a new subparagraph as follows:

"(F) the amounts received in the Treasury under section 4691 of the Internal Revenue Code of 1954.".

(c) STUDY.—

(1) IN GENERAL.—Not later than January 1, 1987, and annually thereafter through 1989, the Secretary of the Treasury, in consultation with the Administrator of the Environmental Protection Agency, shall submit to the Congress a report on the amount of revenues being collected in accordance with subchapter D of chapter 38 of the Internal Revenue Code of 1954 and his recommendations, if any, for changes in the tax imposed under such subchapter in order to—

(A) raise an amount of revenue equivalent to the anticipated amount of revenue from the tax originally imposed under such subchapter,

(B) assure that the tax is discouraging the release of hazardous substances in an environmentally unsound manner, and

(C) assure that the tax is being collected with maximum administrative feasibility.

(2) ADDITION OF CERTAIN SUBSTANCES.—The Secretary of the Treasury shall also study, and recommend to the Congress whether releases of the following should be subject to tax under subchapter D of chapter 38 of such Code.

(A) Pesticides identified for a rebuttable presumption against registration under the Federal Insecticide, Fungicide, and Rodenticide Act.

(B) Chemicals which, according to the International Agency for Research on Cancer, have substantial evidence of carcinogenicity.

(d) EFFECTIVE DATE.—The amendments made by subsections (a) and (b) shall take effect on January 1, 1986.

CORPORATE TAX ON NET RECEIPTS

SEC. 204. CORPORATE TAX ON NET RECEIPTS.

"(a) IN GENERAL.—Chapter 38 of the Internal Revenue Code of 1954 (relating to environmental taxes) is amended by adding at the end thereof the following new subchapter:

"SUBCHAPTER E—TAX ON CORPORATE NET PROFITS

"SEC. 4696. ENVIRONMENTAL NET PROFITS TAX.

"(a) GENERAL RULE.—There is hereby imposed on each corporation a tax equal to .014 percent of the taxable net receipts of such corporation for the taxable year.

"(b) TAXABLE NET RECEIPTS.—For purposes of this section—

"(1) IN GENERAL.—The term 'taxable net receipts' means the excess (if any) of—

"(A) the gross receipts of the taxpayer for any taxable year over

"(B) the sum of—

"(i) the costs of goods sold by the taxpayer for such taxable year, plus

"(ii) $75,000,000.

"(2) AGGREGATION OF CONTROLLED GROUPS.—

"(A) IN GENERAL.—For purposes of this sec-tion, all members of the same controlled group of corporations shall be treated as one taxpayer.

"(B) OTHER GROUPS UNDER COMMON CONTROL.—Under regulations prescribed by the Secretary, a rule similar to the rule of subparagraph (A) shall apply to trades or businesses (whether or not incorporated) which are under common control.

"(C) CONTROLLED GROUP DEFINED.—For purposes of this paragraph, the term 'controlled group of corporations' has the meaning given such term by section 1563(a), except that—

"(i) 'more than 50 percent' shall be substituted for 'at least 80 percent' each place it appears in section 1563(a)(1), and

"(ii) the determination shall be made without regard to subsections (a)(4) and (e)(3)(C) of section 1563.

"(c) SPECIAL RULE FOR TAX-EXEMPT ORGANIZATIONS.—In the case of any taxpayer which is exempt from tax under section 501(a), taxable net receipts shall be computed only by reference to the unrelated business taxable income (within the meaning of section 512) of the taxpayer.

"(d) TERMINATION.—No tax shall be imposed under this section for taxable years beginning after December 31, 1990.".

(b) ALLOCATION OF REVENUES TO TRUST FUND.—Section 221(b)(1) of the Comprehensive, Environmental Response, Compensation and Liability Act of 1980, as amended by part III, is amended by striking out "and" at the end of subparagraph (E), by striking out the period at the end of subparagraph (F) and inserting in lieu thereof ", and", and by adding at the end thereof the following new subparagraph:

"(G) the amounts received in the Treasury under section 4696 of the Internal Revenue Code of 1954.".

(c) CONFORMING AMENDMENT.—The table of subchapters for chapter 38 is amended by adding at the end thereof the following new item:

"SUBCHAPTER E—TAX ON CORPORATE NET PROFITS"

(d) EFFECTIVE DATE.—The amendments made by this section shall apply to taxable years beginning after December 31, 1985.

STUDY OF IMPORTS OF CERTAIN CHEMICALS

SEC. 205. STUDY ON IMPORTED DERIVATIVES.

(a) GENERAL RULE.—

(1) The Secretary of the Treasury shall conduct a study on (A) the economic effects of the tax imposed by section 4661 of the Internal Revenue Code of 1954, and (B) the feasibility and desirability of imposing a tax on imported derivative of substances subject to the tax imposed by section 4661. Such study shall develop the methodology for selecting the list of substances and shall list the substances which would be subject to the tax referred to in subparagraph (B) and their corresponding item numbers in the Tariff Schedules of the United States.

(2) The U.S. International Trade Commission should conduct a study on (A) the trade

effects of the tax imposed by section 4661 with and without the tax on derivatives; and (B) the means of making such a tax on derivatives compatible with current international trade agreements.

(b) REPORT.—

(1) Not later than March 1, 1985, the Secretary of the Treasury shall submit to the Committee on Ways and Means of the House of Representatives and the Committee on Finance of the Senate the list of substances (and corresponding item numbers in the Tariff Schedules of the United States) prepared as part of the study conducted under subsection (a)(1). Not later than June 1, 1985, the Secretary of the Treasury shall submit the report on the study conducted under subsection (a)(1).

(2) The Commission shall submit to the Committee on Ways and Means of the House of Representatives and the Committee on Finance of the Senate its report on the study conducted under (a)(2) within four months from the date of receipt of the Secretary of Treasury's list of substances provided for in paragraph (1), but not before June 1, 1985.

AMENDMENT No. 3

S. 51, the Superfund Improvement Act of 1985, is amended by adding a new section at the end thereof as follows:

"FEDERAL CAUSE OF ACTION

"SEC. 124. (a) Section 107(a) of the Comprehensive Environmental Response, Compensation, and Liability Act of 1980 is amended by striking and at the end of subparagraph (B); by striking the period at the end of subparagraph (C) and inserting in lieu thereof and; and by adding the following new subparagraph:

"(D) damages, as defined in section 101(6)(B), resulting from such a release.".

(b) Section 101(b) of the Comprehensive Environmental Response, Compensation, and Liability Act of 1980 is amended by inserting "(A)" after "damages for" and by adding at the end thereof the following: "and (B)(i) any medical expenses, rehabilitation costs, or burial expenses due to bodily injury; (ii) any loss of income or profits or impairment or loss of earning capacity due to bodily injury; (iii) any pain and suffering due to bodily injury; (iv) any economic loss and any injury to property, including diminution in value, and (v) whenever the court determines such award is appropriate in accordance with section 107(n), taking into account the proportion of the injured class which would benefit from such award, punitive damages;".

(c) Section 107 of the Comprehensive Environmental Response, Compensation, and Liability Act of 1980 is amended by adding the following new subsections:

"(l) In any action for damages under subparagraph (D) of subsection (a), subject to Rules 402 and 403 of the Federal Rules of Evidence, the following evidence relevant to the issue of causation of personal injury shall be admissible:

"(1) increases in the incidence of injury of disease in the exposed population over that which is otherwise probable;

"(2) epidemiological studies;

"(3) animal studies;

"(4) short-term in-vitro studies,

"(5) tissue and toxicologic studies;

"(6) environmental monitoring data; and

"(7) government health effects studies done for the purpose of developing standards or exposure limits.

"(m) The standard of liability for any person for damages under subparagraph (D) of subsection (a) of this section shall be strict liability without limitation to the defenses specified in subsection (b) of this section.

"(n) For the purposes of subparagraph (D) of subsection (a), punitive damages may be awarded in the case of conduct manifesting a conscious, flagrant indifference to the safety of those persons who might be harmed by a hazardous substance, pollutant, or contaminant and constituting an extreme departure from accepted practice.

"(o) In the case of damages under subparagraph (D) of subsection (a), persons liable under paragraph (3) of such subsection shall be liable only with regard to damages resulting from releases of hazardous substances, pollutants or contaminants owned or possessed by such person.".

(d) Section 113 of the Comprehensive Environmental Response, Compensation, and Liability Act of 1980 is amended by adding the following new subsections:

"(e) Jurisdiction of the United States district courts over any action under subparagraph (D) of section 107(a) of this title shall be concurrent with the jurisdiction of the courts of any State over such an action, and nothing in this section shall be construed to affect the jurisdiction of any State court with respect to any action under this title.

"(f) It is the policy of the Congress to encourage certification of class actions in actions under subparagraph (D) of section 107(a) of this title involving common issues of fact or law. In furtherance of that policy, the Congress finds that the requirements of Rule 23 of the Federal Rules of Civil Procedure are met in actions under such subparagraph arising from the same r˕ase and presenting common issues of fact law and involving 30 or more potential cla ˕ts.

"(g) In any action under sut ˕raph (D) of section 107(a) of this title, ˕ants may be added at the request of p s or defendants, without regard to t ˕en-ship of the parties. The United S ˕ all make available to appropriate pa ˕˕r-mation in its possession which is ˕˕ ˕o the identification of other respo ˕-ties who are potential defendants.

[From the Congressional Record, permanent edition, Jan. 22, 1985, pp. 797-800]

SUPERFUND IMPROVEMENT ACT OF 1985

STAFFORD AMENDMENT NO. 7

(Ordered referred to the Committee on Environment and Public Works.)

Mr. STAFFORD submitted an amendment intended to be proposed by him to the bill (S. 51) to extend and amend the Comprehensive Environmental Response, Compensation and Liability Act of 1980, and for other purposes; as follows:

S. 51, the Superfund Improvement Act of 1985, is amended by adding a new title at the end thereof as follows:

"TITLE II

SEC. 201. TAX ON PETROLEUM.

(a) INCREASE IN TAX.—Subsections (a) and (b) of section 4611 of the Internal Revenue Code of 1954 (relating to environmental tax on petroleum) are each amended by striking out "0.79 cent" and inserting in lieu thereof "4.5 cents".

(b) TERMINATION OF TAX.—

(1) Subsection (d) of section 4611 of such Code (relating to termination) is amended to read as follows:

"(d) TERMINATION.—The tax imposed by this section shall not apply after the earlier of—

"(1) September 30, 1990, or

"(2) the date on which the Secretary, in the manner prescribed by regulations, reasonably estimates that the sum of the amounts received in the Treasury of the United States by reason of the taxes imposed by this section and sections 4661, 4691, and 4696 will equal $6,470,000,000.".

(c) EFFECTIVE DATE.—The amendments made by this section shall take effect on January 1, 1985.

SEC. 202. INCREASE IN TAX ON CERTAIN CHEMICALS.

(a) INCREASE IN RATE OF TAX; ADDITIONAL CHEMICALS TAXED.—Subsection (b) of section 4661 of the Internal Revenue Code of 1954 (relating to amount of tax imposed on certain chemicals) is amended by striking out the table contained in such subsection and inserting in lieu thereof the following:

"In the case of	The tax (before any inflation adjustment) is the following amount per ton:	
	Sales during 1985	Sales after 1985
Organic Chemicals.		
Acetylene	8.83	10.23
Benzene	6.60	8.80
Butadiene	9.79	10.23
Butane	4.87	5.60
Butylene	5.15	6.87
Ethylene	6.89	9.19
Methane	3.44	3.44
Naphthalene	6.89	9.19
Propylene	5.87	7.82
Toluene	5.19	6.92
Xylene	7.70	10.23
Inorganic Chemicals:		
Ammonia	2.64	3.52
Antimony	9.34	9.34
Antimony trioxide	7.87	7.88
Arsenic	9.34	9.34
Arsenic trioxide	7.16	7.16
Barium sulfide	4.83	4.83
Bromine	9.34	9.34
Cadmium	9.34	9.34
Chlorine	3.05	4.07
Chromite	1.52	1.52
Chromium	9.34	9.34
Cobalt	9.34	9.34
Cupric oxide	7.54	7.54
Cupric sulfate	3.93	3.93
Cuprous oxide	8.34	8.34
Hydrochloric acid	0.61	0.61
Hydrogen fluoride	8.88	8.88
Lead	8.27	11.03
Mercury	9.34	9.34
Nickel	9.34	9.34
Nitric acid	0.50	0.50
Phosphorus	9.34	9.34
Potassium dichromate	3.55	3.55
Potassium hydroxide	0.46	0.46
Sodium dichromate	3.93	3.93
Sodium hydroxide	0.59	0.59
Stannic chloride	4.45	4.45
Stannous chloride	5.98	5.98
Sulfuric acid	0.55	0.55
Zinc chloride	4.66	4.66
Zinc sulfate	3.99	3.99

"In the case of:	The tax is the following amount per ton:
Other Organic or Inorganic Substances:	
Aceton	$8.64
Barium	0.81
Bis (2-ethylhexyl) phthalate	8.64
Carbon tetrachloride	8.43
Chlorobenzene	27.66
Chloroform	25.93
1,2-Dichloroethane	4.54
Ethylbenzene	27.33
Methylene chloride	21.61
Methyl ethyl ketone	14.26
Pentachlorophenol	28.59
Phenol	44.95
1,1,2,2-Tetrachloroethane	6.05
1,1,2,2-Tetrachloroethene	21.18
Trichloroethylene	60.51
1,1,1-Trichloroethane	39.33
Vinylchloride	11.24

(b) INFLATION ADJUSTMENTS IN AMOUNT OF TAX.—Section 4661 of such Code is amended by redesignating subsection (c) as subsection (d) and by inserting after subsection (b) the following new subsection:

"(c) INFLATION ADJUSTMENTS IN AMOUNT OF TAX.—

"(1) IN GENERAL.—In the case of any taxable chemical sold in a calendar year after 1985 the amount of the tax imposed by subsection (a) shall be the amount determined under subsection (b) increased by the applicable inflation adjustment for such calendar year.

"(2) APPLICABLE INFLATION ADJUSTMENT.—

"(A) IN GENERAL.—In the case of a taxable chemical, the applicable inflation adjustment for the calendar year is the percentage (if any) by which—

"(i) the applicable price index for the preceding calendar year, exceeds

"(ii) the applicable price index for 1984.

"(B) APPLICABLE PRICE INDEX.—For purposes of subparagraph (A), the applicable price index for any calendar year is the average for the months in the 12-month period ending on September 30 of such calendar year of—

"(i) in the case of organic substances, the producer price index for basic organic chemicals as published by the Secretary of Labor, or

"(ii) in the case of inorganic substances, the producer price index for basic inorganic chemicals as published by the Secretary of Labor.

"(3) ROUNDING.—If any increase determined under paragraph (1) is not a multiple of 1 cent, such increase shall be rounded to the nearest multiple of 1 cent (or if the increase determined under paragraph (1) is a multiple of ½ of 1 cent, such increase shall be increased to the next higher multiple of 1 cent).".

"(c) EXEMPTION FOR EXPORTS OF TAXABLE CHEMICALS.—

"(1) Section 4662 of such Code (relating to definitions and special rules) is amended by redesignating subsection (e) as subsection (f) and by inserting after subsection (d) the following new subsection:

"(e) EXEMPTION FOR EXPORTS OF TAXABLE CHEMICALS.—

"(1) TAX-FREE SALES.—

"(A) IN GENERAL.—No tax shall be imposed under section 4661 on the sale by the manufacturer or producer of any taxable chemical for export, or for resale by the purchaser to a second purchaser for export.

"(B) PROOF OF EXPORT REQUIRED.—Rules similar to the rules of section 4221(b) shall apply for purposes of subparagraph (A).

"(2) CREDIT OR REFUND WHERE TAX PAID.—

"(A) IN GENERAL.—Except as provided in subparagraph (B), if—

"(i) tax under section 4661 was paid with respect to any taxable chemical, and

"(ii) such chemical was exported by any person. Credit or refund (without interest) of such tax shall be allowed or made to the person who paid such tax.

"(B) CONDITION TO ALLOWANCE.—No credit or refund shall be allowed or made under subparagraph (A) unless the person who paid the tax establishes that he—

"(i) has repaid or agreed to repay the amount of the tax to the person who exported the taxable chemical, or

"(ii) has obtained the written consent of such exporter to the allowance of the credit or the making of the refund.

"(3) REGULATIONS.—The Secretary shall prescribe such regulations as may be necessary to carry out the purposes of this subsection."

(2) Paragraph (1) of section 4662(d) of such Code (relating to refund or credit for certain uses) is amended—

(A) by striking out "the sale of which by such person would be taxable under such section" and inserting in lieu thereof "which is a taxable chemical", and

(B) by striking out "imposed by such section on the other substance manufactured or produced" and inserting in lieu thereof "Imposed by such section on the other substance manufactured or produced (or which would have been imposed by such section on such other substance but for subsection (e) of this section)".

(d) EXEMPTION FOR SUBSTANCES USED IN THE PRODUCTION OF ANIMAL FEED.—

(1) IN GENERAL.—Subsection (b) of section 4662 of the Internal Revenue Code of 1954 (relating to definitions and special rules with respect to the tax on certain chemicals) is amended by adding at the end thereof the following paragraph:

"(7) SUBSTANCES USED IN THE PRODUCTION OF ANIMAL FEED.—

"(A) IN GENERAL.—In the case of nitric acid, sulfuric acid, phosphoric acid, ammonia, or methane used to produce ammonia, which is a qualified animal feed substance, no tax shall be imposed under section 4661(a).

"(B) QUALIFIED ANIMAL FEED SUBSTANCE.—For purposes of this section, the term 'qualified animal feed substance' means any substance—

"(i) used in a qualified animal feed use by the manufacturer, producer, or importer,

"(ii) sold for use by any purchaser in a qualified animal feed use, or

"(iii) sold for resale by any purchaser for use, or resale for ultimate use, in a qualified animal feed use.

"(C) QUALIFIED ANIMAL FEED USE.—The term qualified animal feed use means any use in the manufacture or production of animal feed or animal feed supplements, or of ingredients used in animal feed or animal feed supplements.

"(D) TAXATION OF NONQUALIFIED SALE OR USE.—For purposes of section 4661(a), if no tax was imposed by such section on the sale or use of any chemical by reason of subparagraph (A), the first person who sells or uses such chemical other than in a sale or use described in subparagraph (A) shall be treated as the manufacturer of such chemical.".

(2) REFUND OR CREDIT FOR SUBSTANCES USED IN THE PRODUCTION OF ANIMAL FEED.—Subsection (d) of section 4662 of such Code (relating to refunds and credits with respect to the tax on certain chemicals) is amended by adding at the end thereof the following new paragraph:

"(4) USE IN THE PRODUCTION OF ANIMAL FEED.—Under regulations prescribed by the Secretary if—

"(A) a tax under section 4661 was paid with respect to nitric acid, sulfuric acid, phosphoric acid, ammonia, or methane used to produce ammonia, without regard to subsection (d)(7), and

"(B) any person uses such substance as a qualified animal feed substance.

then an amount equal to the excess of the tax so paid over the tax determined with regard to subsection (b)(7) shall be allowed as a credit or refund (without interest) to such person in the same manner as if it were an overpayment of tax imposed by this section.".

"(e) EFFECTIVE DATES.—

(1) IN GENERAL.—The amendments made by this section shall take effect on January 1, 1985.

(2) The amendments made by subsection (d) shall take effect on the date of enactment of this Act.

ENVIRONMENTAL TOXICS TAX

SEC. 203. Tax on Hazardous Pollutants.

(a) IN GENERAL.—Chapter 38 of the Internal Revenue Code of 1954 is amended by adding the following new subchapter:

"SUBCHAPTER E—TAX ON THE RELEASE OF HAZARDOUS SUBSTANCES AND DISPOSAL OF HAZARDOUS WASTES.

"Section 4691. Imposition of Tax.
"Section 4692. Definitions.
"Section 4693. Records, Statements and Returns.

"SEC. 4691. IMPOSITION OF TAX.

"(a) GENERAL RULE—There is hereby imposed a tax on—

"(1) the release of any hazardous substance, and

"(2) the receipt of a hazardous waste for disposal at a hazardous waste disposal facility.

"(b) AMOUNT OF TAX.—The amount of the tax imposed by subsection (a) shall be equal to the following:

"(1) $150 for each ton of hazardous waste which is disposed of by landfill, surface impoundment or in waste piles;

"(2) $75 for each ton of a hazardous substance released in compliance with a federally permitted release;

"(3) $150 for each ton of a hazardous substance released in any other way.

"(c) ALTERNATIVE COMPUTATION OF TAX.— Under regulations provided by the Secretary, if the owner or operator of a hazardous waste disposal or hazardous substance handling facility can establish the amount of water of the hazardous waste or substance deposited or released, then such owner or operator may elect to pay, in lieu of the taxes which would otherwise be paid under this section, a tax reduced by the weight of water.

"(d) EXCLUSION FOR CERTAIN WASTES.—No tax shall be imposed under subsection (a) on any of the following:

"(1) The disposal of wastes which are, as of the date of enactment of this section, exempt from regulation as a hazardous waste under Section 3001 of the Solid Waste Disposal Act. In the event that any such waste is determined by the Administrator of the Environmental Protection Agency, following studies as required under section 8002 of such Act, to pose a potential danger to human health and environment, and the Administrator of the Environmental Protection Agency promulgates regulations for the disposal of such waste, then the Administrator shall transmit to both Houses of Congress, along with such regulations, his recommendation for imposing a tax, if any, on the disposal or long-term storage of such waste. A tax shall be imposed under subsection (a) on such waste only when authorized by Act of Congress.

"(2) The disposal of—

"(A) any waste by any person in the course of carrying out any removal or remedial action under the Comprehensive Environmental Response, Compensation, and Liability Act of 1980 if such disposal is carried out in accordance with a plan approved by the Administrator of the Environmental Protection Agency or the State, or

"(B) any waste removed from any facility listed on the National Priorities List (NPL).

"(e) LIABILITY FOR THE TAX.—The Tax imposed by this section shall be imposed on the owner or operator of the hazardous waste disposal facility or hazardous substance handling or treatment facility at which the hazardous waste is disposed of or released.

"(f) CREDIT FOR PRIOR TAX.—

"(1) IN GENERAL.—A credit shall be allowed in the computation of any tax due under this section on the disposal of a hazardous waste for any tax previously paid under this section by the disposer on the long-term storage of such hazardous waste.

"(2) LONG-TERM STORAGE.—In the event that a person who has paid a tax under this section on the long-term storage of a hazardous waste causes such hazardous waste to be delivered to and received by another person who is the owner or operator of a qualified hazardous waste disposal facility, then such person who paid the tax on the long-term storage shall be allowed a credit for such tax in the computation of any tax subsequently due on the long-term storage or disposal of a hazardous waste.

"(3) SPECIAL RULE OF FUNGIBLE WASTE.—For purposes of determining any credit allowances for fungible waste under the provisions of paragraphs (1) and (2), it shall be presumed that the last of such waste placed in a qualified hazardous waste storage facility shall be the first to be removed from such facility.

"(g) FRACTIONAL PART OF TON.—In the case of a fraction of a ton, the tax imposed by this section shall be the same fraction of the amount of such tax imposed on a whole ton.

"(h) PROSPECTIVE APPLICATION OF TAX.— Any taxes imposed by this section shall not apply to the hazardous waste which is received for disposal or hazardous substances received for release before the effective date of this section.

"Sec. 4692. Definitions.

"(a) DEFINITIONS.—For purposes of this subchapter—

"(1) DISPOSAL.—The term 'disposal' means the discharge, deposit, injection, dumping or placing of any hazardous waste into or on any land, air or water so that such hazardous waste may enter the environment.

"(2) WASTE PILE.—The term 'waste pile' is a quantity of hazardous waste heaped together as a means of storage as defined under regulations promulgated by the Administrator of the Environmental Protection Agency pursuant to section 3005 of the Solid Waste Disposal Act.

"(3) SURFACE IMPOUNDMENT.—The term 'surface impoundment' is an impoundment in which quantities of hazardous wastes are collected as a means of storage as defined under regulations promulgated by the Administrator of the Environmental Protection Agency pursuant to section 3005 of the Solid Waste Disposal Act.

"(4) HAZARDOUS WASTE DISPOSAL FACILITY.— The term 'hazardous waste disposal facility' means any disposal facility with respect to which a permit is issued or interim status accorded under section 3005 of the Solid Waste Disposal Act.

"(5) HAZARDOUS WASTE.—The term 'hazardous waste' means any waste:

"(A) identified or listed under section 3001 of the Solid Waste Disposal Act, other than waste the regulation of which has been suspended by Act of Congress, and

"(B) subject to the recording or recordkeeping requirements of section 3002 and 3004 of such Act.

"(6) TON.—The term 'ton' means 2000 pounds.

"(7) RECEIPT.—The term 'receipt' means the act of the owner or operator of a qualified hazardous waste disposal facility by which such owner or operator, at an offsite facility, signs, or is required by regulation to sign, the manifest or shipping paper accompanying the hazardous waste, or at an onsite facility, enters, or is required to do so by regulation, the description and quantity of the hazardous waste in the qualified hazardous waste disposal facility operating record.

"(8) the terms 'release', 'hazardous substance', and 'environment' shall have the meaning assigned to them by the Comprehensive Response, Compensation and Liability Act of 1980.

"Sec. 4693. Records, Statements, and Returns.

"Every person who disposes of, or stores hazardous wastes for one year or more subject to taxation under this subchapter shall keep records, render such statements, make such returns, and comply with rules and regulations as the Secretary may prescribe to ensure proper assessment, payment, and collection of the taxes imposed by section 4691. The Secretary shall consult with the Administrator of the Environmental Protection Agency to assure that records, statements, and returns required to be kept, rendered, and made under this section shall be consistent, to the extent possible, with the reports required to be submitted to the Administrator under the Solid Waste Disposal Act. The Secretary may require any person who generates, transports, disposes of, or stores hazardous wastes, for one year or more, or who releases hazardous substances, and who is required to maintain records under the Solid Waste Disposal Act, the Marine Protection, Research and Sanctuaries Act, the Clean Air Act, the Clean Water Act, the Atomic Energy Act, the Uranium Mill Tailings Radiation Control Act, the Toxic Substances Control Act, or the Safe Drinking Water Act, to submit copies of such reports available to the Secretary as required.".

(b) CONFORMING AMENDMENTS.—

(1) The table of subchapters for chapter 38 of the Internal Revenue Code of 1954 is amended by adding at the end thereof the following new item:

"SUBCHAPTER D—TAX ON DISPOSAL OF HAZARDOUS WASTE OR RELEASE HAZARDOUS SUBSTANCES.".

(2) Section 221(b)(1) of the Comprehensive Environmental Response, Compensation and Liability Act of 1980 is amended by striking out "and" at the end of subparagraph (D), by striking out the period at the end of subparagraph (E) and inserting a comma and "and", and by adding a new subparagraph as follows:

"(F) the amounts received in the Treasury under section 4691 of the Internal Revenue Code of 1954.".

(c) STUDY.—

(1) IN GENERAL.—Not later than January 1, 1987, and annually thereafter through 1989, the Secretary of the Treasury, in consultation with the Administrator of the Environmental Protection Agency, shall submit to the Congress a report on the amount of revenues being collected in accordance with subchapter D of chapter 38 of the Internal Revenue Code of 1954 and his recommendations, if any, for changes in the tax imposed under such subchapter in order to—

(A) raise an amount of revenue equivalent to the anticipated amount of revenue from the tax originally imposed under such subchapter,

(B) assure that the tax is discouraging the release of hazardous substances in an environmentally unsound manner, and

(C) assure that the tax is being collected with maximum administrative feasibility.

(2) ADDITION OF CERTAIN SUBSTANCES.—The Secretary of the Treasury shall also study, and recommend to the Congress whether releases of the following should be subject to tax under subchapter D of chapter 38 of

such Code:

(A) Pesticides identified for a rebuttable presumption against registration under the Federal Insecticide, Fungicide, and Rodenticide Act.

(B) Chemicals which, according to the International Agency for Research on Cancer, have substantial evidence of carcinogenicity.

(d) EFFECTIVE DATE.—The amendments made by subsections (a) and (b) shall take effect on January 1, 1986.

CORPORATE TAX ON NET RECEIPTS

Sec. 204. Corporate Tax on Net Receipts.

(a) IN GENERAL.—Chapter 38 of the Internal Revenue Code of 1954 (relating to environmental taxes) is amended by adding at the end thereof the following new subchapter:

"SUBCHAPTER E—TAX ON CORPORATE NET PROFITS

"Sec. 4696. Environmental Net Profits Tax

"(a) GENERAL RULE.—There is hereby imposed on each corporation a tax equal to .014 percent of the taxable net receipts of such corporation for the taxable year.

"(b) TAXABLE NET RECEIPTS.—For purposes of this section—

"(1) IN GENERAL.—The term 'taxable net receipts' means the excess (if any) of—

"(A) the gross receipts of the taxpayer for any taxable year over

"(B) the sum of—

"(i) the costs of goods sold by the taxpayer for such taxable year, plus

"(ii) $75,000,000.

"(2) AGGREGATION OF CONTROLLED GROUPS.—

"(A) IN GENERAL.—For purposes of this section, all members of the same controlled group of corporations shall be treated as one taxpayer.

"(B) OTHER GROUPS UNDER COMMON CONTROL.—Under regulations prescribed by the Secretary, a rule similar to the rule of subparagraph (A) shall apply to trades or businesses (whether or not incorporated) which are under common control.

"(C) CONTROLLED GROUP DEFINED.—For purposes of this paragraph, the term 'controlled group of corporations' has the meaning given such term by section 1563(a), except that—

"(i) 'more than 50 percent' shall be substituted for 'at least 80 percent' each place it appears in section 1563(a)(1), and

"(ii) the determination shall be made without regard to subsections (a)(4) and (e)(3)(C) of section 1563.

"(c) SPECIAL RULE FOR TAX-EXEMPT ORGANIZATIONS.—In the case of any taxpayer which is exempt from tax under section 501(a), taxable net receipts shall be computed only by reference to the unrelated business taxable income (within the meaning of section 512) of the taxpayer.

"(d) TERMINATION.—No tax shall be imposed under this section for taxable years beginning after December 31, 1990.".

Two pages of text were inadvertently dropped from the amendment.

I am today submitting a new amendment which contains the omitted text and is thus merely a corrected version of the amendment introduced earlier.

I ask unanimous consent that the text of the corrected amendment be printed.

[From the Congressional Record, p 1985, pp. 13647-13649]

SUPERFUND LEGISLATION EXTENSION

BENTSEN (AND STAFFORD) AMENDMENT NO. 224

(Ordered to lie on the table.)

Mr. BENTSEN (for himself and Mr. STAFFORD) submitted an amendment intended to be proposed by them to the bill (S. 51) to extend and amend the Comprehensive Environmental Response, Compensation, and Liability Act of 1980, and for other purposes; as follows:

By adding at the end thereof the following:

"TITLE III—INDEMNIFICATION OF CONTRACTORS

"SEC. 301. (a) The President shall in contracting or arranging for response action to be undertaken under the Comprehensive Environmental Response, Compensation, and Liability Act of 1980, agree to hold harmless and indemnify a contracting party against claims, including the expenses of litigation or settlement, by third persons for death, bodily injury or loss of or damage to property arising out of performance of a cleanup agreement to the extent that any such damages awarded do not arise out of the negligence of the contracting party.

"(b)(1) Amounts expended pursuant to this section shall be considered costs of response to the release with respect to which the contracting party took the action which resulted in liability. Costs incurred in the defense of suits against indemnified parties may be paid in quarterly or other increments but the United States shall not otherwise participate, directly or indirectly, in the defense of contracting parties unless named as a first party defendant. No other amounts shall be expended pursuant to this section until after entry of a judgment or a final order.

"(2) Indemnification contracts entered into pursuant to this section shall not be subject to section 1301 or 1340 of title 31 or section 11 of title 41 of the United States Code.".

● Mr. BENTSEN. Mr. President, I am submitting an amendment today to address the problems faced by contractors and architect/engineering firms involved in the cleanup of Superfund sites. During the reauthorization of the Superfund law, the Committee on Environment and Public Works heard testimony that pollution liability in-

DEFINITIONS

"SEC. 402. (a) As used in this title—

"(1) 'insurance' means primary insurance, excess insurance, reinsurance, surplus lines insurance, and any other arrangement for shifting and distributing risk which is determined to be insurance under applicable State or Federal law;

"(2) 'pollution liability' means liability for injuries arising from the release of hazardous substances, pollutants or contaminants;

"(3) 'risk retention group' means any corporation or other limited liability association taxable as a corporation, or as an insurance company, formed under the laws of any state—

"(A) whose primary activity consists of assuming and spreading all, or any portion, of the pollution liability of its group members;

"(B) which is organized for the primary purpose of conducting the activity described under subparagraph (A);

"(C) which is chartered or licensed as an insurance company and authorized to engage in the business of insurance under the laws of any State; and

"(D) which does not exclude any person from membership in the group solely to provide for members of such a group a competitive advantage over such a person.

"(4) 'purchasing group' means any group of persons which has as one of its purposes the purchase of pollution liability insurance on a group basis; and

"(5) 'State' means any State of the United States or the District of Columbia.

"(b) Nothing in this Title shall be construed to affect either the tort law or the law governing the interpretation of insurance contracts of any State, and the definitions of pollution liability and pollution liability insurance under any State law shall not be applied for the purposes of this Act, including recognition or qualification of risk retention groups or purchasing groups.

"RISK RETENTION GROUPS

"SEC. 403. (a) Except as provided in this section, a risk retention group is exempt from any State law, rule, regulation, or order to the extent that such law, rule, regulation, or order would—

"(1) make unlawful, or regulate, directly or indirectly, the operation of a risk retention group except that the jurisdiction in which it is chartered may regulate the formation and operation of such a group and any State may require such a group to—

"(A) comply with the unfair claim settlement practices law of the State;

"(B) pay, on a nondiscriminatory basis, applicable premium and other taxes which are levied on admitted insurers and surplus line insurers, brokers, or policyholders under the laws of the State;

"(C) participate, on a nondiscriminatory basis, in any mechanism established or authorized under the law of the State for the equitable apportionment among insurers of pollution liability insurance losses and expenses incurred on policies written through such mechanism;

"(D) submit to the appropriate authority reports and other information required of licensed insurers under the laws of a State relating solely to pollution liability insurance losses and expenses;

"(E) register with and designate the State insurance commissioner as its agent solely for the purpose of receiving service of legal documents or process, and, upon request, furnish such commissioner a copy of any financial report submitted by the risk retention group to the commissioner of the chartering or licensing jurisdiction;

"(F) submit to an examination by the State insurance commissioner in any State in which the group is doing business to determine the group's financial condition, if—

"(i) the commissioner has reason to believe the risk retention group is in a financially impaired condition; and

"(ii) the commissioner of the jurisdiction in which the group is chartered has not begun or has refused to initiate an examination of the group; and

"(G) comply with a lawful order issued in a delinquency proceeding commenced by the State insurance commissioner if the commissioner of the jurisdiction in which the group is chartered has failed to initiate such a proceeding after notice of a finding of financial impairment under subparagraph (F) of this paragraph;

"(2) require or permit a risk retention group to participate in any insurance insolvency guaranty association to which an insurer licensed in the State is required to belong;

"(3) require any insurance policy issued to a risk retention group or any member of the group to be countersigned by an insurance agent or broker residing in that State; or

"(4) otherwise discriminate against a risk retention group or any of its members, except that nothing in this section shall be construed to affect the applicability of State laws generally applicable to persons or corporations.

"(c) The exemptions specified in subsection (a) apply to—

"(1) pollution liability insurance coverage provided by a risk retention group for—

"(A) such group; or

"(B) any person who is a member of such group;

"(2) the sale of pollution liability insurance coverage for a risk retention group; and

"(3) the provision of insurance related services or management services for a risk retention group or any member of such a group.

"(d) A State may require that a person acting, or offering to act, as an agent or broker for a risk retention group obtain a license from that State, except that a State may not impose any qualification or requirement which discriminates against a nonresident agent or broker.

"PURCHASING GROUPS

"SEC. 404. (a) Except as provided in this section, a purchasing group is exempt from any State law, rule, regulation, or order to the extent that such law, rule, regulation, or order would—

"(1) prohibit the establishment of a purchasing group;

"(2) make it unlawful for an insurer to provide or offer to provide insurance on a basis providing, to a purchasing group or its member, advantages, based on their loss and expense experience, not afforded to other persons with respect to rates, policy forms, coverages, or other matters;

"(3) prohibit a purchasing group or its members from purchasing insurance on the group basis described in paragraph (2) of this subsection;

"(4) prohibit a purchasing group from obtaining insurance on a group basis because the group has not been in existence for a minimum period of time or because any member has not belonged to the group for a minimum period of time;

"(5) require that a purchasing group must have a minimum number of members, common ownership or affiliation, or a certain legal form;

"(6) require that a certain percentage of a purchasing group must obtain insurance on a group basis;

"(7) require that any insurance policy issued to a purchasing group or any members of the group be countersigned by an insurance agent or broker residing in that State; or

"(8) otherwise discriminate against a purchasing group or any of its members.

"(b) The exemptions specified in subsection (a) apply to—

"(1) pollution liability insurance, and comprehensive general liability insurance which includes this coverage, provided to—

"(A) a purchasing group; or

"(B) any person who is a member of a purchasing group; and

"(2) the sale of—

"(A) pollution liability insurance, and comprehensive general liability coverage;

"(B) insurance related services; or

"(C) management services;

to a purchasing group or member of the group.

"(c) A State may require that a person acting, or offering to act, as an agent or broker for a purchasing group obtain a license from that State, except that a State may not impose any qualification or requirement which discriminates against a nonresident agent or broker.

"APPLICABILITY OF SECURITIES LAWS

"SEC. 405. (a) The ownership interests of members in a risk retention group shall be—

"(1) considered to be exempted securities for purposes of section 5 of the Securities Act of 1933 and for purposes of section 12 of the Securities Exchange Act of 1934; and

"(2) considered for be securities for purposes of the provisions of section 17 of the Securities Act of 1933 and the provisions of section 10 of the Securities Exchange Act of 1934.

"(b) A risk retention group shall not be considered to be an investment company for purposes of the Investment Company Act of 1940 (15 U.S.C. 80a-1 et seq.).

"(c) The ownership interests of members in a risk retention group shall not be considered securities for purposes of any State blue sky law.".

● Mr. STAFFORD. Mr. President, Senator BENTSEN and I are today introducing two amendments which we hope will solve a significant number of insurance difficulties which appear to have arisen with regard to environmental impairment liabilities.

During the reauthorization of the Superfund law, the committee heard from a wide variety of parties that pollution liability insurance was increasingly unavailable. Most of the reasons for this have nothing to do with the Superfund law. However, the unavailability of insurance is frustrating the goals of not only the Superfund law, but other environmental statutes as well. I hope that the two amendments which Senator BENTSEN and I are offering will go a long way toward eliminating these problems.

One amendment, of which I am the prinicipal sponsor, would authorize the creation of risk retention programs for environmental impairment liability. The effect of this amendment would be to allow groups of individuals to insure themselves. If private insurance were available, individuals would still be free to purchase coverage. But if it were not, they would be able to band together to provide their own insurance.

The second amendment would require the Administrator of the Environmental Protection Agency to indemnify persons engaged in Superfund cleanups for damages resulting from nonnegligent actions.●

[From the Congressional Record, Aug. 1, 1985, p. S10946]

COMPREHENSIVE
ENVIRONEMENTAL RESPONSE

COMPENSATION AND LIABILITY
ACT EXTENSION

CRANSTON AMENDMENT NO. 577

(Ordered to lie on the table)

Mr. CRANSTON submitted an amendment intended to be proposed by him to the bill (S. 51) to extend and amend the Comprehensive Environmental Response, Compensation, and Liability Act of 1980, and for other purposes; as follows:

On page 124, line 16, strike out "FUNDS UNSPENT OR $7,500,000,000" and insert in lieu thereof "$10,000,000,000".

On page 125, strike out lines 1 through 18.

On page 125, line 19, strike out "(3)" and insert in lieu thereof "(2)".

On page 125, line 20, strike out "$7,500,000,000" and insert in lieu thereof "$10,000,000,000".

On page 126, line 10, strike out "$7,500,000,000" and insert in lieu thereof "$10,000,000,000".

On page 126, line 13, strike out "$7,500,000,000" and insert in lieu thereof "$10,000,000,000".

On page 126, line 18, strike out "$7,500,000,000" and insert in lieu thereof "$10,000,000,000".

On page 126, line 20, strike out "(4)" and insert in lieu thereof "(3)".

On page 126, line 23 strike out "or (3)".

On page 135, line 16, strike out ".08 percent" and insert in lieu thereof ".115 percent".

On page 135, line 20 and 21, strike out "FUNDS UNSPENT OR $7,500,000,000" and insert in lieu thereof "$10,000,000,000".

On page 136, line 3, strike out "or (3)".

On page 136, line 4, strike out "section 4611(d)(3)" and insert in lieu thereof "such paragraph".

On page 141, line 20, strike out ".08 percent" and insert in lieu thereof ".115 percent".

On page 142, line 2, strike out "$4,000" and insert in lieu thereof "$5,750".

On page 144, line 16 and 18, strike out "$4,000" each place it appears and insert in lieu thereof "$5,750".

[From the Congressional Record, S

SUPERFUND IMPROVEMENT
LEGISLATION

DeCONCINI AMENDMENT NO. 627

(Ordered to lie on the table.)

Mr. DeConcini submitted an amendment intended to be proposed by him to the bill (S. 51) to extend and amend the Comprehensive Environmental Response, Compensation, and Liability Act of 1980, and for other purposes; as follows:

On pages 88-89, strike out section 124 of the bill. On page 118, following the line 8, insert the following:

CONTRACTOR LIABILITY AND INDEMNIFICATION

SEC. . Title I of the Comprehensive Environmental Response, Compensation, and Liability Act of 1980 is amended by adding at the end thereof the following new section:

"CONTRACTOR LIABILITY AND INDEMNIFICATION

"SEC. 119. (a) Notwithstanding the provisions of section 114 of this title, no response action contractor shall be liable under this title or under any other Federal or State law or under common law to any person for injuries, costs, damages, expenses, or other liability (including but not limited to claims for indemnification or contribution and claims by third parties for death, personal injury, illness, loss of or damage to property, or economic loss) which result from any release or threatened release of a hazardous substance or pollutant or contaminant from a facility.

"(b) The exemption from liability provided under subsection (a) of this section shall not apply where—

"(1) a release or threatened release was caused by conduct of the response action contractor which was negligent or reckless or constituted intentional misconduct; or

"(2) the response action contractor is also a person against whom an action could be brought under section 106 with respect to any release or a person who would be liable under section 107(a) with respect to any release or threatened release.

"(c)(1) The Administrator may agree to hold harmless and indemnify any response action contractor meeting the requirements of this subsection against any liability (including the expenses of litigation or settlement) arising out of the contractor's performance in carrying out a response action under this title, but only to the extent that—

"(A) the contractor has made reasonable efforts to obtain liability insurance cover-

[From the Congressional Record, Sept. 19, 1985, p. S11810]

SUPERFUND IMPROVEMENT ACT

GRASSLEY AMENDMENT NOS. 642 AND 643

(Ordered to lie on the table.)

Mr. GRASSLEY submitted two amendments intended to be proposed by him to the bill (S. 51) to extend and amend the Comprehensive Environmental Response, Compensation, and Liability Act of 1980, and for other purposes; as follows:

AMENDMENT NO. 642

On page 5 of amendment No. , line 14, strike the semicolon after "considered", substitute a period, and insert thereafter the following: "The analysis should identify anticipated benefits of each alternative, evaluate the underlying data and information to insure that it is reliable and accurate, and as provided for under the National Contingency Plan, consider the extent to which the benefits of a proposed plan can be achieved through alternative means, and evaluate, in accordance with the National Contingency Plan, the costs associated with the use of such alternative means including potential adverse effects on public health or the environment:"

AMENDMENT No. 643

On page 5, line 24, strike "The administrative record" through "subsection". on page 6, line 1, and insert in lieu thereof the following: "If the President decides to make substantial changes in the proposed action, he shall provide a notice describing these changes and provide the necessary supporting information and analysis.

"The President shall maintain a file for each response action and shall maintain a current index. The file shall constitute the record for purposes of judicial review.

"Any remedial action file shall include, but is not limited to—

"(A) the notice of proposed action and any notice describing changes in the proposed action;

"(B) copies of all comments, criticisms, and new data submitted in written or oral form in connection with the proposed action;

"(C) copies of all verified data, which shall be included in the file once they are available;

"(D) a description of any remedial alternatives, which shall be included in the file as soon as practicable;

"(E) a description of all response action alternatives selected for evaluation in any feasibility study, which shall be included in the file once such alternatives have been selected:

"(F) the President's reponse to each of the significant comments, criticisms, and new data submitted in written or oral presentations;

"(G) the President's careful and full articulation of the basis and purpose of the selected action grounded upon the remedial action file as constituted on the date of final selection of the remedial action, including the reasons behind the selection, the factual and policy determinations which support it, identification of factors considered, an explanation of how information received by the President was developed and evaluated, and citation to the credible and reliable evidence in the record which support his determinations;

"During the interim period while such regulations are being promulgated, where major deficiencies are shown to exist in the administrative record that has been assembled, judicial review of the response in an enforcement or cost recovery action may be de novo."

AMENDMENTS TO H.R. 2817

(5613)

[From the Congressional Record, Nov. 1, 1985, pp. H9617–H9623]

DEFENSE ENVIRONMENTAL RESTORATION PANEL AMENDMENTS

The SPEAKER pro tempore. Under a previous order of the House, the gentleman from Oklahoma [Mr. McCURDY] is recognized for 5 minutes.

(Mr. McCURDY asked and was given permission to revise and extend his remarks, and include extraneous matter.)

Mr. McCURDY. Mr. Speaker, in the near future, the House will consider a bill to reauthorize the Superfund. The rapid and effective cleanup of our hazardous waste sites around the country is one of the most important public health issues before the Congress today.

Several committees of the House have, or will shortly, report legislation to provide for the Superfund reauthorization.

The bill reported by the Committee on Energy and Commerce, H.R. 2817, contains a section that, for the first time in Superfund history, specifically deals with Federal facilities.

As the Members know, the Committee on Armed Services has oversight responsibility for all Department of Defense installations, and would normally ask for referral on the Superfund legislation. In this instance, the committee decided not to request referral but instead created a special panel to review the Defense Department's efforts in this area.

The bipartisan environmental restoration panel, which I chair, has just completed several months of careful review and hard work. We have prepared some sensible and needed legislation dealing with the cleanup of Federal hazardous waste sites.

The panel recently approved a series of amendments, which I propose to offer, which will greatly strengthen our cleanup efforts at military installations, and also would make DOD, the Environmental Protection Agency, and the States more effective partners in this vital national priority.

Mr. Speaker, I have reserved time in today's special orders and I intend to submit the amendments to be printed in the RECORD so that the full extent of its contents may be reviewed by the Members.

Mr. Speaker, I would also like to commend each of the members of the Armed Forces Panel on Environmental Restoration, which spent a number of hours working, hearing witnesses, and preparing the amendments that we will soon offer. Specifically, I would like to commend the gentleman from Michigan [Mr. HERTEL], the gentleman from Georgia [Mr. RAY], the gentleman from Kentucky [Mr. HOPKINS], and the gentleman from Colorado [Mr. KRAMER]. I would also like to commend the gentleman from California [Mr. FAZIO] for his diligent efforts in pursuit of this issue and the very valuable assistance that he provided to the panel by introducing legislation that would also cover Federal facilities. Again I want to commend him for his cooperation because I think we have completely come to an agreement on these amendments and will offer them en bloc.

Mr. Speaker, I submit a report and the amendments to which I referred for printing in the RECORD, as follows:

REPORT OF THE ENVIRONMENTAL RESTORATION PANEL TO THE HOUSE ARMED SERVICES COMMITTEE REGARDING ITS RECOMMENDATIONS CONCERNING H.R. 1940 AND AMENDMENTS TO H.R. 2817, THE SUPERFUND AUTHORIZATION BILL REPORTED BY THE HOUSE COMMITTEE ON ENERGY AND COMMERCE

Mr. McCURDY. Mr. Chairman, as the members will recall, the Environmental Restoration Panel was established on July 29 to study the Department of Defense (DoD) Environmental Restoration Program and make recommendations to the committee to streamline the program and insure its compliance with the Comprehensive Environmental Response, Compensation, and Liability Act of 1980 (CERCLA)—more commonly referred to as the "Superfund Act". The immediate task confronting the panel was to review pending legislation introduced by Mr. Fazio, H.R. 1940. The intent of H.R. 1940 was to clarify DoD responsibilities of the Department of Defense under CERCLA and raised issues involving funding and policy matters ranging across the jurisdiction of at least four subcommittees.

Just two days after the creation of the panel there was a major development that altered its focus and approach. Specifically, the House Committee on Energy and Commerce reported out H.R. 2817, Superfund Amendments of 1985. In addition to authorizing additional funding for Superfund cleanups of toxic waste sites, H.R. 2817, for the first time, specifically addressed cleanups at federal facilities. This affected the panel in two important ways. First, H.R. 2817 would provide a convenient and appropriate legislative vehicle for the provisions contained in H.R. 1940. Second, the nature and impact of the federal facilities provisions contained in H.R. 2817 raised a host of new policy issues to be addressed by the panel in a very short period of time.

Consequently, on September 18th, the panel agreed to explore the feasibility of recommending to this committee amendments to H.R. 2817 that would incorporate its recommendations on the provisions contained in H.R. 1940 along with recommended changes to the federal facilities provisions. On September 26th, the panel received testimony from DoD, and Environmental Protection Agency witnesses along with interested members of Congress regarding toxic waste cleanups and federal facilities. Finally, on October 10th, the panel unanimously approved recommending to the committee the amendments that are before you this morning.

I want to emphasize at the outset that in presenting these amendments, the panel has two primary objectives in mind. One, to provide clear policy and program guidance to DoD in meeting its environmental restoration responsibilities under CERCLA. And two, to establish a process that will streamline program implementation while allowing meaningful state and local participation in the development and execution of cleanup efforts at federal facilities.

In accordance with these dual objectives, the amendments can be broken down into two categories. The first 14 pages contain amendments reflecting the panel's recommendations regarding the DoD specific provisions contained in H.R. 1940. The remaining 12 pages contain amendments reflecting the panel's recommendations regarding the federal facilities provisions of H.R. 2817.

Although the specific provisions are explained in the accompanying section-by-section analysis, I would like to briefly mention a few salient features of the first part of the amendments.

First of all, Sec. 151 requires that the Secretary of Defense carry out a program of environmental restoration and to identify a specific office within OSD having responsibility for program execution. This section also establishes specific program goals that are consistent with CERCLA and overall federal environmental restoration guidelines. To insure that the Environmental Protection Agency (EPA) has input into the development of procedures and program implementation, the Secretary is required to consult with the Administrator of EPA.

Second, Sec. 152 establishes a research, development, and demonstration program to aggressively pursue new technologies for the treatment, disposal and management of hazardous substances used by DoD. Properly supported and managed this program offers the greatest potential return on investment for environmental restoration dollars.

Third, Sec. 153 establishes an Environmental Restoration Transfer Account that will allow the Secretary of Defense to apply available funding in the most timely and effective fashion while giving Congress maximum oversight over budget development and execution.

Finally, Sec. 155 requires DoD to insure that EPA, state and local authorities are kept fully informed about environmental restoration efforts and have adequate opportunity to review and comment on all phases of DoD toxic waste cleanups.

Taken together, these provisions provide the basis for a responsible, flexible and effective DoD program to carry out environmental restoration.

The second category of amendments deals with the issue of state participation in toxic waste cleanups at all federal facilities not just DoD. The issue of state participation in federal facility cleanups has generated a great deal of debate and frustration in recent years. And, frankly, federal agencies—including DoD and the Department of Energy—have not been without fault in their dealing with state and local authorities. In fact, much of the preliminary work done by DoD has suffered due to the failure to work more closely with state and local environmental representatives. In addition, the failure by federal agencies to provide full and timely information to affected communities had fuelled controversy and created a reservoir of suspicion and ill-will that will take years to dissipate.

On the other hand, it is clear that DoD and the Services have made a great deal of progress to remedy these short-comings. In late 1983, DoD signed a memorandum of agreement with EPA that has established a good working relationship between the two agencies in addressing environmental restoration problems within the context of existing federal policy and standards. In addition, new DoD guidance provides for state and local participation in ongoing cleanup efforts and encourages the adoption of promulgated state standards and siting requirements. Basically, DoD has come to recognize that if it wants to be a good neighbor and enjoy the continued support of the communities surrounding its installations, it has become a full partner in efforts to clean up the environment.

Unfortunately, the pendulum is swinging to the other extreme with a vengeance. As reported by the House Energy and Commerce Committee, H.R. 2817 provides that all cleanups at federal facilities be subject to all federal and state permit requirements. In effect, the states will have an absolute veto power over the performance of any future federal cleanup. While this approach effectively addresses the problem of past federal noncooperation, it creates a number of serious new problems.

In the first place, the use of permits for toxic waste cleanups is largely inappropriate. In testimony before the panel, the DoD witness, Mr. Carl J. Schafer, Jr., Director for Environmental Policy, summed it up well:

"Permits are basically a device in which to set a timetable for the installation of technology that has been identified as capable of meeting certain performance standards, and to enforce those standards. It is the lack of those scientific and technological determinations that bring me to the conclusion that permit procedures are inappropriate to the hazardous waste cleanup program."

The fact of the matter is that toxic waste cleanup efforts more closely represent a research and development program with many uncertainties and technical problems. We know too little about many hazardous substances to develop uniform standards to tell us "How clean is clean?" Under the circumstances, the best answers to many of the cleanup problems will come through a process of consultation and negotiation. The imposition of state permit requirements amounts to a single party veto that undercuts meaningful negotiation. I fear that the result will be a dictated solution that may not be environmentally sound or fiscally responsible.

Another problem with state permits is that they represent an uncontrolled variable that is likely to impose significant additional requirements for federal cleanup efforts without being subject to any kind of federal review. If DoD wants to carry out its environmental program, it will have no option but to pay the additional cost to meet applicable state permit requirements. Those requirements may be inconsistent with federal guidelines, be technically infeasible, and could end up delaying response action.

The requirement of state permits may also complicate efforts to secure congressional authorization and appropriation of funds for cleanup efforts. It will be very difficult to recommend the authorization and appropriation of funding for a DoD cleanup absent a state permit. And in this instance, an impasse over state permitting requirements will translate into a one year slip in the initiation of remedial action.

In sum, state permits are inconsistent with the technical uncertainty surrounding hazardous waste cleanup efforts, with the necessity for good faith negotiations, and with efficient and effective management and oversight. I can see no way that the imposition of state permits will not result in delaying federal cleanup programs; increasing costs, and promoting suboptimal response strategies.

Nevertheless, the panel recognizes that any solution to the problems created by the imposition of state permit requirements must provide for full and meaningful state participation in the development and implementation of federal cleanups. That is the basis for the compromise amendment which I will briefly outline:

In return for the elimination of the requirement for state permits, there will be a presumption in favor of promulgated state standards and siting requirements. Thus, in the vast majority of cases where state standards and siting requirements are reasonable and consistently applied, they will be incorporated into response action selected by the Administrator of EPA (at sites on the National Priority List (NPL)) or agency heads (at non-NPL sites). If state standards and siting requirements are incorporated into the response action, the state can go to federal court to enforce that action. In sum, the panel compromise procedure provides the substance of state permits—state standards and siting requirements and enforceability—without subjecting the remedial action to one party veto.

If the Administrator or agency head rejects state standards and siting requirements, he must find that his alternative remedial action provides "substantially equivalent" protection of public health and the environment and that the state standard was inconsistent with the National Contingency Plan (NCP), or is not being consistently applied in other remedial actions in the state. Clearly, rejections will be few and far between to meet this tough criteria. The important thing, however, is that this procedure does afford some protection against unreasonable state standards and siting requirements and encourages a negotiated settlement of these differences.

Even if its standards and siting requirements have been rejected, the state can still insist on its remedial action if it is willing to pay the difference. Subsequently, it can seek to recover all or part of this funding in federal court if it believes that the Administrator or agency head acted wrongly.

Although this process falls short of the level of state control afforded by the imposition of permit requirements, it does largely address state concerns. The panel believes this compromise does provide meaningful participation by EPA and the states in accomplishing the expeditious cleanup of DoD and DoE toxic waste sites. The panel strongly believes that this goal should be paramount and seeks to avoid any "show stoppers" that will impede the timely initiation and completion of remedial actions. We believe it is time to get on with the job and this process does that.

One final issue is the question of a national security exemption that will allow the President to issue such orders as necessary to protect national security and waive the provisions of this act. In addition, to avoid the release of restricted data or national security information, all statutory or executive order requirements will apply to Citizen right-to-know provisions of H.R. 2817.

While the panel recognizes the need to avoid the use of CERCLA provisions to interfere with or jeopardize legitimate national security requirements and strategic program, it is equally sensitive to the possibility that such an exemption could be used to cloak DoD cleanup activities and prevent citizen access to information to which they are legitimately entitled. Consequently, the amendment requires that the waiver authority be site specific, that Armed Services and Appropriations Committees be notified within 30-days regarding the reason for this action, and that the remedial action be resumed as quickly as practicable. The panel recommends such waiver authority in the belief that it represents a prudent hedge against uncertainty and expects that it will be rarely exercised.

On the basis of the panel's review of H.R. 1940, and the fact that it has not been acted upon by the Energy and Commerce and Public Works and Transportation Committees, we recommend that no further action be taken on that bill. Rather, the panel recommends, as an alternative, that the committee support an amendment to H.R. 2817 to be offered by the panel chairman in his name when that legislation is considered by the House of Representatives. The panel also requests that the committee endorse the panel chairman's personal appearance before the Rules Committee when it considers a rule on H.R. 1827. Finally, unless there is some objection we will make any necessary technical and conforming corrections to the amendments as presented today prior to offering them on the floor.

Thank you, Mr. Chairman.

AMENDMENT TO H.R. 2817 (SUPERFUND AMENDMENTS OF 1985) APPROVED BY THE ENVIRONMENTAL RESTORATION PANEL OF THE HOUSE ARMED SERVICE COMMITTEE

(Page and line numbers refer to the bill as reported by the Committee on Energy and Commerce.)

Page 86, line 23, insert "(a) IN GENERAL.—" before "Title I".

Page 95, after line 23, insert the following new subsection:

(b) SPECIAL PROVISIONS FOR DEPARTMENT OF DEFENSE.—Title I of CERCLA is amended—

(1) by inserting before section 101 the following: "Subtitle A—Response, Liability, and Compensation"; and

(2) by adding at the end thereof the following new subtitle:

"Subtitle B—Department of Defense Environmental Restoration Program

"SEC. 151. DOD ENVIRONMENTAL RESTORATION PROGRAM.

"(a) ENVIRONMENTAL RESTORATION PROGRAM.—

"(1) IN GENERAL.—The Secretary. shall carry out a program of environmental restoration at facilities under the jurisdiction of the Secretary. The program shall be known as the 'Defense Environmental Restoration Program'.

"(2) APPLICATION OF SECTION 120.—The program shall be carried out subject to section 120 (relating to Federal facilities).

"(3) CONSULTATION WITH EPA.—The program shall be carried out in consultation with the Administrator.

"(4) DESIGNATION OF ADMINISTRATIVE OFFICE WITHIN OSD.—The Secretary shall identify an office within the Office of the Secretary which shall have the responsibility for carrying out the program.

"(b) PROGRAM GOALS.—Goals of the program shall include the following:

"(1) The identification, investigation, and cleanup of contamination from hazardous substances and wastes.

"(2) Correction of other environmental damage, such as detection and disposal of unexploded ordnance, which creates an imminent and substantial endangerment to the public health, welfare, or environment.

"(3) Demolition and removal of unsafe buildings and structures, including buildings and structures of the Department at sites formerly used by or under the jurisdiction of the Secretary.

"(c) RESPONSIBILITY FOR RESPONSE ACTIONS.—

"(1) BASIC RESPONSIBILITY.—The Secretary shall carry out (in accordance with the provisions of this title) all response actions with respect to releases of hazardous substances from each of the following:

"(A) Each facility or site owned by, leased to, or otherwise possessed by the United States and under the administrative jurisdiction of the Secretary.

"(B) Each facility or site which was under the administrative jurisdiction of the Secretary and owned by, leased to, or otherwise possessed by the United States at the time of action leading to contamination by hazardous substances.

"(C) Each vessel of the Department of Defense, including vessels owned or bareboat chartered and operated.

"(2) OTHER RESPONSIBLE PARTIES.—Paragraph (1) shall not apply to a removal or remedial action if the Administrator has provided for response action by a potentially responsible person in accordance with section 122.

"(3) STATE FEES AND CHARGES.—The Secretary shall pay all fees and charges imposed by State authorities for permit services for the disposal of hazardous substances on lands which are under the administrative jurisdiction of the Secretary to the same extent that nongovernmental entities are subject to fees and charges imposed by State authorities for permit services. This requirement shall not apply where such payment is the responsibility of a lessee, contractor, or other private person.

"(d) SERVICES OF OTHER AGENCIES.—The Secretary may enter into agreements on a reimbursable basis with any other Federal agency, and on a reimbursable or other basis with any State or local government agency, to obtain the services of that agency to assist the Secretary in carrying out any of the Secretary's responsibilities under this section. Services which may be obtained under this subsection include the identification, investigation, and cleanup of any off-site contamination possibly resulting from the release of a hazardous substance or waste at a facility under the Secretary's administrative jurisdiction.

"(e) The provisions of section 119 apply to contractors for response actions under this section.

"(f) FUNCTIONS AT SITES FORMERLY USED BY DEPARTMENT OF DEFENSE.—The Secretary, as part of the Defense Environmental Restoration Program, may provide for the removal of unsafe buildings or debris of the Department of Defense at sites formerly used by the Department.

"SEC. 152. RESEARCH, DEVELOPMENT, AND DEMON-
STRATION PROGRAM.

"(a) PROGRAM.—As part of the Defense Environmental Restoration Program, the Secretary shall carry out a program of research, development, and demonstration with respect to hazardous wastes. The program shall be carried out in consulation and cooperation with the Administrator. The program shall include research, development, and demonstration with respect to each of the following:

"(1) Means of reducing the quantities of hazardous waste generated by activities and facilities under the jurisdiction of the Secretary.

"(2) Methods of treatment, disposal, and management (including recycling and detoxifying) of hazardous waste of the types and quantities generated by current and former activities of the Secretary and facilities currently and formerly under the jurisdiction of the Secretary.

"(3) Identifying more cost-effective technologies for cleanup of hazardous substances.

"(4) Toxicological data collection and methodology on risk of exposure to hazardous waste generated by the Department of Defense.

"(5) The testing, evaluation, and field demonstration of any innovative technology, processes, equipment, or related training devices which may contribute to establishment of new methods to control, contain, and treat hazardous substances.

"(b) SPECIAL PERMIT UNDER SECTION 3005(g) OF RCRA.—The administrator may use the authorities of section 3005(g) of the Solid Waste Disposal Act to issue a permit for testing and evaluation which receives support under this section.

"(c) CONTRACTS AND GRANTS.—The Secretary may enter into contracts and cooperative agreements with, and make grants to, universities, public and private profit and nonprofit entities, and other persons to carry out the research, development, and demonstration authorized under this section. Such contracts may be entered into only to the extent that appropriated funds are available for that purpose.

"(d) INFORMATION COLLECTION AND DIS-
SEMINATION.—

mines to be the most widely used unregulated hazardous substances at facilities under his administrative jurisdiction. The notification shall be of not less than the 25 most widely used such substances.

"(2) DEFINITION.—For the purposes of this subsection, the term 'unregulated hazardous substance' means a hazardous substance—

"(A) for which no standard is in effect under the Toxic Substances Control Act, the Safe Drinking Water Act, the Clean Air Act, or the Clean Water Act; and

"(B) for which no water quality criteria are in effect under any provision of the Clean Water Act.

"(b) TOXICOLOGICAL PROFILES.—The Administrator of the Agency for Toxic Substances and Disease Registry shall take such steps as necessary to ensure the timely preparation of toxicological profiles of each of the substances that the Administrator is notified of under subsection (a). The secretary shall transfer to such Agency such toxicological data and such sums as may be necessary to prepare the profiles of such substances. The profiles on such substances shall include each of the following:

"(1) The examination, summary, and interpretation of available toxicological information and epidemiologic evaluations on a hazardous substance in order to ascertain the levels of significant human exposure for the substance and the associated acute, subacute, and chronic health effects.

"(2) A determination of whether adequate information on the health effects of each substance is available or in the process of development to determine levels of exposure which present a significant risk to human health of acute, subacute, and chronic health effects.

"(c) HEALTH ADVISORIES.—

"(1) PREPARATION.—At the request of the Secretary, the Administrator shall in a timely manner prepare health advisories on hazardous substances. Such an advisory shall be prepared on each hazardous substance—

"(A) for which no advisory exists;

"(B) which is found to threaten drinking water; and

"(C) which is emanating from facilities under the administrative jurisdiction of the Secretary.

"(2) CONTENT OF HEALTH ADVISORIES.—Such health advisories shall provide specific advice on the levels of contaminants in drinking water at which adverse health effects would not be anticipated and which include a margin of safety so as to protect the most sensitive members of the population at risk. The advisories shall provide data on 1-day, 10-day, and longer-term exposure periods where available toxicological data exist.

"(3) TRANSFER OF NECESSARY DATA.—The Secretary shall transfer to the Administrator such toxicological data as are available and may be necessary to prepare such health advisories.

"SEC. 155. NOTICE OF ENVIRONMENTAL RESTORATION ACTIVITIES

"(a) EXPEDITED NOTICE.—The Secretary shall take such actions as necessary to ensure that the regional offices of the Environmental Protection Agency and appropriate State and local authorities for the State in which a facility under the Secretary's administrative jurisdiction is located receive prompt notice of each of the following:

"(1) The discovery of releases or threatened releases of hazardous substances at the facility.

"(2) The extent of the threat to public health and the environment which may be associated with any such release or threatened release.

"(3) Proposals made by the Secretary to carry out response actions with respect to any such release or threatened release.

"(4) The initiation of any response action with respect to such release or threatened release and the commencement of each distinct phase of such activities.

"(b) COMMENT BY EPA AND STATE AND LOCAL AUTHORITIES.—

"(1) RELEASE NOTICES.—The Secretary shall ensure that the Administrator and appropriate State and local officials have an adequate opportunity to comment on notices under paragraphs (1) and (2) of subsection (a).

"(2) PROPOSALS FOR RESPONSE ACTIONS.—The Secretary shall require that an adequate opportunity for timely review and comment be afforded to the Administrator and to appropriate State and local officials after making a proposal referred to in subsection (a)(3) and before undertaking an activity or action referred to in subsection (a)(4). The preceding sentence shall not apply if the action is an emergency removal taken because of imminent and substantial endangerment to human health or the environment and consultation would be impractical.

"(c) TECHNICAL REVIEW COMMITTEE.—Whenever possible and practical, the Secretary shall establish a technical review committee to review and comment on Department of Defense actions and proposed actions with respect to releases or threatened releases of hazardous substances at installations. Members of any such committee shall include at least one representative of the Secretary, the Administrator, and appropriate State and local authorities and shall include a public representative of the community involved.

"SEC. 156. COMPLIANCE WITH NATIONAL ENVIRONMENTAL POLICY ACT.

"Removal or remedial actions selected or taken pursuant to this subtitle or secured under section 106 constitute fulfillment of the requirements of section 102 of the National Environmental Policy Act of 1969 (Public Law 91-190, 83 Stat. 852).

"SEC. 157. ANNUAL REPORT TO CONGRESS.

"(a) REPORT ON PROGRESS IN IMPLEMENTATION.—The Secretary shall furnish an annual report to the Congress for each fiscal year which commences after the date of the enactment of this Act. The report shall describe the progress made by the Secretary during the fiscal year in implementing the requirements of this Act.

"(b) MATTERS TO BE INCLUDED.—The report under this section shall include the following:

"(1) A statement for each facility under the administrative jurisdiction of the Secretary of the number of individual facilities at such installation at which a hazardous substance has been identified.

"(2) The status of response actions contemplated or undertaken at each such facility.

"(3) The specific cost estimates and budgetary proposals involving response actions contemplated or undertaken at each such facility.

"SEC. 158. MILITARY CONSTRUCTION FOR RESPONSE ACTIONS.

"(a) AUTHORITY.—Subject to subsection (b), the Secretary may carry out a military construction project not otherwise authorized by law if necessary to carry out a response action under this Act.

"(b) CONGRESSIONAL NOTICE-AND-WAIT.—

"(1) NOTICE TO CONGRESS.—When a decision is made to carry out a military construction project under this section, the Secretary shall submit a report in writing to the appropriate committees of Congress on that decision. Each such report shall include—

"(A) the justification for the project and the current estimate of the cost of the project; and

"(B) the justification for carrying out the project under this section.

"(2) OVERSIGHT PERIOD.—The project may then be carried out only after—

"(A) the end of the 21-day period beginning on the date the notification is received by those committees; or

"(B) each such committee approves the project, if the committees approve the project before the end of that period.

"SEC. 159. DEFINITIONS.

"As used in this subtitle:

"(1) SECRETARY.—The term 'Secretary' means the Secretary of Defense.

"(2) ADMINISTRATIVE JURISDICTION OF THE SECRETARY.—The term 'administrative jurisdiction of the Secretary' includes the administrative jurisdiction of the Secretary of Defense and the Secretaries of the military departments.".

[AMENDMENTS RELATING TO FEDERAL FACILITIES].

Page 87, line 11, after the period, insert the following new sentence: "Nothing in this section shall be construed to affect the liability of any person or entity under sections 106 and 107.".

Page 87, line 14, strike out "procedures".

Page 88, line 1, strike out "procedures".

Page 88, line 13, after the period insert the following new sentence: "This subsection shall not apply to the selection of response action where a State standards which is more protective of human health and the environment may be applicable in accordance with section 121(k).".

Page 88, strike lines 14 through 20.

Page 92, lines 21 and 22, strike out ", including construction design".

Page 93, strike out lines 3 through 5.

Page 93, after line 21, insert the following new paragraph:

"(5) ACTION BY OTHER PARTIES.—If the Administrator, in consultation with the head of the relevant department, agency, or instrumentality of the United States, determines that RIFS or remedial action will be done properly at the Federal facility by another potentially responsible party within the deadlines provided in paragraphs (1), (2), and (3) of this subsection, the Administrator may enter into an agreement with such party providing for assumption of the responsibilities set forth in those paragraphs. Following approval of the agreement by the Attorney General, the agreement shall be entered in the appropriate United States district court as a consent decree under section 106 of this Act.".

Page 94, line 1, strike out "Administrator" and insert "President" in lieu thereof.

Page 94, line 17, insert ", to the extent such information is reasonably available" after "place" and before the period.

Page 95, line 10, insert ", to the extent such information is reasonably available," after "shall contain".

Page 95, line 23, strike out the period and closing quotation marks.

Page 95, after line 23, insert the following new subsections:

"(j) FEDERAL AGENCY SETTLEMENTS.—The head of each department, agency, or instrumentality or his designee may consider, compromise, and settle any claim or demand under this Act arising out of activities of his agency, in accordance with regulations prescribed by the Attorney General. Any award, compromise, or settlement in excess of $25,000 shall be made only with the prior written approval of the Attorney General or his designee. Any such award, compromise, or settlement shall be paid by the agency concerned out of appropriations available to that agency. The acceptance of any payment under this paragraph shall be final and conclusive, and shall constitute a complete release of any claim under this Act against the United States and against the employees of the United States whose acts or omissions gave rise to the claim or demand, by reason of the same subject matter.

"(k) NATIONAL SECURITY.—

"(1) SITE SPECIFIC PRESIDENTIAL ORDERS.—The President may issue such orders regarding response actions at any specified site or facility of the Department of Energy or the Department of Defense as may be necessary to protect the national security interests of the United States at that site or facility. Such orders may include, where necessary to protect such interests, an exemption from any requirement contained in this title or under title III of the Superfund Amendments of 1985 with respect to the site or facility concerned. The President shall notify the Committees on Armed Services and Appropriations of the House of Representatives and the Senate within 30 days of the issuance of an order under this paragraph providing for any such exemption. Such notification shall include a statement of the reasons for the granting of the exemption. It is the intention of the Congress that whenever a waiver is issued under this paragraph the response action shall proceed as expeditiously as practicable. The Committees on Armed Services and Appropriations of the House of Representatives and the Senate shall be notified periodically of the progress of any response action with respect to which a waiver has been issued under this paragraph.

"(2) CLASSIFIED INFORMATION.—Notwithstanding any other provision of law, all requirements of the Atomic Energy Act and all Executive orders concerning the handling of restricted data and national security information, including 'need to know' requirements, shall be applicable to any grant of access to classified information under the provisions of this Act or under title III of the Superfund Amendments of 1985.".

Page 101, beginning on line 5, strike out "private parties" and insert in lieu thereof "potentially responsible parties".

Page 103, strike out "Nothing" and all that follows through line 11.

Page 106, line 13, strike out the period and closing quotation mark.

Page 106, after line 13, insert:

"(k) ONSITE CLEANUP OF FEDERAL FACILITIES.—

"(1) FEDERAL AND STATE PERMITS.—For any response action undertaken at any facility owned or operated by a department, agency, or instrumentality of the United States, to the extent that such action does not involve the transfer of a hazardous substance or pollutant or contaminant from the facility at which the release or threatened release occurs to an offsite facility, the only permits which may be required are those applicable pursuant to section 118 of the Clean Air Act and section 313(a) of the Federal Water Pollution Control Act. Nothing in the preceding sentence shall affect the authority of any State to impose, after remedial action is completed, any requirement (including a fee) with respect to any operation and maintenance activities required with respect to a hazardous substance or pollutant or contaminant. Nothing in this subsection shall affect any requirement of Federal or State law to the extent that such requirement applies to response action involving the transfer of a hazardous substance from the facility at which the release or threatened release occurs to an offsite facility.

"(2) REMEDIAL ACTION SELECTED FOR NPL SITES.—The Administrator shall select the remedial action to be undertaken under this Act at any facility on the National Priorities List that is owned or operated by a department, agency, or instrumentality of the United States. All other remedial actions at facilities owned or operated by a department, agency, or instrumentality of the United States shall be selected pursuant to a memorandum of understanding between the Federal agency established under paragraph (4) of this subsection. The Administrator shall provide an opportunity for appropriate State and local officials to participate in the remedy selection process, including but not limited to an opportunity to review and comment on each proposed remedial action and to consult with the Federal agency and the Administrator concerning each proposed action. The Administrator shall also provide prompt notice and explanation of each decision under paragraph (9) on compliance with promulgated State standards or siting requirements, to the State in which the facility is located.

"(3) STATE STANDARDS.—Except as provided in paragraph (9), the Federal agency or the Administrator, in selecting remedial action to be undertaken under this Act at any facility that is owned or operated by a department, agency, or instrumentality of the United States, shall require that the remedial action conform to both of the following:

"(A) The promulgated State standard relating to the level or standard for control of the hazardous substance concerned where such standard is more protective of public health or the environment.

"(B) Any State law regarding the siting of a facility.

Such remedial action, including the promulgated State standard or siting requirement, shall be incorporated into the interagency agreement required under section 120(e) of this Act. The State may bring an action to enforce any promulgated State Standard or siting requirement incorporated into an intergency agreement in the United States district court in which the facility is located.

"(4) NON-NPL SITES.—with respect to remedial actions to be undertaken under this Act at facilities that are owned or operated by a department, agency, or instrumentality of the United States but are not on the National Priorities List, the Federal agency shall enter into a memorandum of understanding with the Administrator. The memorandum of understanding shall provide for each of the following:

"(A) Consultation between the two agencies sufficient to ensure that all proposed remedial actions meet the requirements of this Act and the National Contingency Plan and provide protection of public health and the environment.

"(B) Compliance with any applicable promulgated State standards relating to the level or standard for control of the hazardous substances concerned and any State law regarding the siting of facilities, except as provided in paragraph (9).

"(C) Prompt notice and explanation of each proposed action, including an explanation regarding the decision on compliance with promulgated State standards or siting requirements, to the State in which the facility is located.

"(D) An opportunity for appropriate State and local officials to participate in the remedy selection process, including but not limited to an opportunity to review and comment on each proposed remedial action and to consult with the Federal agency and the Administrator concerning each proposed action.

"(5) STATE NOTIFICATION.—Within 30 days after the close of the required comment period on the selected remedy, the State shall notify the Federal agency and the Administrator that it concurs or does not concur with a decision not to comply with a promulgated State standard or siting requirement. If the State concurs in the decision, the remedial action selected by the Federal agency and the Administrator shall proceed through completion. If the State fails to act within 30 days after the close of the comment period such failure shall be deemed concurrence for purposes of this paragraph.

"(6) STATE PAYMENT.—If the State notifies the Federal agency and the Administrator within 30 days of the close of the comment period that it does not concur with the decision under paragraph (9) not to comply with a promulgated State standard or siting requirement, and within 90 days after close of the comment period provides assurances deemed adequate by the administration that the State will pay or assure payment of the additional costs attributable to compliance with the State standard or requirement, as determined by the Federal agency and the Administrator, the remedial action shall comply with such State standard or requirement and shall proceed through completion. If the State fails to provide such assurances within 90 days, the remedial action selected by the Federal agency and the Administrator shall proceed through to completion.

"(7) RECOVERY OF ADDITIONAL COST.—In an action under section 107 against responsible persons, including any responsible department, agency, or instruméntality of the United States, the State may recover any additional remedial cost incurred by the State under this paragraph, if the State can establish, based on the administrative record, that the determination under paragraph (9) regarding the promulgated State standard or siting requirement was not supported by substantial evidence.

"(8) ATTORNEY AND WITNESS FEES.—Whenever a State recovers its additional costs under paragraph (7) from the Federal department, agency, or instrumentality, such department, agency, or instrumentality shall be liable for the costs incurred by the State in such action, including reasonable attorney and witness fees. Whenever the court upholds a determination under paragraph (9), the State which brought the action under paragraph (7) shall be liable for the costs incurred by the Administrator

and the Federal department, agency, or instrumentality in such action, including reasonable attorney and witness fees.

"(9) REJECTION OF STATE STANDARDS.—A remedial action at a facility owned or operated by a department, agency, or instrumentality of the United States that does not conform to a promulgated State standard or siting requirement referred to in paragraph (3) may be selected under this section only if one or both of the following applies:

"(A) The remedial action selected provides protection of public health and of the environment which is substantially equivalent to the protection provided by the State standard and compliance with the promulgated State standard or siting requirement is not consistent with the National Contingency Plan.

"(B) The Administrator determines that the State has not consistently undertaken previous remedial actions (or made plans to undertake future response action at facilities) within that State using the more protective State standards.

Mr. VOLKMER. Mr. Speaker, will the gentleman yield?

Mr. McCURDY. I am glad to yield to the gentleman from Missouri.

Mr. VOLKMER. Mr. Speaker, I commend the gentleman from Oklahoma [Mr. McCURDY] for his remarks in regard to the Superfund.

As the gentleman knows, we are addressing ourselves today to the major issue of reducing the deficits, and another major issue is to try to continue to keep the Government running without divesting the Social Security funds which most of our senior citizens rely on for assistance.

Just so the House knows what the gentleman from Pennsylvania objected to, not permitting the bill to be taken up by the gentleman from Illinois, I would like to read the language that the gentleman from Illinois sought to take up in order to protect that Social Security fund from divestment so our senior citizens would be able to receive their Social Security checks without problems in the future.

The language was that:

During the period beginning on the date of enactment of this act and ending on November 6, 1985, the public debt limit set forth in subsection (b) of section 3101 of title 31, United States Code, shall be increased by an amount determined by the Secretary of the Treasury as necessary to permit the United States to meet its obligations without divesting the Social Security trust funds or any other trust funds established pursuant to Federal law.

It says that no increase shall result in a public debt limit in excess of $1,840-some billion.

Now, what this means to me, by the gentleman's objecting, is that undoubtedly he does want to divest the Social Security trust funds in order to use those funds for maybe tanks and planes, et cetera, in this Government. I think our senior citizens should know that later on today we are going to have the opportunity hopefully to bring up a rule that will make this language in order. We are going to need a two-thirds vote, and I would hope that everyone who favors continuing that Social Security fund and providing that it not be used for other Government programs will vote favorably on that rule, because if they do not and we are not able to take it up, then Treasury says that we are going to go ahead and divest the Social Security fund and use it for other things other than Social Security.

□ 1440

So I would urge everyone to make sure we get a two-thirds vote on the rule when it comes up to make this language in order.

I thank the gentleman for yielding.

Mr. McCURDY. Mr. Speaker, I thank the gentleman for his statements and comments.

Again, Mr. Speaker, I hope my colleagues and all the Members will review the amendments that I have placed in the RECORD on the environmental restoration provisions of the Superfund bill and ask for their support.

Mr. FAZIO. Mr. Speaker, I rise today to join with my colleague from Oklahoma, Mr. McCURDY, in introducing an amendment to the Superfund reauthorization bill to accelerate the cleanup of toxic waste sites at military bases and for other purposes relating to the cleanup of other Federal sites.

The amendment that Mr. McCURDY and I are proposing reflects months of work by the House Armed Services Task Force on Environmental Restoration and several years of my own efforts to investigate and document the weaknesses and strengths of the military's cleanup program. Through hearings by the Appropriations Committee, on which I sit, and several investigations by the General Accounting Office, conducted at my request, we have developed a far greater understanding of the problems associated with the cleanup of toxic dumps at military bases. Again, Mr. Speaker, Mr. McCURDY's panel has also played an invaluable role in building the record in this regard.

Our investigations, Mr. Speaker, indicate that over the years the Department of Defense has improperly disposed of literally billions of gallons of poisonous chemicals in nearly every State in the Nation. Hazardous pollutants have been found at more than 4,000 sites at some 473 military bases across the country.

From one end of the Nation to the other, the Defense Department has polluted surface and ground water, contaminated drinking water and fouled open waterways.

From McClellan Air Force Base in my own district in Sacramento, where cancer-causing solvents, waste oils, paint thinners, strippers, and sludges have contaminated the ground water both on and off base, to Homestead Air Force Base in Homestead, FL, where contaminants are thought to threaten major municipal drinking water supplies, the Department of Defense has left its mark on communities.

The fences and barbed wire that surround our military bases cannot contain the poisons that are, as we speak, leaching into the water supply of surrounding communities. It is an intolerable situation that we must squarely address. The Federal Government can no longer clean up its sites to a different standard, under less scrutiny, and without any oversight from Federal and State health and environmental officials. Indeed, the Federal Government should and must set the standard by which all cleanups occur.

The problem of military toxics may be dwarfed by the cleanups that will be required at private sites, if only in sheer numbers. But in a very real sense the struggle to get our Federal property cleaned up is just as important. The Federal Government cannot demand from the private sector what it cannot itself do. We have one set of environmental laws and they should apply to all equally—whether they are the largest Federal agency or the smallest corporation—the laws should be applied in the same manner with the same commitment to protecting the public health and environment.

Mr. Speaker, while the Pentagon has recently made some improvements in its cleanup program, more needs to be done. The amendment we are prepared to offer to the Superfund reauthorization bill incorporates most of the provisions of H.R. 1940, the Defense Environmental Restoration Act of 1985.

Among other things, the amendment:

Requires greater DOD coordination with Federal, State, and local health and environmental authorities. The military will be mandated to coordinate all aspects of the cleanup program—from the identification of any possible contamination to the details of the final, permanent cleanup phase. In addition, as in H.R. 1940, our proposal would require DOD to establish Technical Review Committees or task forces made up of representatives of the military, EPA, local citizens, and State and local regulatory agencies to review DOD cleanup plans.

Requires DOD cleanups to meet any and all State standards for pollutants or contaminants which are more protective of the public 'health or environment than the applicable Federal standard.

Sets up the mechanisms necessary to ensure that adequate funding will be available to finance the cleanup program. As in H.R. 1940, the amendment sets up a special central account to finance all aspects of the environmental cleanup program, including military construction. Congressional investigations have identified the cumbersome DOD funding process as a major obstacle to an accelerated cleanup effort.

Requires the Agency for Toxic Substances and Disease Registry to generate fundamental health risk assessment data on the most commonly used DOD contaminants.

Requires DOD to establish a research, development, and demonstration program to develop innovative and cost-effective cleanup technologies. Appropriate research and development is the only way the ultimate price tag of the cleanup program, now expected to cost between $5 and $10 billion over the next 10 years, can be reduced.

Requires DOD to seek input from the general public on all cleanup plans. As in H.R. 1940, our amendment would require DOD to publish a notice and brief analysis of all cleanup proposals for all sites, NPL and non-NPL alike, as well as provide the general public with an adequate opportunity to comment on the plans.

Mr. Speaker, our proposal' is a very modest but important one. I urge my colleagues to consider it carefully. And once again, Mr. Speaker, I commend the work of Mr. MCCURDY and the other members of the task force and urge my colleagues favorable consideration of our proposal.

[From the Congressional Record, Nov. 14, 1985, pp. E5183-E5185]

SUPERFUND AMENDMENT AL-LOWING VICTIMS OF HARM TO SUE FOR DAMAGES

[NOTE.- The text of the amendment appears in debate in Vol. 5 at p. 4313]

HON. BARNEY FRANK
OF MASSACHUSETTS
IN THE HOUSE OF REPRESENTATIVES
Thursday, November 14, 1985

Mr. FRANK. Mr. Speaker, I intend to offer an amendment to the Superfund reauthorization that would allow persons injured by hazardous substances to sue in Federal court for damages. The original enactment of Superfund was a recognition by the Federal Government that the problem of hazardous waste is a national one and that there should be a national response. I believe that this national response should encompass those most damaged by hazardous substances, victims of actual harm.

Last year a provision for a Federal cause of action was narrowly defeated on the House floor. In response to many of the concerns raised by those who supported a mechanism by which victims could sue for damages under Superfund but were concerned that some provisions in last year's language might result in excessive liability for those with minimal or no actual responsibility for injuries, I have redrafted the amendment to insure that it deals fairly with innocent parties. For instance, my amendment states clearly that victims must show by "a preponderance of the evidence" that the damages claimed were caused by the hazardous substance in question. Furthermore, defenses from liability have been included for de minimus contributors and innocent landowners. Moreover, the amendment explicitly states that joint and several liability will not apply where the harm is shown to be divisible and that the court can apportion damages among defendants once liability is found. Lastly, the amendment specifically protects sovereign immunity, preventing suits against the United States or any State or local government.

It is clear to me that we need a Federal cause of action in the Superfund law. I have tried, in my amendment, to respond to constructive criticism of last year's language. What follows is the current draft of the amendment and I welcome suggestions on how it might be further improved.

[From the Congressional Record, Dec. 3, 1985, pp. H10701-H10702]

AMENDMENTS

Under clause 6 of rule XXIII, proposed amendments were submitted as follows:

H.R. 2817

By Mr. BLILEY:

(As reported by the Committee on Ways and Means.)

—Page 261, strike out line 1 and all that follows through line 13, and insert in lieu thereof the following:

"(2) EQUIVALENT OF INCINERATION.—For purposes of subparagraph (A), a method, technique, or process shall be treated as the equivalent of incineration on land if—

"(A) such method, technique, or process has been shown to achieve a destruction and removal efficiency for the hazardous waste involved at least equivalent to the destruction and removal efficiency applicable to incineration on land, and

"(B) such method, technique, or process meets any applicable detailed performance standards established by the Environmental Protection Agency."

By Mr. McKERNAN:

(Union Calendar No. 216.)

—Page 365, strike out lines 20 through line 2 on page 366.

—Page 365, strike out lines 23 through 25 and insert in lieu thereof the following:

"503(a), except that any State which on the date of enactment has in effect a statute that requires".

By Mr. VENTO:

(Union Calendar No. 216.)

—Page 45, after line 2, insert the following:

(3) In paragraph (3) insert before the period at the end thereof the following: "; except that if any groundwater which is used as a water supply source by any municipality or the residents of any municipality is contaminated as a result of a release of a hazardous substance from a federally owned facility and if the United States is not the only potentially responsible party with respect to such release, money in the Fund, made available pursuant to authorizations of appropriations for fiscal years beginning after September 30, 1986, shall be available for reimbursement of any costs incurred after December 11, 1980, by such muncipality for provision or acquisition of alternative water supplies".

(As reported by the Committee on Energy and Commerce.)

—Page 39, after line 14, insert the following:

(3) In paragraph (3) insert before the period at the end thereof the following: ";

except that if any groundwater which is used as a water supply source by any municipality or the residents of any municipality is contaminated as a result of a release of a hazardous substance from a federally owned facility and if the United States is not the only potentially responsible party with respect to such release, money in the Fund, made available pursuant to authorizations of appropriations made by this bill, shall be available for reimbursement of any costs incurred after December 11, 1980, by such muncipality for provision or acquisition of alternative water supplies".

(As reported by the Committee on Public Works and Transportation.)

—Page 445, line 24, strike out "and". Page 446, after line 4, strike out the period and insert in lieu thereof "; and".

(3) In paragraph '(3) insert before the period at the end thereof the following: "; except that if any ground water which is used as a water supply source by any municipality or the residents of any municipality is contaminated as a result of a release of a hazardous substance from a federally owned facility and if the United States is not the only potentially responsible party with respect to such release, money in the Fund, made available pursuant to authorizations of appropriations for fiscal years beginning after September 30, 1986, shall be available for reimbursement of any costs incurred after December 11, 1980, by such municipality for provision or acquisition of alternative water supplies.".

[From the Congressional Record, Dec. 4, 1985, pp. H10856-H10857]
Amendment to H.R. 2817

By Mr. KANJORSKI:

(As reported by the Committee on Energy and Commerce.)

—Page 34, line 25, strike out the quotation marks and last period, and add the following after line 25:

"(d) AWARDS.—The Administrator of the Environmental Protection Agency may pay an award of up to $10,000 to any individual who provides information leading to the arrest and conviction of any person for a violation subject to a criminal penalty under this Act, including any violation under section 103 and under this section. The Administrator shall be regulation prescribe criteria for such an award and may pay any award under this subsection from the Fund, as provided in section 111.

Page 42, after line 13, add the following new subsection:

(j) AWARDS.—Section 111(c) of CERCLA is further amended by striking out "and" at the end of paragraph (8) (as added by subsection (c) of this section), by striking out the period at the end of paragraph (9) and substituting ", and", and by adding the following new paragraph at the end thereof:

"(10) the costs of any awards granted under section 109(d).".

By Mr. RAHALL:

(As reported by the Committee on Ways and Means.)

—Section 417 is amended by redesignating subsection (e) as subsection (f) and by inserting after subsection (d) the following new subsection:

"(e) Any amount for which a taxpayer would but for this sentence be liable under subchapter E of chapter 38 (relating to su perfund excise tax) shall be reduced by amounts paid by the taxpayer after the effective date of this section under title IV of the Surface Mining Control and Reclamation Act of 1977 (P.L. 95–87) and not previously taken into account under this sentence."

(As reported by the Committee on Ways and Means.)

—Section 413(d) is amended by striking out paragraph (1).

5628

[From the Congressional Record, Dec. 5, 1985, p. H11150]

AMENDMENTS

Under clause 6 of rule XXIII, proposed amendments were submitted as follows:

H.R. 2817

By Mr. McKERNAN

(Amendment to the amendment in the nature of a substitute.)

—Page 336, beginning on line 20, strike out "for a period of three years beginning on the effective date of this section, any State which on such date" and insert in lieu thereof the following: "any State which on the date of enactment of this section".

APPENDIX IV

STATEMENTS INSERTED IN THE CONGRESSIONAL RECORD AFTER PASSAGE MMENTING ON OR CLARIFYING CERTAIN PROVISIONS

(5629)

[From the Congressional Record, Oct. 17, 1986, pp. S16590-S16591, S17136-S17139, S17212-S17214]

Mr. LAUTENBERG. Mr. President, today the President has signed the Superfund bill. In the past week, we have marshaled our forces to convince the White House to sign this bill. We sent the letter to the President with 81 cosignors from the Senate, urging him to sign the bill. I was joined by 56 of my colleagues in a letter to Senator DOLE expressing our will to stay in session as long as it took to ensure a veto override, should one have been necessary.

All these efforts, combined with clear public support for this bill, made the difference. And I believe a new era of environmental protection has begun.

In this bill, we have an historic piece of legislation.

The Superfund Program has been on the books for 6 years. We have spent $1.6 billion. We have barely touched the surface. We want that changed. We think this bill will do the job.

New Jersey stands to gain a minimum of $500 million under this bill, and maybe much more.

This bill will ensure that the job is done right. It includes tough, new cleanup standards. At Lipari landfill in Pitman, NJ, the most hazardous site in the country, the EPA has proposed a cleanup plan that fails the test. The Lipari cleanup should be done right, and the 98 other sites in New Jersey should be done right. The cleanup standards in this bill serve that goal.

Mr. President, this bill gives citizens the right to know about the chemicals present in their communities, and the right to know about the toxics being released into their air and water. New Jersey experiences constant chemical spills and releases, and the air is despoiled by toxic emissions.

Mr. President, after the incident in Bhopal, India, I introduced legislation to insist that in America we inventory our chemicals and alert emergency response personnel to potential dangers in their communities. And, that we plan for the worst but insist on the best prevention. That legislation survived the conference. It's an enormous achievement, and important for New Jersey.

This bill contains my radon legislation, to set up a comprehensive program for radon detection and mitigation at EPA. In New Jersey, unfortunately we discovered radon. Now it is important that we lead the effort to abate it. This bill assures that these efforts will continue. A significant portion of these funds will go to New Jersey.

This bill also includes an important underground storage tank cleanup program, critical to protecting the drinking water supplies in New Jersey, and guarantees citizens the right to sue if EPA is not doing the job.

If the President had vetoed this bill, work would have stopped at over 100 sites across the Nation and at 16 sites in New Jersey. It never would have started at the remaining 83 New Jersey sites. That was unacceptable. We are prepared to stay in session as long as need to be to force final congressional action on this bill. I am gratified that the President signed this bill.

Mr. President, the enactment of this bill breathes new life into this program. $1.5 billion of funding will become available almost immediately for Superfund, which has been starved for more than 1 year. In the Appropriation Committee, I fought hard for the highest funding level. New Jersey has gotten $1 of every $5 of Superfund money. Every dollar added to the program helps our State.

A bold new program is in place. Resources are dedicated to do the job. The challenge is immense. Now we can get on with the job.

Mr. President, with the signing of Superfund today, this Nation embarks on a bold new program of environmental protection. In addition to its many new provisions, the bill contains a new community right-to-know program that greatly enhances the health and safety of this Nation. As the author of the Senate provisions, I would like to take this opportunity to clarify some features of the right-to-know program.

In doing so, I would like to commend the chairman of the Environment and Public Works Committee for his determination, patience, and commitment to protecting the environment. Without the labors of the distinguished senior Senator from Vermont we would not have had a reauthorized Superfund. His devotion to the bill as a whole, and to the right-to-know program, was an inspiration to all of the conferees, and I thank him.

Mr. President, given Senator STAFFORD's leadership role on this bill and contribution to right to know, I would welcome his views on the clarifications I am about to discuss.

Mr. President, I would like to begin by noting that the overriding goal of the title is to provide long absent information on the management of toxic chemicals to the public—as well as to firefighters, State and local officials, health professionals, and others. To that end, the information must be usable. Units of measurement must be consistent, descriptions of and identities must be uniform among the various reporting forms so that data can be cross-checked and tracked adequately.

Where volumes are to be reported in ranges, those ranges must be established so the information is valuable and not so broad that it is impossible to determine anything of relevance. In addition, it is extremely important to ensure that specific chemicals names are present on all forms since that information is needed to use many reference sources. This is a requirement which means EPA should be extremely vigilant in implementing and enforcing its trade secret obligation to ensure that the public is granted this meaningful data.

Mr. President, the public should be able to gain easy access to the information collected under this title. Information coordinators at the State and local level, as well as at EPA, must provide data to the public and it is expected that the public will be able to view reporting forms at specified locations and gain access through the mails—with costs reimbursed if appropriate. Moreover, while public access to tier II information is mandated if a hazardous chemical is stored in an amount in excess of 10,000 pounds or if the information has already been requested of the facility, it is the intention that the public should also have access to information regarding chemicals of lesser volumes. In short, information requests should be denied only

if there are compelling reasons to do so.

Mr. President, requests for information must be met in a timely fashion. Under this title, facilities are allowed to provide lists of chemicals for which material safety data sheets are available, but then they must provide the actual MSDS's upon request. Additionally, in section 312, tier II information must also be made available upon request. It is the firm intention of this title that, when such requests are made, they shall be complied with as quickly as possible. Similarly, all information requests should be met in a timely fashion.

Mr. STAFFORD. Mr. President, I would associate myself with the remarks the junior Senator from New Jersey has made about the goal of public availability of the right-to-know title. It is essential that information collected be usable, easily accessible, and made available in a timely fashion.

Mr. LAUTENBERG. Mr. President, I would also like to comment on the issue of State and local authority. The community right-to-know and emergency planning provisions in the bill represent a milestone: The first Federal program addressing those essential needs. At the same time, however, it is recognized that States and localities have been active in this arena previously and will continue to act to serve their citizens. States and localities retain their authority to enact and implement community right-to-know programs, which are not preempted by these Federal provisions.

Mr. STAFFORD. Mr. President, again I concur with Senator LAUTENBERG. I worked with the junior Senator from New Jersey to ensure that State right-to-know programs would not be preempted by the provisions in this title. The ability of States to go forward with their own programs is vital, and that ability has been clearly preserved in this legislation.

Mr. LAUTENBERG. Mr. President, I would also like to touch briefly on the trade secret provisions in the title. The title does give facility owners and operators the ability to withhold only the specific chemical name or identity if various requirements and procedures are met. Those requirements and procedures are intended to set a high standard for trade secret claims and review, with the presumption that this information should be made available to the public except in very narrow circumstances. In particular, chemical identities which are readily discoverable through reverse engineering cannot be claimed as trade secrets under this title.

Mr. President, I would make a final point about the discretion of the EPA. The title does provide the Agency with discretion in terms of setting thresholds, adding chemicals to the list of those who must report. In implementing this title, the EPA must remember and abide by the overriding purpose of this program and act to ensure that as much meaningful and usable information as possible be made available. This is essential not just so that the public will have access to this data but so that EPA itself will be better informed on the toxic picture in this country.

Mr. STAFFORD. Mr. President, again I concur with Senator LAUTENBERG'S statements about the title's trade secret provisions, and the intent of Congress to guide EPA in implementing this right-to-know program. The right-to-know program is an important step forward in protecting the environment and public health, and I look forward to its implementation.

Mr. LAUTENBERG. Mr. President, I thank the distinguished chairman for his observations on the right-to-know program. Again, I wish to express my gratitude to Chairman STAFFORD for his support and leadership in crafting the right-to-know provisions and the Superfund reauthorization package.

SUPERFUND

Mr. DOLE. Mr. President, let me indicate that the President signed the Superfund legislation on Air Force One this morning on the way to North Dakota. So we are making progress.

Let me add, Mr. President, I understand he is signing the Superfund primarily on the strength of a letter he received late last evening signed by 50 Senators.

So I want to thank my colleagues who were willing to sign that letter which indicated to the President very properly in my view that if there is an effort next year to expand the program and raise the taxes that we would stand by the President if he were required to veto any such efforts.

So I think the President was pleased to have the letter. I thank my colleagues for their assistance. I think he did the right thing in signing the Superfund.

I suggest the absence of a quorum.

The PRESIDING OFFICER. The clerk will call the roll.

The legislative clerk proceeded to call the roll.

□ 1330

Mr. DOLE. Mr. President, I ask unanimous consent that the order for the quorum call be rescinded.

The PRESIDING OFFICER. Without objection, it is so ordered.

Mr. STENNIS. Mr. President, may we have order? This is important.

The PRESIDING OFFICER. The point is well taken. The Senate will be in order.

---

* * * * * * * * *

p. S17136

FURTHER CLARIFICATION OF SUPERFUND PROVISIONS

Mr. STAFFORD. Mr. President, it has been said that the Superfund Amendments and Reauthorization Act of 1986, which has already acquired the affectionate nickname of "SARA" among some Washington lobbyists, is "fuzzy" and not a clear congressional directive.

While this Senator would agree that the bill approved by the Superfund conference, which the Senate passed by a vote of 88 to 8, is not a perfect example of lucidity and precision, he would not go so far as to call it "fuzzy." Admittedly, however, neither the bill nor the statement of managers necessarily provides all of the guidance which might be desired. It is for this reason that Members on both sides, as a matter of routine, explain and elaborate on particular provisions contained in conference reports.

These explanations are offered by Members for the purpose of clarifying ambiguities or filling blank spots. In some cases, attempts are made by special interests groups to create the basis for later legal challenges as part of the administrative or judicial processes, but such attempts at revisionism are the exception.

But in every case, the language of the conferees, as set forth in the statement of managers, is the best and surest expression of the intent of the House and Senate. Whenever the statement or the Member conflicts with either the legislative language or the narrative explanation of the conference report, the statement of the Member must yield.

Having said that, there nonetheless remain ambiguities in virtually any legislation of more than a few pages in length. The original Superfund law of 1980 was no exception, and neither is SARA. Where such ambiguities exist, individual Members can and legitimately do offer guidance. It is to be expected that in some cases where such guidance is offered, there may be differences of opinion between Members.

This Senator is in a somewhat unusual, but by no means unique, position. When the legislation which lead to the enactment of Superfund was introduced in the 95th Congress as S. 2900, he was an original cosponsor, together with its primary author, Senator Muskie of Maine. Together, we helped see that proposal through Senate approval under the number S. 2083, but it died when the other body failed to act.

When the successor to S. 2900 was introduced in the following Congress, it bore the number S. 1480. Again, this Senator was privileged to be a primary cosponsor and to play a large part in the bill's development due to his position as the ranking minority member of both the full committee and the subcommittee.

Late in the 96th Congress when Superfund appeared dead, it was my privilege to collaborate with my good friend, Senator RANDOLPH of West Virginia, in several successive compromise bills. Essentially, these compromises were pared down versions of S. 1480 as reported from the Committee on Environment and Public Works. The changes were worked out in private, closed door meetings with a wide variety of Senators with various concerns. In a sense, these meetings were not unlike the "small group" meetings that characterized the conference of SARA.

Due in large measure to the efforts of Representative FLORIO, the House passed S. 1480 exactly as it had been approved by the Senate. And within days of the time Superfund was signed into law, the Committee on Environment and Public Works began overseeing the law's implementation. Eventually, this lead to the resignation of senior Agency officials and their replacement by new appointees, one of whom was Mr. Lee Thomas.

In April 1984, the Committee on Environment and Public Works began the process of reauthorizing Superfund. It has now stretched over 31 months, consuming tens of thousands of hours.

Mr. President, I belabor this point for a purpose:

First to make it clear that even if this Senator had closed his eyes and ears at every possible opportunity, he still would have acquired a great familiarity with the Superfund law.

Second, to make it clear that this Senator's eyes and ears were not shut. Even had he cared to avoid the Superfund program, it would ahve been impossible to do so and still serve adequately as the ranking minority member and then the chairman of the Committee on Environment and Public Works. But mere duty could never have compelled the attendance at uncounted hurs of hearings, markups, closed door negotiations, conference committee meetings, and subgroup meetings. Attendance was because of interest, not obligation.

I sincerely believe, Mr. President, that this Senator's understanding of the Superfund law, the programs it established and the latest set of amendments is as good as any, and better than most. Therefore, if there are errors in what I say, they are honest mistakes. I do not believe there are any such mistakes in this statement or that which I made on October 3, 1986, although I will freely admit that some did not necessarily agree with or like what was said.

Mr. President, for the record, I would like to review some of the areas of the conference report and share my views on them.

The question of timing—usually referred to as "pre-enforcement review"—was one of the central issues throughout the Superfund debate, and apparently the cause of some continuing confusion. The question is when and under what circumstances a Superfund cleanup may be reviewed in court.

The statement of mangers, at page 40, explains that two of the House provisions adopted by the conferees "explicitly provide for circumstances in which judicial review can be obtained prior to implementation of the response action." On page 41, the statement directly explains the conference substitute as follows:

In new section 113 (h)(4) of the substitute, the phrase "removal or remedial action taken" is not intended to preclude judicial review until the total response action is finished if the response action proceeds in distinct and separate stages. Rather an action under section 310 would lie following completion of each distinct and separable phase of the cleanup. For example, a surface cleanup could be challenged as violating the standards or requirements of the Act once all the activities set forth in the Record of Decision for the surface cleanup phase have been completed. This is contemplated even though other separate and distinct phases of the cleanup, such as subsurface cleanup, remain to be undertaken as part of the total response action. Similarly, if a response action is being conducted at a complex site with many areas of contamination, a challenge could lie to a completed excavation or incineration response in one area, as defined in a Record of Decision, while a pumping and treating response activity was being implemented at another area of the facility. It should be the practice of the President to set forth each separate and distinct phase of a response action in a separate Record of Decision document. Any challenge under this provision to a completed stage of response action shal not interfere with those stages of the response action which have not been completed.

New section 113(h) is not intended to affect in any way the rights of persons to bring nuisance actions under State law with respect to releases or threatened releases of hazardous substances, pollutants, or contaminants.

Although known as a "pre-enforcement review" issue, this shorthand is a misnomer. The issue highlighted is more accurately referred to as "pre-implementation review." It is clear that while the Conference Committee sought to extinguish "pre-enforcement review", the opportunities for citizens and responsible parties to seek "pre-implementation review" were not extinguished. This is true under both Superfund and under State nuisance law.

Courts, where it is consistent with the law and the circumstances at a given site, should allow citizen challenges early in the process.

This statement is not inconsistent with either the conference bill or the statement of managers, nor with any agreement that Members would withhold floor statements explaining these provisions.

It has been said that 113(h) covers all lawsuits, under any authority, concerning the response actions that are performed by EPA and other Federal agencies, by State pursuant to a cooperative agreement, and by private parties pursuant to an agreement with the Federal Government. Such a construction would be inconsistent with the evolution of the "preenforcement review" provisions, as well as the explicit language of the bill and report.

As passed by both the House and Senate, section 113(h) began as follows:

"No court shall have jurisdiction to review any challenges * * *"

But as approved by the conferees, the bill now begins as follows:

"No *Federal* court shall have jurisdiction *under Federal law other than under section 1332 of Title 28 of the United States Code (relating to diversity of citizenship jurisdiction) or under State law which is applicable or relevant and appropriate under section 121 (relating to cleanup standards)* to review any challenges . . . .".

As originally drafted, each bill purported to extinguish the jurisdiction of any court to review any challenge. Clearly, the conference bill no longer does this. Rather, it purports to extinguish the juridiction of specified courts to review challenges arising out specified laws. What was a sweeping prohibition in the House and Senate versions has become much more narrow and targeted. An illustration of this change is the differing impacts which the bills would have on challenges based on State laws, such as nuisance (which was discussed at length in my October 3 statement).

Clearly, under either the House or Senate version of H.R. 2005 a complaint based on State nuisance law would fall within the phrase "no court shall have jurisdiction to review any challenge". But equally clearly, such a claim would not be barred by the conference language, which would permit a suit to lie in either Federal court (where jurisdiction could be based on diversity of citizenship) or in State court. This construction is confirmed by the statement of managers explanation that—

New section 113(h) is not intended to affect in any way the rights of persons to bring nuisance actions under State law with respect to releases or threatened releases of hazardous substances, pollutants or contaminants.

Whether or not a challenge to a cleanup will lie under nuisance law is determined by that body of law, not section 113, because section 113 of CERCLA governs only claims arising under the act.

Section 113 (a) and (b) are drawn directly from S. 1480 of the 96th Congress, which I mentioned earlier in this statement. They are identical to sections 9 (a) and (b) of S. 1480, both as it was introduced and as it was reported. The committee report accompanying S. 1480 stated that the subsections "provide for jurisdiction and venue of actions brought under this act." The report noted that the Federal district courts would have "exclusive original jurisdiction over all other causes of action *arising under this act*" (emphasis added). Thus, it is clear that reach of 113 is restricted to suits "brought under" CERCLA or "arising under" it. Similarly, new subsection (h) governs only the suits filed under the circumstances enumerated in paragraphs (1) through (5) for the review of "challenges to removal or remedial action selected under section 104, or to review any order issued under 106(a)." Nowhere in the original law, in the version or H.R. 2005 approved by the conferees or in the statement of managers is there support for the proposition that "any controversy over a response action selected by the President, whether it arises under Federal law or State law, may be heard only in Federal court and only under circumstances provided" in section 113. Such a statement in contrary to the express legislative language and the statement of managers.

Such a construction would also be inconsistent with the provisions of CERCLA and SARA relating to preemption of State laws and displacement of Federal laws.

CERCLA, as enacted in 1980, contained only one arguably preemptive provision, which was section 114(c). SARA has repealed even that provision due to its misconstruction by the U.S. Supreme Court. Thus, the law as amended by SARA will leave unalloyed the statement contained in 114(a) that—

Nothing in this act shall be construed or interpreted as preempting any State from imposing any additional liability or requirements with respect to the release of hazardous substances within such State.

This policy of leaving State laws undisturbed is also reflected in 302(d) of the original law.

Nothing in this act shall affect or modify in any way the obligations or liabilities of any person under other Federal or State law, including common law, with respect to releases of hazardous substances or other pollutants or contaminants. The provisions of this act shall not be considered, interpreted, or construed in any way as reflecting a determination, in part or whole, of policy regarding the inapplicability of strict liability, or strict liability doctrines, to activities relating to hazardous substances, pollutants, or contaminants or other such activities.

The bill approved by the committee of conference continues and confirms this policy of nonpreemption. It does attempt to establish a process of integrating the requirements of State laws into the decisionmaking process of Superfund. The statement of managers explains that while the cleanup standards contained in section 121 "create circumstances in which State requirements can be avoided, it does not establish a system of preemption."

To state, as some have done, that the cleanup standards provisions of SARA preempt Federal and State cleanup standards and Federal and State permitting requirements is to suggest that the requirements of section 121 are a nullity. Both in substance and procedure, they were painstakingly developed for the purpose establishing a cleanup system which is required, by law, to accommodate itself to the requirements of Federal and State laws, but allow some of the financial or other burdens to be shifted to States. It is, in effect, a system that allows for the uniform application of stringent standards, but imposes some of the incremental costs on either the responsible parties or the State government, rather than the Superfund. While the system established by section 121 will bring pressure to bear on States to yield when there is conflict between their standards and the cleanup intentions of the Superfund, it does not provide a mechanism that allows them to be unilaterally overridden. Nowhere in section 121 is there authority for the Federal Government to preempt, for good reasons or bad, applicable and appropriate State laws.

Section 121(d)(2)(C) (i) allows the application of clause (ii). Since clause (ii) provides for the nonapplicability of a "State standard * * * which could effectively result in the Statewide prohibition of land disposal of hazardous substances, pollutants or contaminants • • • ", it appears to provide for preemption of such State laws. It does not. Instead it establishes an admittedly complex, and very probably confusing, mechanism which allows for the preservation of these laws and prevents unilateral action to override them.

Clause (i) never becomes available until the requirements of 121(b)(1) have been satisfied with respect to the site or release in question. Section 121(b)(1) requires, in turn, that the President determine that a remedial action which permanently and significantly reduces the volume, toxicity or mobility of the hazardous substances, pollutants or contaminants cannot be undertaken at the site or release in question. Such determinations are to be made on a case-by-case, site specific basis, and are described in more detail in the paragraph's third, fourth, fifth, sixth and seventh sentences.

Specifically, the President must conduct an assessment of permanent solutions and alternative treatment technologies or resource recovery technologies. The technologies must include any which would, in whole or part, result in a permanent and significant decrease in the toxicity, mobility, or volume of the hazardous substance, pollutant, or contaminant. And, in making the assessment, the President must at a minimum take into account certain factors, listed as (A) through (G). Finally, the President must select a remedial action which protects human health and the environment. In no circumstance, whether with respect to cleanups to which clause (ii) might apply or to any other, may the President select a remedial action which fails to protect human health and the environment. Of those solutions which are protective of human health and the environment, the President must select one which is cost effective and utilizes permanent solutions and alternative treatment technologies to the maximum degree possible.

It will be burdensome for the President to comply with these requirements on a case-by-case basis. Nevertheless, the burden imposed on the President is justified because of the serious consequences of proposing land disposal as the remedial action, when such action would be in violation of State law.

When the President has exhausted all alternatives and the only remaining option is land disposal within a State where that would, in fact, be contrary to State law, then and only then does clause (ii) becomes applicable. Although clause (ii) appears to state unequivocally that such a State requirement would be inapplicable, it is followed immediately by clause (iii) which provides for the continued application of such requirements.

If such a State standard, requirement, criteria, or limitation meets the conditions contained in (I), (II), and (III), it remains applicable and must be complied with by the President. Conditions (I) and (II) are attempts to describe, for lack of a better term, State statutes which are "Not In My Back Yard" laws and which have no legitimate reason for their enactment. In some areas of all States, and in all areas of some States, prohibitions on the land disposal of hazardous wastes are not only defensible, but the soundest possible public policy. Indeed, the Congress itself adopted in the Hazardous and Solid Waste Amendments of 1984 a band on the land disposal of liquid hazardous wastes to apply throughout the United States.

State laws which satisfy condition (II) would include those establishing comprehensive land use programs, even when in the opinion of some they merely protect "esthetics." Such laws, many of them statutes, exist in many States for the purpose of protecting natural resources ranging from fragile ecosystems to unblemished views and vistas. Indeed, the Clean Air Act protects such values. The judgment of whether a law was adopted by the legislature or courts of a State for reasons unrelated to protection of human health or the environment is to be made from the perspective of the State and its interests, for it is its citizens and officials who are best situated to define what is appropriate environmental protection within such State's borders.

Finally, a State must arrange for the disposition of the materials, both financially and otherwise, elsewhere. But while the State is left to its own resources in making nonfinancial arrangements, it may recover the incremental costs through use of CERCLA, State laws, or other Federal laws for example the Clean Water Act, the Safe Drinking Water Act and the Resource Conservation and Recovery

Act . Section 107 expressly authorizes the recovery of such response costs by State and local governments, unless they are inconsistent with the National Contingency Plan (NCP). Costs incurred in compliance with State laws described in condition (II) are consistent with SARA and are, therefore, consistent with the NCP, absent some independent and unrelated reason for disqualifying them.

Mr. President, such a system—designed to encourage an accommodation between two systems, not the capitulation of one of them—can scarcely be described as preemption. Ultimately, State laws and standards remain in full force and effect. If such laws yield when they could be applied, it is because State officials made that choice.

Mr. President, there are several other areas regarding the Superfund reauthorization which require a very brief further explanation. They are as follows:

THE SUPERFUND LIABILITY STANDARD

While CERCLA does not explicitly state that the liability is strict, joint, and several, it does incorporate in the definition of "liable." the standard of liability under section 311 of the Clean Water Act. Both section 311 and CERCLA have been held to impose strict, joint and several liability, which was the outcome that was expected by myself and others in 1980.

LIABILITY FOR UNDERGROUND TANKS

SARA establishes a new program for response to releases from underground tanks. To the extent that response costs exceed the mandated financial responsibility requirements, the Administrator may take that into account in deciding whether the equities demand the recovery of costs exceeding the insurance or other financial responsibility instrument. But compliance with the financial responsibility requirement is not determinative of the equities.

HEALTH ASSESSMENTS

While the language in SARA does not contain the phrase "medical testing," health assessments are to include morbidity and mortality data. To accumulate such data may require some medical testing, if the Administrator of the Agency for Toxic Substances and Disease Registry considers it necessary.

Neither the health assessment nor the health study provisions were included for the purpose of providing litigants with information to be used in law suits. However, the information collected would be admissible, or not, into evidence or otherwise used in a court as it would without respect to the provisions of SARA or CERCLA. Neither of the laws affects whether or not the information may be used.

USE OF MCLG'S

Section 121 provides a mechanism for compliance with State and Federal laws and standards. This mechanism applies to sources of water, surface as well as subsurface, whether or not the water is now, is projected to be, or is capable of consumption by human beings. Potability is only one of several considerations to be taken into account and the fact that water either is not presently used, or is not projected to be used, as a drinking water supply does not automatically determine whether MCLG's are to be considered. If it is appropriate, MCLG's should be taken into account; if it is not, they should not be.

SELECTION OF PERMANENT REMEDIES

SARA establishes, among those remedies which are protective of human health and the environment, a preference for those which permanently and significantly reduce the volume, toxicity or mobility of the hazardous substances, pollutants, and contaminants. In some cases, this requirement may very well constrain the President's flexibility in the selection of remedies, but as to choosing one of several which satisfy the preference, the President's flexibility is retained.

RESPONSE ACTION CONTRACTORS

The statement of managers accompanying SARA states that "the conferees urge States to take note of the Federal standards and review their own standards of liability." According to the "Random House College Dictionary," a review is "a second or repeated view of something." According to "Webster's Third New International Dictionary," to review is to "to examine again: make a second or additional inspection of: study anew." Also according to Webster's a review (the noun) is "a looking over or examination with a view to amendment or improvement."

Mr. President, if the word "review" suggest a change, it does not suggest one in any particular direction or the other, nor in favor of one particular interest group or the other. The sentences immediately preceding that which I quoted refer not just to the liability standard for contractors, but to the "existing standard of liability for responsible parties under CERCLA" as well.

Without belaboring this point, Mr. President, it is the view of this Senator that the statement of managers does not urge States to necessarily change their own standards of liability, with respect to responsible parties or any other group, or to change them in any particular direction. Of course, these are the views of just this Senator—as I made clear at the outset of these remarks—but I made them known at the time of the conference to the other body. If there is some disagreement, this Senator regrets it. But the language of the conferees, as set forth in the statement of managers, is the best and surest expression of the intent of the House and the Senate on this and all other matters.

* * * * * * * * *

p. S17212

SIGNING OF H.R. 2005, SUPERFUND AMENDMENTS AND REAUTHORIZATION ACT OF 1986

● Mr. MITCHELL. Mr. President, I want to express my strong approval of the President's acton today in signing the Superfund Amendments and Reauthorization Act of 1986, H.R. 2005. I and many colleagues in the Senate and House spent long hours over many months in developing this legislation, and its enactment is vital to the protection of the health of Americans in many parts of the Nation. With the signing of this legislation, containing the programmatic changes and the taxing authorities necessary to support an expanded program, and action today on the fiscal year 1987 appropriation for this program, progress on cleanups may resume at an accelerated pace. I want to express my appreciation to my colleagues who have joined me in efforts to persuade the President to sign this critically important legislation.

I would also like to take this opportunity to clarify some of my earlier remarks regarding the Superfund conference report.

Cleanup standards have been a major issue of concern to me, which is why I devoted so much of my time during the conference developing a satisfactory provision. My primary interest in this provision has been to assure what every American wants at Superfund sites: adequate protection of the public health. Public health protection is the essence of Superfund and of all of our environmental laws. Any provision that dilutes or diminishes this goal would be unacceptable to me.

Section 121, the standards provision, permits limited use of a regulatory process for setting alternate concentration levels [ACL's]. As I stated at the subconference meetings, I do not believe the ACL process is sound policy under subtitle C of the Solid Waste Disposal Act [RCRA] nor do I believe that it is authorized by law. RCRA does not mention nor envision a mechanism such as ACL's, which are used to diminish the amount of protection we are providing to the public. I cannot conceive that congressional silence on a concept developed by EPA after enactment of the Solid Waste Disposal Act can constitute approval of such a process.

I am willing to authorize use of the ACL process in setting Superfund cleanup standards, but only when other standards are not applicable. Since the ACL process is used to provide less protection to public health, any other outcome would be to admit that we cannot protect the public around Superfund sites as well as we protect other citizens. It has and continues to be my opinion that all citizens deserve equal protection under the law. Children drinking water that originates from a Superfund site should not be exposed to higher concentrations of contaminants than other children. The reason is fairly simple: The adverse effect on human health remains the same and we cannot in good conscience knowingly endanger the public health.

Some of my colleagues in the House appear to argue that the mention of the ACL process opens up the standards provision to a free for all that is controlled by cost. I cannot disagree more strongly with this position. Superfund is not a cost-saving mechanism; it is a health protection mechanism. We have not spent so much time and so much debate on this bill to finally conclude that we will protect people only so long as such protection is cheap.

One of my colleagues stated that, "The most important standards in section 121 requires the Administrator to select cost-effective remedies that protect the public health. * * * The Administrator must select the most cost-effective remedy that achieves this level of protection."

This is not a program that is intended to be a bargain-hunter's paradise for the simple reason that cleaning up contaminated ground water that people drink is not cheap. Removing contaminated soil is not cheap. These are expensive activities that we as a society have decided must be undertaken to protect people from toxic substances. This is the primary purpose of Superfund, and the only reason that justifies the tremendous scope and funding level of the Superfund Program.

Similarly, there are some who argue that the selection of a remedial action can be made by considering costs only. It is disappointing to hear some of my colleagues, with whom this issue was discussed during the conference, revisit this issue and direct EPA to consider cost first and protection of public health second. I was reluctant to include any mention of cost effectiveness in this section, in part because compliance with the National Contingency Plan already takes into account cost effectiveness. Repetition of the provision concerned me, but I was assured that protection of the public health clearly was the first priority. It is my belief, and on this basis I support section 121, that EPA must first select a remedial action that protects the public health. Only after that decision has been made may the Agency then determine which is the least costly alternative to implement that remedial action.

Similarly in selection of remedial action, EPA is to select the remedial action that serves the purpose of protecting the public health. Only after the basic need has been determined and a solution selected can EPA choose the most cost-effective alternative. Protection of public health is meaningless if cost overrules all other considerations.

If EPA selects a remedial action, what happens to the hazardous substances that are to be removed from the Superfund site? Clearly it is no improvement if they are transported to another site that is environmentally unsound. In order to prevent this outcome, we included in section 121(d) a provision that incorporates and strengthens EPA's offsite policy. Hazardous substances from a Superfund site can only be transferred to a facility operating in compliance with sections 3004 and 3005 of the Solid Waste Disposal Act, for example. The unit receiving the substances, as my colleagues in both Chambers agree, cannot be leaking substances into the ground or surface water or soil. Similarly, all releases from other units must be controlled by a corrective action program. Clearly the intent of this provision is to assure that only the most secure facilities receive the hazardous substances from a Superfund site, or we have just compounded our problem by creating more Superfund sites.

As I stated earlier, "such facilities can ordinarily only meet the second requirement if the corrective action has already been performed." One of my House colleagues appeared startled by my observation that in the ordinary course of things such an approach would be applied; I did not state this as a mimimal requirement in the offsite policy, but included it as a practical and, in my view, obvious result of this requirement.

Do we want to suggest to EPA that it is good policy to transfer hazardous substances to a facility that is in the process of controlling releases, but has not quite managed to do so? I do not believe this is the kind of public health protection we were elected to provide. They expect that hazardous substances taken from a Superfund site should be transferred to a facility that all agree will not leach contaminants into ground water or the soil. Anything less exacerbates an already serious national problem.

There also seems to be some confusion about EPA's obligation to meet the section 121 standards provision in the 30 days after enactment. As I stated earlier, there is a nondiscretionary duty on the Administrator to apply the requirements of section 121 in selecting remedial actions during the 30-day period following enactment. This was a difficult issue to resolve and I agreed to the compromise based on the understanding that this was a nondiscretionary duty: EPA must apply the section 121 standards in the 30 days after enactment and must certify in writing that such requirements have been complied with to the maximum extent practicable. One of my House colleagues suggests that the language "to the maximum extent practicable" makes this duty discretionary. I disagree with this view and would note that elsewhere in the bill where we have imposed a nondiscretionary duty, it has been clearly stated. The provision states clearly that the Administrator "must" certify in writing, not "may" or "should".

One last issue strikes very close to home, and this is the issue of preemption. Two of my House colleagues argued that Superfund is a preemptive law. Nothing could be farther from the truth. In fact, one of the motivations for reauthorization was the opportunity to correct the Supreme Court ruling in Exxon versus Hunt, in which the Court held that New Jersey's Superfund was preempted. H.R. 2005 corrects that misinterpretation and section 114(c) so that discussion need not be repeated here. The sole reason offered for concluding that preemption was part of the Superfund scheme is that "[it] could not be otherwise given the structure of the statute." I strongly disagree, as do a clear majority of conferees. None of our other environmental statutes, with a limited exception in the Clean Air Act, are preemptive. This is an issue of great importance to many of us, and we have stated repeatedly in this bill that there is no preemption. Any other conclusion is wholly without foundation.

These House Members suggested that section 113(h) covers all lawsuits under the authority of any law, State or Federal, concerning the response actions that are performed by EPA and other Federal agencies, by States pursuant to cooperative agreements, and by private parties pursuant to an agreement with the Federal Government. Under this suggestion, section 113 would become preemptive in a way never contemplated or intended by the Congress, in any case in which the executive branch took or endorsed response action. Such a construction would be inconsistent with the evolution of the "preenforcement review" provisions, as well as the explicit language of the bill and Statement of Managers and of sections 114 (a) and 320 (d) of existing law.

As passed by both the House and Senate, section 113(h) began as follows:

No court shall have jurisdiction to review any challenges. * * *

Because of a concern about the very result urged by my two House colleagues, the language was changed to read as follows:

No Federal court shall have jurisdiction under Federal law other than under section 1332 of title 28 of the United States Code (relating to diversity of citizenship jurisdiction) or under State law which is applicable or relevant and appropriate under section 121 (relating to cleanup standards) to review any challenges. * * *

An interpretation of the original text may have been to extinguish the jurisdiction of any court to review any challenge. Clearly, the conference substitute no longer does this. It limits the jurisdiction of specified courts to review challenges arising out of specified laws. The final language has become much more narrow and targeted. Clearly preserved, for example, are challenges to the selection or adequacy of remedies based on State nuisance law, or actions to abate the hazardous substance release itself, independent of Federal response action.

The conference language would permit a suit to lie in either Federal court—where jurisdiction could be based on diversity of citizenship—or in State court, where based on nuisance law. This construction is confirmed by the statement of managers explanation that "New section 113(h) is not intended to affect in any way the rights of persons to bring nuisance actions under State law with respect to releases or threatened releases of hazardous substances, pollutants or contaminants."

Section 113 of CERCLA governs only claims arising under the act. Whether or not a challenge to a cleanup will lie under nuisance law is determined by that body of law, not section 113. New subsection (h) governs only the suits filed under the circumstances enumerated in paragraphs (1) through (5) for the review of "challenges to removal or remedial action selected under section 104, or to review any order issued under section 106(a)". There is no support whatsoever in the original CERCLA law, in H.R. 2005 as now signed by the President, or in the statement of managers for the proposition that "any controversy over a response action selected by the President, whether it arises under Federal law or State law, may be heard only in

Federal court and only under circumstances provided" in section 113. That statement is contrary to the express legislative language and the statement of managers.

The view of the courts on this reauthorization will not be known for some time. Some try to discount the views that have been expressed in floor statements to the extent the floor statements do not coincide with their view. I do not believe that courts will go wrong if the purpose of Superfund is kept clearly in mind: protection of public health and the environment. I have repeatedly stated the public health concern since that is the most salient issue.

Superfund can ony work if the sites are cleaned up enough that people need not live in fear of the sites any longer and if the environment is no longer threatened. Our ability to overcome the threat posed by hazardous substances that are found at Superfund sites are limited, as amply demonstrated by the all-too familiar stories of children with leukemia and other diseases. A program that does not recognize this delicate balance is a failure for which we and generations to come will have to pay. Such an outcome is unacceptable and is the main reason why I have fought so hard for a strong Superfund program.●

SECTION-BY-SECTION INDEX

THE COMPREHESIVE ENVIRONMENTAL RESPONSE, COMPENSATION, AND LIABILITY ACT OF 1980 (CERCLA, SUPERFUND), PUBLIC LAW 96-510

as amended by

THE SUPERFUND AMENDMENTS AND REAUTHORIZATION ACT OF 1986 (SARA), PUBLIC LAW 99-499

TITLE I - HAZARDOUS SUBSTANCES RELEASES, LIABILITY, COMPENSATION

SECTION 101. DEFINITIONS

SECTION 102.
REPORTABLE QUANTITIES AND ADDITIONAL DESIGNATIONS

SECTION 103. NOTICES, PENALTIES

SECTION 104. RESPONSE AUTHORITIES

SECTION 106. ABATEMENT ACTION

SECTION 107. LIABILITY

SECTION 109. CIVIL PENALTIES AND AWARDS

SECTION 110. EMPLOYEE PROTECTION

SECTION 111. USES OF FUND

SECTION 112. CLAIMS PROCEDURE

SECTION 113. LITIGATION, JURISDICTION, AND VENUE

SECTION 114. RELATIONSHIP TO OTHER LAW

SECTION 115.
AUTHORITY TO DELEGATE, ISSUE REGULATIONS

SECTION 116. SCHEDULES

SECTION 117. PUBLIC PARTICIPATION

SECTION 118. HIGH PRIORITY FOR DRINKING WATER SUPPLIES

SECTION 121. CLEANUP STANDARDS

SECTION 122. SETTLEMENTS

SECTION 123. REIMBURSEMENT TO LOCAL GOVERNMENTS

SECTION 124. METHANE RECOVERY

SECTION 125. SECTION 3001(b)(3)(A)(i) WASTE

SECTION 126. INDIAN TRIBES

TITLE II - HAZARDOUS SUBSTANCE
RESPONSE REVENUE ACT OF 1980

SECTION 201. SHORT TITLE; AMENDMENT OF 1954 CODE

Subtitle A - Imposition of Taxes on Petroleum and Certain Chemicals

SECTION 211. IMPOSITION OF TAXES

[Subtitle B - Establishment of Hazardous Substance Response Trust Fund
Repealed by Section 517 of SARA]

[SECTION 221. ESTABLISHMENT OF HAZARDOUS SUBSTANCE RESPONSE TRUST FUND
Repealed by Section 517 of SARA]

[SECTION 222. LIABILITY OF UNITED STATES
LIMITED TO AMOUNT IN TRUST FUND
Repealed by Section 517 of SARA]

[SECTION 223. ADMINISTRATIVE PROVISIONS
Repealed by Section 517 of SARA]

[Subtitle C - Post-Closure Tax and Trust Fund
Repealed by Section 514 of SARA]

[SECTION 231. IMPOSITION OF TAX
Repealed by Section 514 of SARA]

[SECTION 232. POST-CLOSURE LIABILITY TRUST FUND
Repealed by Section 514 of SARA]

TITLE III - MISCELLANEOUS PROVISIONS

SECTION 301. REPORTS AND STUDIES

SECTION 302. EFFECTIVE DATES, SAVINGS PROVISION

[SECTION 303. EXPIRATION, SUNSET PROVISION
Repealed by Section 511 of SARA]

SECTION 304. CONFORMING AMENDMENTS

SECTION 308. SEPARABILITY

SECTION 309. ACTIONS UNDER STATE LAW FOR DAMAGES FROM EXPOSURE TO HAZARDOUS SUBSTANCES

SECTION 310. CITIZENS SUITS

SECTION 311.
RESEARCH, DEVELOPMENT, AND DEMONSTRATION

SECTION 312. LOVE CANAL PROPERTY ACQUISITION

TITLE IV. POLLUTION INSURANCE

SECTION 401. DEFINITIONS

SECTION 402. STATE LAWS; SCOPE OF TITLE

SECTION 403. RISK RETENTION GROUPS

SECTION 404. PURCHASING GROUPS

SECTION 405. APPLICABILITY OF SECURITIES LAWS

PROVISIONS OF SARA WHICH DO NOT AMEND CERCLA

SECTION 1. SHORT TITLE AND TABLE OF CONTENTS

SECTION 2. CERCLA AND ADMINISTRATOR

SECTION 3. LIMITATION ON CONTRACT AND BORROWING AUTHORITY

SECTION 4. EFFECTIVE DATE

TITLE I-PROVISIONS RELATING PRIMARILY TO RESPONSE AND LIABILITY

SECTION 118. MISCELLANEOUS PROVISIONS

SECTION 120(b).
FEDERAL FACILITIES: LIMITED GRANDFATHER

SECTION 127.
LIABILITY LIMITS FOR OCEAN INCINERATION VESSELS
[Amending CERCLA, sections 101, 107, and 108, and the
Marine Protection, Research and Sanctuaries Act of 1972.]

TITLE II. MISCELLANEOUS PROVISIONS

SECTION 203(b). STATE PROCEDURAL REFORM: EFFECTIVE DATE

SECTION 209(a).
RESEARCH, DEVELOPMENT, AND DEMONSTRATION: PURPOSE

SECTION 211. DEPARTMENT OF DEFENSE
ENVIRONMENTAL RESTORATION PROGRAM

SECTION 213(a). LOVE CANAL PROPERTY ACQUISITION: CONGRESSIONAL FINDINGS

TITLE III - EMERGENCY PLANNING AND COMMUNITY RIGHT-TO-KNOW

SECTION 300. SHORT TITLE; TABLE OF CONTENTS

SUBTITLE A - EMERGENCY PLANNING AND NOTIFICATION

SECTION 301. ESTABLISHMENT OF STATE COMMISSIONS, PLANNING DISTRICTS, AND LOCAL COMMITTEES

SECTION 302. SUBSTANCES AND FACILITIES COVERED AND NOTIFICATION

SECTION 303. COMPREHENSIVE EMERGENCY RESPONSE PLANS

SECTION 304. EMERGENCY NOTIFICATION

SECTION 305. EMERGENCY TRAINING AND REVIEW OF EMERGENCY SYSTEMS

SUBTITLE B - REPORTING REQUIREMENTS

SECTION 311. MATERIAL SAFETY DATA SHEETS

SECTION 312. EMERGENCY AND HAZARDOUS
CHEMICAL INVENTORY FORMS

SECTION 313. TOXIC CHEMICAL RELEASE FORMS

SUBTITLE C - GENERAL PROVISIONS

SECTION 321. RELATIONSHIP TO OTHER LAW

SECTION 322. TRADE SECRETS

SECTION 323. PROVISION OF INFORMATION TO HEALTH PROFESSIONALS, DOCTORS, AND NURSES

SECTION 324. PUBLIC AVAILABILITY OF PLANS, DATA SHEETS, FORMS, AND FOLLOWUP NOTICES

SECTION 325. ENFORCEMENT

SECTION 326. CIVIL ACTIONS

SECTION 327. EXEMPTION

SECTION 328. REGULATIONS

SECTION 329. DEFINITIONS

SECTION 330. AUTHORIZATION OF APPROPRIATIONS

TITLE IV - RADON GAS AND INDOOR AIR QUALITY RESEARCH

SECTION 401. SHORT TITLE

SECTION 402. FINDINGS

SECTION 403. RADON GAS AND INDOOR AIR QUALITY RESEARCH PROGRAM

SECTION 404. CONSTRUCTION OF TITLE

SECTION 405. AUTHORIZATIONS

TITLE V - AMENDMENTS OF THE INTERNAL REVENUE CODE OF 1986

SECTION 501. SHORT TITLE

Part I - Superfund and Its Revenue Sources

SECTION 511. EXTENSION OF ENVIRONMENTAL TAXES

SECTION 512. INCREASE IN TAX ON PETROLEUM

SECTION 513. CHANGES RELATING TO TAX ON CERTAIN CHEMICALS

SECTION 514. REPEAL OF POST-CLOSURE TAX AND TRUST FUND

SECTION 515. TAX ON CERTAIN IMPORTED SUBSTANCES DERIVED FROM TAXABLE CHEMICALS

SECTION 516. ENVIRONMENTAL TAX

SECTION 517. HAZARDOUS SUBSTANCE SUPERFUND

Part II - Leaking Underground Storage Tank Trust Fund and Its Revenue Sources

SECTION 521. ADDITIONAL TAXES ON GASOLINE, DIESEL FUEL, SPECIAL MOTOR FUELS, FUELS USED IN AVIATION, AND FUELS USED IN COMMERCIAL TRANSPORTATION ON INLAND WATERWAYS

SECTION 522. LEAKING UNDERGROUND STORAGE TANK TRUST FUND

Part III - Coordination With Other Provisions Of This Act

SECTION 531. COORDINATION

PROVISIONS OF SARA
WHICH AMEND THE SOLID WASTE DISPOSAL ACT

SARA SECTION 205. CLEANUP OF PETROLEUM
FROM LEAKING UNDERGROUND STORAGE TANKS
[Amending SWDA Subtitle I - Regulation of Underground Storage Tanks]

[Amending SWDA Subtitle C Used Oil Provisions]

[Amending SWDA Section 3019,
Exposure Information and Health Assessments]

[Requiring the Section 8002(m) Drilling Fluids Study
to Commence Within 6 Months]

PROVISIONS OF SARA WHICH AMEND THE MARINE PROTECTION, RESEARCH, AND SANCTUARIES ACT OF 1972

SECTION 127(d).
LIABILITY LIMITS FOR OCEAN INCINERATION VESSELS
[Amending MPRSA Section 106, Relationship to Other Laws]

SELECTED PROVISIONS NOT ENACTED

VICTIMS ASSISTANCE,
AND FEDERAL CAUSE OF ACTION

WASTE END TAX, AND
WASTE MANAGMENT TAX

SENSE OF THE SENATE RELATING TO THE VALUE ADDED TAX

TITLE III - LEAD FREE DRINKING WATER

SECTION 301. SHORT TITLE

SECTION 302. SAFE DRINKING WATER ACT AMENDMENTS
[Prohibition on Use of Lead Pipes, Solder, and Flux]

SECTION 303. BAN ON LEAD WATER PIPES, SOLDER, AND FLUX IN VA AND HUD INSURED OR ASSISTED PROPERTY

SECTION 304. LEAD SOLDER AS A HAZARDOUS SUBSTANCE

REFERENCES TO OIL POLLUTION LIABILITY AND COMPENSATION, AND THE OIL SPILL LIABILITY TRUST FUND

Lightning Source UK Ltd.
Milton Keynes UK
UKHW010947180119
335792UK00009B/273/P